HEALTHY
MARRIAGE
HANDBOOK

D0778371

THE HEALTHY MARRIAGE HANDBOOK

From the Editors of *Marriage Partnership*, a Christianity Today International Publication
Louise A. Ferrebee, General Editor

Chapter introductions by Marc Maillefer, Associate Pastor of Christian Education,
College Church in Wheaton, Illinois

HOLMAN
BIBLE PUBLISHERS

Nashville, Tennessee

The Healthy Marriage Handbook
© 2001 Broadman & Holman Publishers
Nashville, Tennessee
All rights reserved

0-8054-9054-X

Dewey Decimal Classification: 306.81
Subject Heading: Marriage
Library of Congress Catalog Number: 01-025760

Library of Congress Cataloging-in-Publication Data
The healthy marriage handbook / Louise A. Ferrebee, general editor.
    p. cm.
"From the editors of Marriage partnership, a Christianity today international publication."
Includes bibliographical references and index.
ISBN 0-8054-9054-X (alk. paper)
    1. Marriage. 2. Marriage--Religious aspects--Christianity. I. Ferrebee, Louise A., 1960-
II. Marriage partnership.

HQ734 .H44 2001
306.81--dc21   2001025760

Printed in the United States
2 3 4 5 05 04 03 02
R

CONTENTS

CONTENTS

CONTENTS

INTRODUCTION

There are few guarantees in marriage, except maybe one: Every couple will have plenty of questions about how to weave two lives into one successfully. And yet, when it comes to asking questions about the most personal, intimate human relationship we'll ever have, we often become surprisingly reserved.

Why this hesitancy, even though we often desperately want answers? Revealing the nitty-gritty concerns and insecurities we have about our marriages takes a kind of vulnerability most of us don't possess. And so we continue to drift along—learning by trial and error and hoping for the best.

Well, drift no more. Within the pages of this handbook are the answers to more than 200 confidential, personal questions from people just like you. It's almost like having a trusted, wise couple come alongside you—ready at a moment's notice to help you safely clear the inevitable hurdles you'll encounter on the road to marital happiness. The advice is time-tested, offered with compassion and understanding, and, most important, based on the counsel of God's word, the Bible. Indeed, it is only upon this rock that you can experience marriage as God intended it to be experienced. And to that end, we encourage you to read on.

CHAPTER 1

COMMUNICATING
WITH
CONFIDENCE

COMMUNICATING
WITH
CONFIDENCE

Good communication is at the heart of a strong marriage, but even the strong confess it's not easy! Why? Well, it's more than just "gender wiring." James tells us our speech is imperfect, and is one of the many ways in which we stumble (Jms. 3:2). Our tongues have been tainted because our hearts are marred by sin. Jesus said out of the overflow of the heart the mouth speaks (Mt. 12:34); and because our hearts are sinful it is possible for both curses and blessings to flow from our mouths. Wild animals can be tamed, "but no man can tame the tongue. It is a restless evil, full of deadly poison" (Jms. 3:8-10). No wonder someone has said that communication in marriage is like a "dialogue of the deaf."

But Jesus has given us new hearts, made us new creatures so we can honor Him with every word we speak. Tongues that were once poisonous as vipers can now be full of grace, seasoned with salt (Rm. 3:13; Col. 4:6) because we have His Spirit. The fruit of the Spirit is love, kindness, gentleness, self-control... (Gl. 5:22). Love, for example, keeps us from selfishness and causes us to consider others better than ourselves (Php. 2:3). Kindness helps us speak to each other with respect. Gentleness cultivates a soft answer, diffusing an angry volley (Pr. 15:1). And self-control gives us the ability to hold our tongues and avoid strife (Pr. 11:12; 20:3). Thus, joyous communication is one of the signs of being filled with the Spirit (Eph. 5:18-19).

As God's people we are to be "speaking the truth in love" (Eph. 4:15). We are not to give false testimony against our neighbor (Ex. 20:16): "The Lord detests lying lips, but he delights in men who are truthful" (Pr. 12:22, NIV).

"Speaking the truth in love" means we are never brutally honest, or lovingly dishonest. It means our yeses are yes and our noes no. Timing is everything. You can say the right thing at the wrong time and miss the mark. "Timely advice is as lovely as golden apples in a silver basket" (Pr. 25:11, NLT). Jesus spoke the truth in love, and "did not commit sin, and no deceit was found in His mouth" (1 Pt. 2:22).

> PRAYER: Lord, help me to be quick to hear, slow to speak and slow to anger (Jms. 1:19). Like Isaiah my lips are unclean (Is. 6:5). Touch my mouth, O God, and purify it so that no rotten talk comes out, but only what is helpful for building up others according to their needs, that it may benefit those who listen (Eph. 4:29). Let the words of my mouth and the meditation of my heart be favorable before You, O Lord, my Rock and my Redeemer (Ps. 19:14). Amen.

1.1 EXPRESSING A BAD MOOD

My husband is under a lot of pressure at work—facing deadlines and dealing with sticky personnel issues. Four out of five nights he comes home grouchy and stays like that most of the evening. His moods are beginning to affect the entire family. I want to be sympathetic to his problems, but at the same time I want to tell him he needs to temper his reactions. Is there a gentle way I can do that?

I have to admit there have been times when I've been guilty of this sort of thing. In fact, I suspect most families face a problem like yours at one time or another. Depending on whether your situation is a short-term or a long-term problem, there are two options open to you.

First, let's consider the short-term situation. Husbands and wives both go through times at work or home that create pressures and problems that carry over into their relational life. If this is a short-term situation your husband is going through (let's say six months or less), he may just need understanding, time, and a little space to work through it. Be patient; go slow about laying on any guilt.

Husbands and wives both go through times at work or home that create pressures and problems that carry over into their relational life.

But be honest with him when something he says or does is hurtful or frustrating to you. Treat him as you normally do. And remember (maybe even remind him) that the cycle will change—things will improve again.

However, if this situation has gone on for longer than six months it needs a more serious response: a trusted Christian friend, a pastor. Remember that your husband might benefit from counseling regarding personal or career issues. And you might encourage him to seek it. Your husband may be in a job that is over his head. Or perhaps he's in a harness that doesn't really fit.

If that's the case, he may feel so overwhelmed that the thought of seeking help or a job change feels like more than he can handle. But I'd encourage him to consider it nonetheless. People harnessed into unhappy work situations for long periods of time can be helped a great deal by making some changes—even if those changes bring additional short-term pain.

So if the problem is short-term, try to go easy. Pray for your husband and try to make his family life as pleasant as you can. Let him brood a little and don't transform this into an unnecessary crisis. But if it is a long-standing difficulty, encourage your husband to take the steps necessary to deal with it. And promise to stick with him through the cure, even if it involves some added pain and struggle for you and your family.

Jay Kesler

1.2 HELPING A QUIET SPOUSE OPEN UP

A lot of husbands have a tough time with the areas of emotional expression and verbal communication.

How can I get my husband to talk to me? I try to be interested in the things he likes to do. For instance, when we get home from work, I ask him about his day. But he says he'd rather not talk about it, that he leaves his work at the office. How can I get him to open up and share his life with me?

There can be a great difference between a husband not wanting to talk to you and a husband not wanting to talk about his work. Many men want to escape the pressures and demands of work when they come home. Talking about work can seem like more work. So I'd suggest you pursue another tack.

Books on communication talk about the various levels of intimacy in conversation. You start with things like facts, events, people and experiences, and then become more intimate as you share ideas, dreams, aspirations and feelings.

The most fulfilling communication, the kind of interaction you long for, takes the commitment and involvement of two people. That's easier said than accomplished, because a lot of husbands have a tough time with the areas of emotional expression and verbal communication. Yet there are some unilateral moves you can make that could move you closer to your goal.

First, instead of pressing your husband to talk about his work, look for some areas of common interest. And then share your own ideas, dreams, aspirations and feelings about the topic(s). I'm not suggesting a continuous monologue of your deepest thoughts. But if you regularly make it a point to express your feelings about topics you both care about, your example may show your husband the way toward better communication.

Sometimes a couple will tell me, "We have nothing to talk about." My advice is simple: find something you can do and enjoy together. Every couple should be able to find some activity they can enjoy sharing. It could be a hobby: gardening, birdwatching, painting, reading, tennis, biking, walking, doing some household task. Often, as a couple begins to share in the pursuit of a hobby or some other pastime, communication improves and begins to carry over into other areas of their lives.

Every couple should be able to find some activity they can enjoy sharing.

Unfortunately, the solution isn't always that simple. If you have tried, but can't find any areas in which to make progress, marriage counseling might be recommended. Or a marriage enrichment weekend with a chance to focus on your relationship for a day or two might help get some communication started. However, the person who has a hard time opening up and communicating is often the most reluctant to consider counseling or a marriage retreat.

I'd encourage you to also develop one or more friendships with a woman your own age. You need that kind of sharing, too. And it may take away some of the pressure you feel as you wait for your husband to open up.

Jay Kesler

1.3 NOT FEELING UNDERSTOOD

Whenever my wife brings up an issue that's bothering her and I offer my advice, she gets mad and says, "You don't care, you never listen!" But I did listen—otherwise I wouldn't have been able to come up with a solution. Why is she so frustrated? What am I doing wrong?

When a woman brings up a subject or area of conflict, her primary desire is usually to be heard and understood. She's most concerned about the relationship. She wants to see that her comments and ideas are well received, and then the problem solving can begin. Here are a few tips that will improve your communication with your wife.

Cherish her. Express the many thoughts and feelings you have about her. Even a simple "I'm totally exasperated with work, but it's great to see your face at the end of the day" can make a huge difference.

Take the initiative. Most wives will fall over with delight when a husband says, "I want to talk to you." Discuss your expectations regarding your relationship.

Talk to your wife. Some men find it easier if "talk time" is scheduled—say, an hour of uninterrupted time once a week. This way they don't have to wait for "inspiration" to check in with their wives, and they don't need to feel guilty that it's not happening.

Lower your defenses. Often husbands become defensive due to their own sense that they are not as verbally skilled as their wives are or because of the way their wives approach communication. If you find yourself becoming defensive, try instead to relax for a moment to hear your wife's concern. This is hard to do, but when your wife knows that you care about how she feels, she is more likely to listen to you and your ideas for resolving a situation.

> *When your wife knows that you care about how she feels, she is more likely to listen to you.*

Take time out. If you're too upset or need time to sort out your feelings, say so, and take time to collect your thoughts. Tell your wife, "I need a break to think this through; let's talk tomorrow at 6:00." Your commitment to resolve the issue will satisfy your wife, and she will probably respect your expressed need for space.

Karen L. Maudlin

1.4 EXPRESSING LOVE IN THE RIGHT WORDS

A few weeks ago I bought my husband a surprise gift. I thought he'd be thrilled but he only said, "That's nice." I was crushed. This isn't the first time my efforts at expressing love have met with a flat response. Why are my actions and words only mildly effective? What am I doing wrong?

Many couples have told me they try to demonstrate love but keep missing the mark. To eliminate misunderstanding, it is necessary to share with one another your needs, wants, and desires in a specific yet non-demanding manner.

One of the most effective ways of meeting each other's love needs is to practice the "Cherishing Days" exercise. Each partner makes a list of simple cherishing behaviors that he or she would enjoy receiving from the other. These requested behaviors should have four characteristics:

1. They must be specific and positive. For example, Janice would like Jim to sit next to her on the couch as they watch the news. She has made a positive request for a desired behavior instead of complaining, "You ignore me and are preoccupied with the TV."

2. The cherishing behaviors must not be related to past conflicts or old demands.

3. The positive behaviors must be such that they can be accomplished on an everyday basis.

4. The behaviors must be achievable—they can't require excessive time or expense.

Think back to the most satisfying times of your courtship and marriage to come up with ideas for your list. Even if the behaviors seem trivial or embarrassing, include them on your list as long as they reflect valid personal wants or needs.

Once your list of 15 to 20 cherishing behaviors is completed, exchange lists with your spouse and discuss what you are requesting from each other. Be sure to tell your spouse how you would like each behavior performed. For example, if you request a back rub at bedtime, specify light skin rub or deep muscle massage, with lotion or without. As you discuss your written behaviors, feel free to add others to the list as you think of them.

After your discussion, declare the next seven days to be "Cherishing Days." Make a commitment to put your partner's list into practice. Try to accomplish as many of the behaviors as possible each day. Focus your attention and energies on what you do for your spouse, not on what he or she does for you. At the end of seven days you can evaluate whether you will continue the exercise for another week.

Why does this exercise encourage love and romance? Because the list of positive behaviors consists of requested, discussed and agreed-upon acts of love. The guesswork of "What shall I do for him? Will she like it?" is eliminated. Also, the commitment is short term—you are only responsible for seven days. And because the behaviors are simple and easily achievable, the margin of failure is greatly reduced.

As each person gives and receives positive loving acts, the bond of love will grow stronger.

Another important factor in the success of this exercise is the commitment of each individual to the "I must change first" principle. You are not keeping score of your spouse's efforts. You are too busy concentrating on accomplishing his or her list. And with each behavior comes a positive response that encourages the giver to continue. As each person gives and receives positive loving acts, the bond of love will grow stronger.

Most couples decide to continue the exercise after completing the initial seven-day commitment. They find that the benefits of filling each other's wants and needs eliminate the negatives of love-recessive behavior patterns.

H. Norman Wright

1.5 FORGOTTEN ANNIVERSARIES

This may sound trivial, but for me (and I suspect a lot of other women) it's very important: my husband often forgets occasions that are important to me—my birthday or our anniversary, for example. I don't want to have to remind him because then if he does something, it's not going to be a sincere show of affection. Why don't men realize that these things matter?

Maybe the reason men forget special days is somehow tied to recent findings about the different ways men and women's brains work. Scientists are telling us the corpus callosum connecting the two halves of our brains is more developed in women. Maybe that's why we men sometimes have a harder time getting a handle on our emotions and connecting our feelings with facts—such as important dates. Maybe that's why, when it comes to our emotions, so many of us men are slow learners. I'm merely speculating here; I can't give you a definitive "why" answer. But I can give you some suggestions on what you might do about it.

First, you need to let your husband know how you feel. You may not cure a severe case of forgetfulness; but if you communicate your feelings, he should never again forget and think you won't mind. If you don't know what to say, ask him to read this portion of the book. When you talk about it, try not to focus on his shortcomings, but emphasize your feelings of disappointment and how much his remembering would mean to you.

I understand your reluctance to remind your husband of special occasions. Most of us know what it feels like to fish for recognition and affirmation and then feel as if it doesn't mean as much because it wasn't spontaneous. But you may want to try a generic type of reminder. If you don't have a monthly family calendar, start one. Post it on the

If you don't have a monthly family calendar, start one.

refrigerator and write in special days—not just your birthday and anniversary, but also those of your extended family. Put your kids' schedule of events on it as well as yours. And when you post it each month, go over it with the entire family. Then you can say, "This month we've got Grandpa's birthday, my sister's anniversary, Johnny's piano recital on the 12th, and my birthday on the 15th." Your special days will be part of the bigger picture, he'll have a reminder, and you won't have to say, "My birthday's coming up and I hope you've got something planned."

Chances are your husband will begin to catch on. When he does remember, let him know you appreciate it. Tell him. Show him. Reinforce his positive behavior.

But don't use positive reinforcements as a way to manipulate him. You shouldn't think about your husband as if he's one of Pavlov's dogs who you'll condition into doing what you want. None of us likes to be manipulated; but many of us can learn our lessons a little quicker if positive reinforcement rewards our efforts.

Jay Kesler

1.6 FEELING EMOTIONALLY SHUT OUT

Often my husband seems upset by something and when I ask him what's wrong he says, "Nothing." And yet, his body language sure says something else! I know he's upset, so why is he so reluctant to talk about it?

No matter how much we try verbally to present ourselves in a particular way, we can't really keep our feelings hidden—especially from our spouse. We may deny we are angry, but the sharp edge on our words will betray us. We may insist we aren't discouraged, but the dullness in our eyes will contradict us. We may say that we're not hurt by our spouse, but the deepened lines of our face will say otherwise.

Perhaps God has made us that way in an effort to minimize the possibilities of secrets in marriage.

We can control what we say, but we can never totally control our nonverbal signals. Perhaps God has made us that way in an effort to minimize the possibilities of secrets in marriage. Willing for us to become one flesh, He made sure that we would give off signals to reveal something of our feelings even when our words give a different message.

If you or your mate have trouble expressing feelings, keep in mind that honest sharing of feelings is crucial to building intimacy in marriage. Then work together on learning how to share your feelings. Here are two techniques we recommend.

First, affirm your spouse whenever he or she shares feelings with you. If your spouse says, "I feel a little down today," don't respond with "Oh, you shouldn't feel that way," or "But you have so much to be thankful for." Your mate doesn't need a rebuke or sermon, he or she needs an appreciative and supportive listener. So you might say something like, "I noticed you looked down. I'm glad you told me; I need to know so I won't assume you're mad at me or disappointed with me. Do you know what has made you feel that way? What can I do to help?"

Second, practice sharing your feelings. Choose a time when you can talk without outside interruptions for about thirty minutes. Take turns sharing your feelings with each other. Have the spouse who finds it easier to talk about his or her feelings to go first, to encourage the other to share honestly.

During these sessions, try one or more of the following approaches:

- Choose an event or incident from the past and try to reconstruct how you felt at the time.
- Think about a particular kind of feeling—anger, joy, satisfaction, jealousy, pride, embarrassment or disappointment—and talk about a time when you felt it keenly.
- Talk about how you are feeling at the moment or how you felt the previous night; or try to give the full range of feelings you have experienced that day. Remember to mention positive feelings as well, so the sessions won't focus exclusively on the uncomfortable feelings many of us find difficult to express.

Most people who find it difficult to talk about their feelings have been that way throughout their lives. Changing the pattern will take time. However, the rewards for doing so are well worth the effort.

Jeanette C. and Robert H. Lauer

1.7 WHEN LIES ERODE TRUST

I can't trust my husband because he repeatedly lies to me about little things. For example, last week he told me he had called the cable guy. But when the cable guy never showed up, my husband admitted he hadn't called. And recently when I found a hamburger wrapper in the car, he lied about having already eaten until he saw the evidence in my hands. I want to restore trust between us, but I'm finding it hard to believe anything my husband tells me.

Lying is a serious problem, a sin. Your husband needs to stop, and you can't be responsible for that. But *the goal is for your husband to feel comfortable being vulnerable and accountable in your marriage,* and there are things you can do to help him reach that goal.

First, affirm the things that he really does do. If he says he's going to pick up the dry cleaning and he does, be sure to thank him. Second, mention things once and then leave them alone. If he says he'll take care of something, let cause and effect run their course. When the two of you are watching TV and the picture barely comes in, you can say, "Hey, the cable guy never came," but not, "Hey you didn't call the cable guy!" This gives your husband a chance to get on the ball and contact the repairman.

Some couples have success posting a "to-do" list for each spouse on the refrigerator. My wife and I talk about which things I'm going to be responsible for, and which things she's going to take care of. Then we post the lists. That way each of us is responsible without either of us having to check up on the other.

Try to keep things light.

Also, try to keep things light. You say your husband ate a hamburger right before dinner, and you felt he shouldn't be eating before a meal. My wife and I are always dieting, always trying to eat healthy foods at the right times. Any time either of us goes to the refrigerator after the other has gone to bed, we feel a little guilty. But we laugh about it as we remind each other. My wife might say, "Ah, ha! Someone had a bowl of cereal last night!" but not, "I caught you in a lie!" A little humor is always helpful.

As your husband feels less like he's being checked up on, he may drop the deceptions and the withdrawing. Over time, as his performance improves, you may be able to start trusting him again.

Jay Kesler

1.8 CONFIDING MARRIAGE WOES TO A FRIEND

From time to time, I get upset about my marriage and end up confiding in a friend. It feels great at the time to vent, but later, when I'm feeling much more positive about my marriage, I feel a little guilty about sharing my frustrations so openly. When is it okay to vent and when should I keep my thoughts to myself?

Before you open your mouth, here are a few questions to consider.

Is it premature to talk to someone else? Sometimes it's tempting to tell others about an incident before you've had a chance to cool off, pray about the problem and then work through it with your spouse.

"I encourage people not to act on impulse," says counselor Carla Schemper. "If you're struggling, it's easy to think, 'I have to talk to someone!' and then blurt out your whole story without thinking through the implications. A lot of people tell me with great regret about times they chose to talk about a certain crisis and then down the road wished they hadn't."

What is my goal? Before you air negative feelings and information about your spouse, be sure you understand what you're trying to accomplish. If you're trying to get advice to solve a problem, make sure the problem really needs to be solved. As one husband puts it, "Marriages partly last because you don't choose to confront your spouse about every little thing."

There's nothing inherently wrong with seeking relief from negative emotions, as long as you don't make the problem worse in the process. But if, after challenging your own motivations, you realize you're trying to get back at your spouse—or you're unloading on a friend as a substitute for tackling an issue directly with your partner—put a lid on that steam.

What are appropriate boundaries? The first rule is "do no harm." This principle may mean different things in different situations. One woman going through a serious crisis in her marriage chose not to share her painful struggle with her parents and siblings. Her reasoning was simple: "If my marriage survives, I would have given my family information about my husband that would affect how they see him for the rest of their lives. I don't want our marriage to have that kind of burden."

If you need to unburden yourself, but are concerned about the potential fallout, determine in advance how much detail you will share. Schemper observes, "When you choose someone to confide in, say, 'I need to talk to someone and I trust you to keep my confidences, but I think it's in my best interest not to share all the specifics. Some things have happened between my spouse and me that have put a strain on our relationship and I'm having trouble handling my anger. Since you know me, maybe you can help me find a way to handle my resentment.'"

A good guideline to use is that the depth of revelation should be appropriate to the depth of the relationship. Another rule of thumb: try to talk about the problem instead of the person. There's no harm in occasional griping about irritations in your marriage as long as you're not labeling and judging your spouse in the process.

Depending on the setting, you may want to get your spouse's permission before talking to a friend about your marriage. Keep in mind that your marriage is your priority relationship.

The depth of revelation should be appropriate to the depth of the relationship.

To whom should I talk? I took an informal survey and came up with mixed results on this question. One point of disagreement centered on whether you should talk to someone who knows your spouse well. The obvious down side is that your venting could permanently alter the opinion your friend or relative has of your spouse. On the other hand, close friends and relatives are usually the people who have earned our deepest trust, have our good in mind and, knowing our weaknesses, have some perspective on how we might be contributing to any marriage conflicts.

Another point in debate is whether it's better to spout off to someone who says, "You poor thing" or someone who will hold your feet to the fire. "When I've got a major head of steam going, the last thing I need is someone helping me build up more steam," says one husband. "So I try to seek out friends who will let me vent, but who will also hold me accountable and call me to prayer." *Janis Long Harris*

1.9 HOW HONEST IS TOO HONEST?

I was talking with a friend the other day and I mentioned that my husband and I believe in total honesty. To my surprise, she cautioned me and said that too much honesty nearly wrecked her marriage. I've always believed that honesty is the best policy, but now I'm confused. Just how candid should I be with my spouse?

Honesty is necessary to create strong bonds between a husband and wife, however there are several reasons you should think before you speak.

First, many of our thoughts and feelings are only transitory—they don't represent the way we really feel. Bill, a salesman facing a lot of pressure at work, told us: "I get frustrated because of my work, and unfortunately I take my frustrations out on my wife, Jan. When that happens, the thought may come into my mind that it would be nice to be single again. That would be one less problem in my life." Bill went on to say that he never expresses that thought to his wife. "I love being married, I know I don't really want to be without her. And I know it would hurt Jan if I said that I wished I were single again. So I just bite my tongue, and pretty soon the feeling passes."

Second, total openness is harmful if it masks, rather than illuminates, your problems. Often, the feeling we have at the moment isn't the root of the problem. Nancy was going through a series of stressful events that caused her to explode in rage against everything in her life, including her husband, Tim. In the middle of a heated argument, Nancy told Tim she hated him. At that moment she felt like she "hated" not only her husband, but also her mother, her best friend, her boss and the paperboy, because they were a part of the general situation that was causing her so much stress. Understandably, Tim was devastated, and it took Nancy several weeks to reassure him that she still loved him and that her hateful words had nothing to do with him.

Third, total openness is harmful when it leads us to say hurtful things to others. We always need to consider whether what we say in an effort to be honest is the product of an "unbridled tongue" rather than an example of "speaking the truth in love." In the New Testament, James suggests the tongue should be a monitor, rather than an open channel, of our thoughts (Jms. 1:26). Perhaps we can't keep hurtful thoughts from coming into our minds, but we can refuse to speak those thoughts that might bring pain to another.

Jeanette C. and Robert H. Lauer

1.10 A SPOUSE WHO DOESN'T LISTEN

I've noticed that when I'm talking with my husband, he doesn't really seem to be listening. In fact, I almost feel as though he's ignoring me. How can I get him to listen with his heart and his head?

The roots of this communication pattern actually go back to adolescence. As boys proceed through normal development, they become more independent by testing limits and disregarding their mothers. To become his own person, a boy actually learns not to listen. In contrast, adolescent girls separate from their mothers in a verbal way, often launching an all-out verbal offensive. This can be painful at the time but if

To become his own person, a boy actually learns not to listen.

all goes well, it results in moms and daughters relating with separate but still connected status. Along the way, young women learn to value cooperation, empathy and developing and maintaining relationships. This glaring gender difference is at the root of the communication problem between husbands and wives, but you can increase the likelihood of your husband listening if you consider this basic advice.

Stick to one topic at a time. Women tend to look for connections, so each issue may seem related to another. But only one topic can be effectively discussed at a time.

Identify and state directly how you feel and what you want. Women are trained to look out for other people's needs and not their own. Often women need to stop and think hard to answer the question, "What do I want and need?" Do this before starting a discussion with your husband. More often than not, wives figure out their needs verbally while reviewing several topics out loud with their husbands. Unfortunately, this process tends to overwhelm husbands with too much information. By the time a woman's need is clear to her, she's lost her listener.

Be selective. Give some thought to which issues are important, at what time to discuss them, and to what extent. More is not better.

Slow down. Women usually talk faster, interrupt more, and talk over their husband's words. Give him time to collect and share his thoughts.

Often men can't identify their feelings as quickly as women do.

Don't assume bad motives—that because he doesn't know what he feels, or doesn't share what he feels, that he's trying to hurt you. Often men can't identify their feelings as quickly as women do, and once they do they might be unsure of how to communicate them. Listen to yourself: If you sound like a nagging mother to you, you probably sound that way to him.
Karen L. Maudlin

1.11 LIVING WITH A LOW-MAINTENANCE SPOUSE

I'll admit it—I'm always analyzing my marriage and thinking "Is it working?" or "What can we improve on?" I know it drives my husband nuts, but I can't change my way of thinking. How can I tell my husband my concerns without overwhelming him?

If you've had the feeling that your husband wasn't investing enough in your relationship, you might have sent the message that he just doesn't measure up. With a new approach you can restore your mate's confidence.

1. Use disarming disclaimers. When you want to bring up a touchy subject, begin with a statement such as, "I know I'm coming across as high-maintenance, but could we talk about...."
2. Replace negative assumptions with requests for specific actions. Instead of complaining that "we never talk anymore," express your desires in specific terms: "I wish we could talk for 15 minutes at the end of the day." Making specific requests helps prevent your spouse from feeling defensive.
3. Reinforce the things your mate does right. Pour on the meaningful praise when you notice a behavior that you'd like to see more of. Tell your partner specifically what he or she did that helped you.
4. Don't forget to meet the needs on your mate's maintenance list. A low-maintenance mate is not a no-maintenance mate.

Tim Sutherland

1.12 CONFRONTING A SELF-CENTERED SPOUSE

I can't seem to talk with my wife about any of my personal concerns. It's not that I'm not willing; it's just that she's so self-centered that every conversation turns into a discussion about her needs and struggles. We can talk endlessly, but I feel cut off and lonely anyway.

This is a major problem, since Scripture teaches us to bear one another's burdens, not to bear just one person's burdens. It appears that you have been stewing about the problem without directly confronting your wife. You need to talk things out, but when you do, avoid accusations and words such as "self-centered" and "selfish." Instead, quietly explain your feelings: "I feel shut out and lonely because somehow you don't seem interested in my concerns. You seem to be concerned only about your own struggles."

Your wife might deny she is preoccupied with herself. But whether or not she is self-centered, the point is that you feel cut off from her. Some people are insensitive to an appropriate balance of conversation, the give-and-take that we expect and desire. If she has been hurting you inadvertently, when she becomes

Some people are insensitive to an appropriate balance of conversation.

aware of your feelings she may immediately respond by wanting to become a better listener.

It might help to establish some ground rules for your conversations. Even if it feels awkward and mechanical, you may have to say, "You share for this many minutes, and then let me share." In the end, you will have done your wife a favor by making her more aware of her listening habits. Many people with "I" trouble (they use the first-person pronoun too much) have lost the balance of good conversation. As a result, they wonder why people avoid them. They need a loved one to tell them, "Hey, this isn't working."

Jay Kesler

1.13 UNCOMFORTABLE WITH CONSTANT RELATIONSHIP TALKS

My wife loves to talk about our relationship. "Are we close enough?" "Do we still love each other?" "What should we be working on in our marriage?" Frankly, I think all this analysis is unnecessary. How can I let her know I love her and value our marriage, even if I don't always want to evaluate our love?

It's not unusual for a husband to operate on the "if-it-ain't-broke-don't-fix-it" assumption. A wife, meanwhile, may wonder in frustration, "Why can't we talk about the most basic and important areas of our marriage? Something must be terribly wrong."

"To many women, the relationship is working as long as they can talk things out," explains Deborah Tannen, author of *That's Not What I Meant!* (William Morrow). "But to many men, the relationship isn't working if they have to continue talking it over."

Bob Berkowitz, host of the nightly talk program "Focus," comments: "A woman's ability to discuss sensitive subjects, while at times painful to her, is a way to deal with reality." But men may prefer golden silence as their way to deal with reality.

A husband's frustration with discussing the marriage, therefore, may stem from his idea that discussing something means there's a problem with it. Otherwise, why would his wife say, "We have to talk about this"? And who wants to admit there's a problem with his marriage, his kids, or his ability to provide for his family?

Simply being aware of this key difference can help. When a wife brings up a topic, rather than pulling into a sort of mental turtle shell, a husband can say to himself: "She isn't nagging. Yes, she has said this over and over, but maybe that's because she likes relationships where you can actually talk back and forth about things."

A wife, for her part, might cushion the blow of her conversation by starting with, "Can I talk with you about our trip next weekend? There's no big problem, but I just wanted to hear what you think about this." A phrase such as "there's no big problem" signals to men that this is safe conversational territory.
Kevin A. Miller

1.14 SQUEEZED OUT OF A SPOUSE'S SCHEDULE

My wife has many talents, so she's called on to fill more and more roles. She helps out at our son's school, teaches piano, directs the choir at church, and holds down a part-time job. The problem is I feel like everyone else gets the best of her energy, and I only get the little that is left over. I'm facing some uncertainty at work, and I've tried to talk with my wife about it. But I get the impression she's only willing to pay attention to my troubles when it fits into her schedule. I feel squeezed out of her life just at a time when I really need her input. What should I do?

It's astonishing how easily work and other outside concerns encroach on the relationships we value most. I got my own wake-up call the morning I saw my son's name on my daily appointment list. When he arrived at my office, I asked him, "Why would you make an appointment? We can talk at home." And he told me, "You're so busy, Dad. But I noticed you always make room for anyone who has an appointment. I want as much time as you would give one of those people." I realized then that my family needed more than just "equal time"; they needed to be a primary focus. It changed my life.

I realized then that my family needed more than just "equal time"; they needed to be a primary focus.

Go to your wife and express, with humility and vulnerability, how much you need her. And tell her you feel "squeezed out" by her many activities. She'll probably understand how you feel. In the early years of marriage, it's common for women to feel what you are describing. When the husband is happy, busy and fulfilled in his work, he often becomes preoccupied and doesn't feel an urgent need for his wife's partnership. As a result, a pattern of independence, rather than healthy *interdependence*, develops. Acting in self-defense, a woman may fill her life with fulfilling activities separate from her husband. Then, when her husband realizes how much he needs her closeness and support, he becomes resentful of the many facets of her life that sap her time and energy.

As you talk with your wife about your desire for her companionship, be prepared to listen carefully. And again be ready to humble yourself and admit that you needed her all along—even if you didn't show it. Remind each other why you got married in the first place: because you loved one another and wanted to build a lifelong partnership. Then be patient as the two of you work together to build a real partnership.

Jay Kesler

1.15 FRAZZLED BY A HIGH-ENERGY SPOUSE

My husband loves to be busy, in fact, too busy in my opinion. He always has some project or involvement that needs his urgent attention. For instance, I was looking forward to a relaxing Friday evening at home only to learn he planned to run errands, work out, and then wanted my help to finish washing the windows. How can I keep my cool when he's always interrupting my life with last-minute plans and a jam-packed schedule?

When it comes to coping with stress, we all have our limits. However, some people seem to be able to handle a much higher level of stress than others. So what happens when someone with a low stress tolerance marries someone who seems to thrive on chaos?

"You want me to be like you, but I can't."

First, we need to understand and accept our spouse for who he or she is, and then willingly adjust to his or her "uniquenesses." For example, my wife and I are at opposite ends of the energy poles. For years, I couldn't understand her need for sleep. I thrived on five hours a night, while she required much more. I tried everything to get her to change, and in doing so created a lot of stress for her. She would say, "You want me to be like you, but I can't." Finally, I learned to accept her need for sleep and adapt to it.

Notice my wife said I wanted her to be like me. Whenever you try to force your spouse to function in life like you do, you raise his or her stress level. And if a person lives at the peak of their chaos threshold too long, eventually the marriage will suffer.

Interestingly, the one thing more difficult than dealing with a spouse who is your opposite is dealing with a spouse whose personality is too similar to your own. Such couples can't offer each other the balance they need to coexist in a healthy manner.

For example, I'm counseling a couple in their mid-20s who are both high-energy types. They thrive on constant stimulation and can't tolerate being bored. When they started dating, they felt a strong attraction to each other because they were so alike. But they mistook their alikeness for intimacy. Now, nine months into their marriage, there's nothing but chaos. Both of them run their own businesses, so they're faced with heavy demands at work. And instead of having a spouse to come home to who is a good listener, or who can help the other see things more objectively, they both have the same hard-nosed, hot-headed personality. So neither of them holds the other accountable for his or her abusive behavior. If one of them had a lower chaos threshold, he or she might say, "Enough. I can't keep living like this."

That's one of the benefits of having different personalities and stress-tolerance levels. You're better able to set limits on your spouse's behavior. You have a right to call a halt to behavior that creates an unhealthy level of stress in your life.

Though the process of discovering who your spouse is can be frustrating at times, it helps to remember that God put the opposites of his creation together for a reason. He knew that out of a man's and woman's differences, growth would take place. Perhaps when we look at it in this light, we can feel grateful for the unique way our mate functions, and look to marriage as a place to grow.

Archibald Hart

1.16 TOO STRESSED TO TALK

I keep hoping that the pace of our life will slow down, but it never seems to change. If anything, now that we have grade-school age kids, life is a complete blur. I know in my heart that the stress of such a busy lifestyle isn't good for our marriage. We seldom have time for one another and our communication has been reduced to sharing the facts about schedules or responsibilities. Is there a way to regain our sense of equilibrium?

One of the biggest mistakes newlyweds make is not to consider the long-term ramifications of the decisions they make today.

We live in a culture-of-the-moment. Our focus is today—with little thought for tomorrow. It's not surprising, then, that one of the biggest mistakes newlyweds make is not to consider the long-term ramifications of the decisions they make today.

I regularly see the fallout of such shortsightedness firsthand in my office. Couples come to me around their tenth year of marriage all stressed out because they're in debt way over their heads. They're under tremendous pressure to meet a mortgage payment on a house they can't afford. Or they're struggling to make payments on two cars. Their past decisions have made them feel trapped today. Consequently, they feel they have no other choice but to stay on the treadmill.

That's why it is so extremely important in the early years of marriage to establish a common value system—priorities, if you will—upon which you can mutually base your decision-making. For example, perhaps you have decided that having a strong family is an important value that the two of you share. From there, you need to discuss exactly what a strong family means to both of you, and what steps you'll have to take to achieve that goal. Will one of you forgo pursuing a career to stay at home with the kids? Will you live in a rural area so you can afford a house or enjoy a certain quality of life?

I once counseled a man in his late 30s who was a successful businessman. However, he paid a high price for his achievement. For years he would leave the house at six in the morning and come home at nine at night. He and his wife had two small children, but he spent little time enjoying them. In order to continue climbing the career ladder, he felt he had no choice but to stay at the office until everyone else had gone home. On top of that, he was active in his church. So he would often rush straight from work to a meeting at church, then back to the office to get more work done. Finally he fell into a serious depression.

When I first started counseling him, I had to help him apply some of the basic principles he used in business to his personal life—managing time, delegating tasks, setting priorities. Finally, after three or four months of therapy, he came in and said, "I've made my decision. If this is what it costs to be successful in business, I'm not willing to pay the price." He now leaves the office at five o'clock every day so he can have time with his children before they go to bed. He made other decisions that will reduce his financial success in the long run. But when he weighed the tradeoff between money and his family, he was willing to sacrifice some monetary gain.

This man's family was important enough to him that he made decisions with them in mind. However, such shared values alone are not enough. It's also critical to be *actively* in touch with each other and with God on an issue that demands a critical decision. If one spouse is off making all of the big decisions without consulting his or her mate, there's bound to be anger and hostility (even if the decision is based on mutually shared values).

Prayer is also the key to good decision-making. But sometimes even when you've prayed and prayed, the two of you end up on opposite sides of the fence. At that point you need to seek the help of friends. You need the wisdom of people you respect. I have a son-in-law who quite often comes to me and says, "I need some of your wisdom on a matter." He knows another person can offer valuable perspective.

Keeping stress at bay is a lifelong task. That's why it's good to get in the habit of reviewing your goals with your spouse and making sure you are both operating from a common set of values. If you consult God for His perspective on your life, and you make critical decisions together, then the choices you make should create an atmosphere of intimacy rather than chaos.

Archibald Hart

1.17 IMPOSSIBLE-TO-PLEASE MATE

My wife is always complaining about our marriage. For example, she says things like, "We're not close enough" or "When's the last time we really talked about our relationship?" I think our marriage is just fine. Why is she is so dissatisfied?

It seems like marriage often unites two opposites. We're all familiar with the morning person who hooks up with a night owl. Or the neat freak that joins her life to a man who is overly comfortable with clutter.

Even if you don't realize it, you have a list of all the things you want and need out of marriage.

But there is one common difference between spouses that is rarely talked about—a couple's conflicting "maintenance requirements." Even if you don't realize it, you have a list of all the things you want and need out of marriage. Like the maintenance schedule in your car's owner's manual, your list describes what you expect to happen in order to feel that your marriage is running well.

Your mate has his or her own list, and it's certain to be different from yours. But beyond the particulars of what's on each list, the differences are complicated by how many items are included on them. One partner's list is always longer (we'll call that spouse "higher-maintenance"—and, contrary to popular myth, this is not always the wife), while his or her mate's list is much shorter (the "lower-maintenance" spouse).

If you don't take your maintenance differences into account, your relationship will suffer. This is what a couple sounds like when they don't handle each other's maintenance needs very effectively.

HIGHER: "Something's been bugging me about our marriage."

LOWER: "Really?" *(Here we go again!)*

HIGHER: "I wish we were, you know ... *closer.*"

LOWER: "I think we've already got a good marriage. Why can't you just be satisfied?"

HIGHER: "Our marriage is okay, but it could be a lot better. I can't pretend to be satisfied with things the way they are."

LOWER: "I think you expect too much."

HIGHER: "Well, you don't expect enough!"

Lower-maintenance spouses might conclude that their partners are too needy or are simply impossible to please. They sometimes interpret their mates' longer maintenance list as a sign of insecurity, and they may feel they're being pressured or scrutinized.

Higher-maintenance spouses react negatively, too. Being higher-maintenance myself, I used to think my wife didn't care as much about me as I did about her. It was easy to feel that no matter what I said or did, my needs weren't going to be met. Of course, she was equally frustrated. She felt that no matter what she said or did, it would never be enough for me.

> *It was easy to feel that no matter what I said or did, my needs weren't going to be met.*

Once you identify the problem as a difference in maintenance needs, how do you solve it? Begin by looking out for what some marriage experts call "hot thoughts"—thoughts that fuel conflict. It's easy to think of a lower-maintenance spouse as "insensitive" or "unresponsive." It's equally easy to see a higher-maintenance partner as "insecure" or "impossible to please." These interpretations, often inaccurate, can become "hot thoughts" that lead you to criticize your mate rather than dealing constructively with your differences.

Instead of assuming negative traits, think of your spouse's objectionable actions (or inaction) as being primarily a matter of maintenance requirements. For my wife and me, it seemed that every few months I'd get dissatisfied with some aspect of our marriage and we'd end up having "The Big Discussion." It seemed to me that she didn't care as much about our marriage as I did, and it seemed to her that I was just an over-critical husband. Once I realized it wasn't about how much she cared but that she was lower-maintenance than I am, and she realized that my dissatisfaction was simply my being higher-maintenance, we could both deal with our differences effectively.

If a husband's maintenance list is shorter, which explanation feels better: "He cares less about our marriage than I do" or "He needs less 'relational mainte-nance' than I do"? If your wife's maintenance needs are greater than your own, how would you prefer to view her words and actions: "There's just no pleasing her" or "She's just higher-maintenance than I am"? Something as simple as taking a nonjudgmental view of your spouse can open the door to better communication and more constructive attitudes.

Tim Sutherland

1.18 HANDLING SUBTLE PUT-DOWNS

My wife has a way of putting me down in subtle ways. Whenever I mention it to her, she says it's just my imagination. But I know it's more than that: there is a tone in her voice and certain phrases she uses that don't indicate acceptance. Is there any way I can help her realize what she's really communicating?

> *"When you say [or do] that, I feel as though you're cutting me down."*

Obviously if your wife is making you feel put-down, something is happening. Yet it could be that she doesn't mean what she's saying, or that she doesn't realize that she's saying it. The only way to deal with this problem is to face it directly and immediately when it happens. The next time your wife makes one of these comments, stop, and as calmly as possible say, "That's an example of what I've been talking about. When you say [or do] that, I feel as though you're cutting me down. And I want to understand what prompted it."

If it happens in public you may not be able to talk right then, but there should be a signal—a look you give her, a certain touch—that says, "That's what I'm talking about." And then as soon as you're alone you should talk about it.

People usually make critical comments because of one of three reasons. Sometimes there's a sense of competition that has developed between two people and when one of them feels the other is getting ahead, he or she responds with criticism aimed at knocking the other person down a peg or two.

A second circumstance that can give rise to criticism is when one spouse is unhappy or dissatisfied about something in the other person. Criticism can be one of the ways we attempt to chisel others into the people we want them to be (often trying to make them more like us).

The third reason is anger, which is usually prompted by pain, frustration or fear. It could just be that when your wife becomes angry (for whatever reason), she responds by aiming cutting remarks at those around her.

If after discussing a few specific situations you think you see a pattern, you might say, "When you say something like that I feel as if you're angry with me"; or "When you say something like that it makes me feel as if you want to change me into something I'm not."

If you can concentrate on how your wife's behavior makes you feel, she won't be as likely to get defensive. And if you can pinpoint and discuss a few of these incidents as soon as they happen, you both may be able to see what is motivating

Criticism can be one of the ways we attempt to chisel others into the people we want them to be.

them and correct the situation. Criticism can quickly become a habit. And it can eat away at the foundation of a relationship. The key to dealing with it is to face it immediately when it happens.

Jay Kesler

1.19 CURBING DISPARAGING REMARKS

When we were out with friends recently I unintentionally made a remark about my husband that he later told me was very upsetting. I was only joking, or so I thought. How can I prevent this from happening again?

To keep myself from falling into the trap you're describing, I judge any potential "joking remark" by a few criteria:

Would I make this remark about someone who wasn't my spouse? Amazingly, most of us treat others—even total strangers—with more respect, courtesy and sensitivity than we accord our life partners.

Regardless of my intention, could this remark hurt or embarrass my husband? One person's harmless joke can come across as a cruel put-down to another.

Will this remark diminish others' opinion of my mate or make him or her look silly? We owe it to our spouses to help others see their good points.

And whether you're alone with your mate or in the company of others, here's the final step toward mastering the art of encouragement and avoiding put-downs: *look for opportunities to build up your spouse.* Keep asking yourself, "Is there a supportive or encouraging remark I can make about my spouse right now?" It doesn't need to be anything fancy, just simple, honest affirmation:

"Jan just redecorated the baby's room, and it looks really professional." Or "I was so tired after work the other night when Tom volunteered to do the laundry, I felt like I'd just won a Caribbean cruise!"

Alicia Howe

1.20 AFFIRMING A SPOUSE'S DREAMS

My husband has always dreamed of living in the country and operating a small farm. He thinks now is the time to make the dream a reality. But frankly, I'm worried that making such a move at this time will ruin us financially. How can I support his dreams and yet help him balance those dreams with reality?

First, *it is important to affirm without inflating.* As I listen to such visionaries in counseling, I hear a common theme emerging: the need to prove something to somebody—to show parents, family, friends or self that he is special. Interestingly, we've seen quests launched by both negative and positive input. The most common source is the message that says, "You'll never make it." And what a myriad of shapes that takes! The dreamer-errant might hear the echo of a too-perfectionistic father snarling, "Can't you do anything right? Here, let me do it!" Or a stressed-out mother: "I wish you'd never been born."

We're amazed at how often that sad song is joined by a teacher who humiliated a fragile child: "Well, students, look what Jenny did. I don't want anyone else being so stupid." Short stature, freckles, learning disorders—any large or small deviation from some imagined ideal—can contribute to the child's shaky self-esteem. This etches the damaged self-concept on the child's soul: *I'm not okay.* And he may spend his life proving to the teacher or a coach or neighborhood bully that he *is* okay.

On the other hand, too much affirmation is equally risky. Many visionaries battle their way through life against the challenge of unlimited potential. The message they received sounds benign enough: "You can do anything you want to do!" Sounds great!

The problems with that statement are twofold. The first is that "doing anything" becomes equated with stardom. It's not enough to enjoy a vigorous game of tennis—you will be Wimbledon champion! Not only will you be accepted into college, you will lead your class at Yale *and* join a think-tank upon graduation.

The second problem with the unlimited-potential idea is that it's just not true. Not everyone can do everything, and that's all right. But to the dreamer hooked by the message of being capable of anything, it's *not* all right. Somewhere out there beckons the impossible dream, and achieving it will prove that he *can* do anything. But alas, "anything" is a constantly moving target.

So how can you help a person driven by that compulsive need to prove his worth? Affirm him—but don't inflate his expectations. Don't perpetuate either lie ("you're not okay" or "absolutely anything is possible"). Offer specific praise. And don't forget a simple "you're special to me" or "I love you."

Second, the spouse of the dreamer has to help the visionary *maintain a hold on reality.* This can best be done with penetrating "search talk"—mostly questions and comments that help a person sort something out for himself. And don't forget its companion, sensitive listening.

One of the first lessons counselors learn is not to give any answers that you can help a person to find for himself. Besides, offering solutions doesn't usually work: When a person is not ready to ask the right questions, answers are ignored. So it's much more pragmatic and satisfying to help him in the quest for the questions. That takes search talk.

When a person is not ready to ask the right questions, answers are ignored.

"Tell me more about this new adventure." Then I would try to listen carefully—even between the lines. I would try to hear the details, discover the omitted facts. I would ask about potential pitfalls: "What do you see as the obstacles? How can you investigate the need for a computerized page turner, or the history of these sorts of ventures?"

Stop yourself from making statements disguised as questions: "You don't really believe that would work, do you?" Put your own ideas on hold at this stage. Often enough, the questions alone can redirect your spouse's energy toward more constructive, well-conceived goals.

Patience is critical to this process. *Don't* throw a wet blanket on the dream immediately. Such a negative response may fuel your husband's need to prove himself. It may kick his quest into overdrive—just what you don't want to have happen!

Notice something else: the listener has not uttered one word of criticism during this conversation. He or she *has* challenged the visionary with some reality testing. And it may surprise you how often that gentle nudge will cool the visionary fires.

The first step is *not* for you to confront the dreamer and say, "Get real!" Rather, you need to identify to yourself what your concerns are. Asking an outside party to help clarify your feelings would be useful. Is your own childhood experience creating unreasonable fears? How do your expectations (which heretofore may not have been well articulated) influence your thinking? What values do you hold most dear? You need to see if any of *your* attitudes (for instance, reflexive predictions of failure) contribute to your mate's pattern of behavior. When you are confident that you understand your own feelings and opinions, take them to the dreamer.

There may come a time when the kindest thing you can say to your dreamy spouse is "Enough!" In other words, you need to *set limits*. These limits need to be laid down in as clear and unemotional language as possible. You might say, "There are some very important things I need to say because our relationship is the most important thing in the world to me. I have carefully considered your latest idea, and I know how excited you are. My problem is that I'm just too tired to go into it at this time. I see the costs and the risks—and I'm frightened. I don't like the odds and I don't have the energy to see you take those risks."
Louis McBurney, M.D.

1.21 FINDING THE PERFECT GIFT (WITHOUT MIND-READING)

I'm embarrassed to admit this but even though I love my wife very much, I'm often stumped about what to get her for anniversaries or birthdays. She's offended when I ask her for specific ideas or a list. Since I can't read her mind, I can't win! How can I figure out what my wife really wants when it comes to gift-giving time?

Try asking each other the following questions to talk together about your expectations when it comes to Christmas, birthdays and your wedding anniversary.

- What was the best gift you ever received? What made it so great?
- What was the most disappointing gift anyone ever gave you? Why was it so awful?

- When you were growing up, what was gift giving like in your family? Did birthdays differ significantly from Christmas? Did you receive one present or many? Were the gifts homemade or purchased, costly or inexpensive?
- In your view, what makes an ideal gift? Does it fit into any particular category, such as personal items, work-related gifts or hobby-related items?
- When our anniversary approaches, what do you hope for?
- What are the other occasions during the year (besides your birthday, our anniversary and Christmas) when you would like to receive a gift?
- If I only had ten dollars to spend, what type of gift would you like me to give you?

Eileen Silva Kindig

1.22 ASKING A SPOUSE TO CHANGE

I'd really like my wife to pay more attention to her appearance—it has slid a bit now that we have kids and she's running a carpool rather than heading to the office each day. However, I hesitate to say anything because I don't want to hurt her feelings. How can I best communicate that I'd like to see her make some changes?

While we advocate change in marriage, we realize there are many inappropriate and even damaging ways to try to bring about change. Note the differences between the inappropriate comments and the more positive, helpful statements that follow.

Inappropriate: "You always think it's my fault." This statement demonstrates the danger of over generalizing. Using words like "always" or "never" is unlikely to characterize the situation accurately.

Better: "Sometimes when we argue I get the feeling that it's all my fault. I'm sure I'm misreading you, but I need to know how you feel about that."

Inappropriate: "Stop being such a slob at the table." This is a command, and we can't bring about changes in our spouse by commanding him or her.

We can't bring about changes in our spouse by commanding him or her.

More constructive: "You're not a messy person, but people might get that impression when they watch you eat. Could I make a few suggestions?"

Inappropriate: "You ought to be more careful when you're driving." This declaration comes across as moralizing. We all tend to get defensive when someone tells us we "ought" to do something.

Instead, try expressing emotion: "When you drive this fast, I get very uncomfortable. It would really help me enjoy the ride if you would drive more slowly."

Inappropriate: "You're so dumb when it come to money matters." Because this comment ridicules, the response is not likely to be: "Gee, you're right. I'd better sharpen my financial skills."

Better: "I'm concerned about the way we handle our money. Let's talk about it."

Inappropriate: "You shouldn't feel that way." Such a statement creates feelings of guilt or inadequacy about the emotions someone is experiencing. Even if anger, frustration or disappointment is not the most appropriate reaction to a situation, you can't stop feeling that way simply because someone tells you it's wrong.

More constructive: "Why do you think you feel that way? What can I do to help?"

Open-ended, positive statements lay the basis for constructive change.

Each of the five negative statements is badly put, but they may actually identify a situation in which change is needed. When that is the case, open-ended, positive statements lay the basis for constructive change. Without accusing or threatening, they show concern, sensitivity and a willingness to help. And those are the characteristics of gentle and effective persuasion, no matter what type of change is needed.

Jeanette C. and Robert H. Lauer

1.23 BEING OPEN ABOUT PROBLEMS

I come from a family of "talkers" who can easily open up about anything, but my husband is just the opposite. His idea of dealing with a problem is to keep it to himself.

He says he doesn't want to trouble me with his problems. His reluctance to talk hurts me, and I know it's not healthy for my husband to keep all these things inside. I want to work out our differences before it gets any worse. Do you have any suggestions?

The two of you need to find some middle ground. It's true that your husband needs to communicate more. But since you've brought up the subject already, I'd suggest you not continue to confront it head-on. Rather, try to create an atmosphere in which it will be easier for him to open up. Males learn early on that it's not safe to talk about feelings; there is danger in exposure. So a wife needs to help break down this fear by assuring her husband, "Around here, you won't be considered weak if you ask for help with your problems."

One way to create this atmosphere is to set aside time when you can both unwind and talk about your day. It might be at night before you go to sleep, or right after you come home from work.

I can identify with your husband's approach. By nature I tend to avoid burdening my wife with the things that happen to me during the day; when I come home I want to escape those things. Yet I've learned she *does* want to share my burden, and she wants to hear even the things I think are trivial.

Another way my wife helped me was to share her own problems and ask for my perspective. In a sense she modeled what it is to share one another's burdens by asking me to share hers, and letting me see that it made me feel needed and wanted, not burdened.

It may also help if your husband can see from other men that it's all right to talk about problems. This often happens at couples' retreats, marriage seminars, or in a Sunday school class that focuses on communication. If any of these opportunities are available to you, you might suggest that it would be fun to attend. Men often find a new freedom in expressing themselves with their wives when they hear other men sharing how they learned to be more open. But this kind of intimate communication is a gradual, learned thing, so be patient.

Jay Kesler

This kind of intimate communication is a gradual, learned thing, so be patient.

1.24 TALKING AT DIFFERENT LEVELS OF INTIMACY

When we were dating, we talked about anything and everything with such ease. I felt like we really connected. Now, after a few years of marriage, it seems like that most of the time when we talk, we're communicating on different wavelengths. Why can't we talk as openly and deeply as we once did?

Once a couple gets married they tend to talk on different levels. The wife tells how she feels about something, while her husband offers solutions. The wife wants to relate, but her husband wants to solve the problem. This can be confusing to the woman, since they didn't relate this way when they were dating. Back then they would sit in front of her dorm for hours and just talk. She saw him as a wonderful conversationalist. He seemed to talk just for the sake of talking.

In reality, he was trying to win her heart, and he knew that meant relating to her. He was working hard to "make the sale"—to win her hand in marriage. But once that goal was accomplished, he couldn't see why they still needed to sit and talk for hours. After all, "the sale" had already been made.

Problems arise when spouses talk to each other at different levels of intimacy. The husband might be talking about how the food tasted at the restaurant and how it was a great meal at a great price. But his wife is talking about how she felt at the restaurant and the fact that it was so loud they didn't have a good chance to talk. She didn't feel it was much of a date. He thought it was a great time.

Communication between spouses can be broken down into three levels. To have a growing and fulfilling marriage, a couple needs to develop the skills of "Level Three" communication. But many people, primarily husbands, begin the process at the first level.

Level One: The Grunt Level. The shallowest level of communication involves an obligatory response to make verbal contact with another person. For example, you pass a person in the hall at work and offer the obligatory, "Hi! How ya doing?" But you don't really listen for that person's response.

Think what would happen if, instead of the customary response of "Fine," the person said, "I'm nearly suicidal." We'd never hear them! We're so accustomed to this "grunt-level" communication that we'd probably respond with, "That's great! Good to see you." Then we'd walk on down the hall. Sadly, many couples approach each other at this level. They say the required things but never really listen to one another. If this goes on for too long, they won't even know each other anymore.

Level Two: The Journalist Level. One step above grunt-level communication is the Journalist Level. When talking with his spouse, the Journalist can easily express his opinions. Unfortunately, he rarely talks about anything other than fact and his opinions about those facts. Stating an opinion and sticking to it protects him from having to talk at a deeper level.

Once I was talking to a couple in my counseling office. The wife said that after seven years of marriage, she still didn't know much about her husband. "I know his opinions about other people, politics, the church, just about everything," she said. "But it stops there. I don't really know who he is."

Her husband responded with an interesting comment. "I guess I thought that having an opinion would mean I wouldn't have to discuss the subject at hand," he said. "It was as if I was saying, 'There's my opinion! Now we can move on to other things since this is so black and white to me.'"

Men generally know how to state the facts as they see them, but they don't know how to go any deeper. Often the Journalist uses opinions as a guard to keep from having to communicate at an intimate level. In contrast, most women are comfortable moving on to the next level of communication.

I can remember my wife saying to me, "Could we just sit out on the porch and talk tonight?" My response was, "What do you want to talk about?" I wanted to get my opinions ready. But then she baffled me by saying, "I don't want to talk about anything in particular; I just want to talk."

She just wanted to share feelings with me. But I couldn't see how you could talk about feelings and ever know when you reached the end of the conversation. At least when a person offers a solution to a problem, you know you're finished.

Level Three: The Feelings Level. A couple reaches this level when each spouse feels safe enough to share areas of weakness or feelings that may put him or her in a bad light.

About four years into our marriage, my wife and I were sitting in a restaurant talking about how we differ in our opinions of what it means to be romantic. "You think romance is a preamble to sex," she said. "It wouldn't be romantic to you if we didn't make love somewhere in close proximity to a time of romance."

As we continued to talk about our differences, I also learned that it's okay to say I don't know how to do something.

My basic response was, "You mean it's not?" As we continued to talk about our differences, I also learned that it's okay to say I don't know how to do something and then ask for my wife's help. Up to that point, I had been so insecure that I found it difficult to admit weakness.

Taking the step of freely discussing your feelings is risky. You never know what the other person will say or do in response. But it's still a risk well worth taking.

Think of it as a long bridge that stands between communicating at the level of opinions and communicating at a much deeper level by freely sharing your feelings. In many marriages one person is sitting on the other side of that bridge waiting for a spouse to cross over. Until that bridge is crossed, those two spouses will continue to be very lonely people.

Robert and Rosemary Barnes

CHAPTER 2

WORKING
THROUGH
CONFLICT

WORKING
THROUGH
CONFLICT

"Anger," wrote C. S. Lewis, "is the fluid that love bleeds when you cut it" (*Letters to Malcolm: Chiefly on Prayer*, p. 97). How true! Time and time again, the sparks of romance can erupt into flames of discord and loving words into sharp barbs.

Our failure to obey God's Word in thought, word, and deed lies at the heart of most marital skirmishes. We still wrestle with our old nature (cf. Rm. 7:14-25). James 4:1 says wars and fights come from the cravings that are at war within us. We were made to give ourselves to God and to each other, not to evil or ourselves. We quarrel when we don't get the things we want (Jms. 4:2). Frustration mounts when we look to others for things that only God can provide. When our needs are unmet, we are "cut" as Lewis described it. And when we do ask God, it's often with wrong motives, seeking our pleasure before God's or our spouse's. So what can we do?

James gives the perfect remedy (Jms. 4:7-10): Submit to God and keep his will number one in your life. Resist the devil—deflect the fiery darts with the "shield of faith" (Eph. 6:16), and draw near to God—remain in Christ and allow His word to grow in your heart (Col. 3:16).

Finally, confess sin—wash and purify, grieve and mourn, humble yourself before the Lord. Marriage uncovers sin and selfishness. If we do not repent before God, we will not confess our sins to our spouses. But our ongoing commitment to confess sin and offer forgiveness will grant peace, grace, and harmony.

Marriage is to reflect the relationship of Christ and his church (Eph. 5:31-33), and that involves the peace and reconciliation that we have in Christ. If our relationship with God is not in order, we cannot expect our marriages to be. "You cannot get second things by putting them first; you can get second things only by putting first things first" (C. S. Lewis, *God in the Dock*, "First and Second Things," p. 281). As conflicts arise we must not let the sun go down on our anger, but "speaking the truth in love" we must be kind, tenderhearted, forgiving each other just as in Christ God has forgiven us (Eph. 4:15, 26, 32). Proverbs 17:14 likens starting a quarrel to breaching a dam (releasing water), so hold off so you both don't get washed away. It is a mark of honor to avoid a fight (Pr. 15:18, NLT), but loving a quarrel is sin (Pr. 17:19). Our anger does not bring about the righteous life that God desires (Jms. 1:20). Rather, people need to see God's grace and righteousness reflected in our marriage.

> *Prayer: Lord, my anger does not achieve the righteous life that You desire (Jms. 1:20). Help me to be a peacemaker (Mt. 5:9). Give me strength to make every effort to do what leads to peace and mutual edification (Rm. 14:9). Give me grace to confess my sins and forgive others. May my answers be gentle (Pr. 15:1), and my memory of a wrong suffered short (1 Co. 13:5). May our marriage reflect your grace to the world. Amen.*

2.1 FIGHTING FAIR

Last night my wife and I got into an argument about the kids' bedtime routines. Before I knew it, we were trading barbs and far from reaching any resolution. When we disagree, how can we make sure we fight fair?

Here are a few scripturally based ground rules for marital battles:

Commit yourselves to honesty and mutual respect. At the altar we made certain vows. But have we committed ourselves, verbally and honestly in our souls, to being authentic and honest with our partners—viewing them with respect? This should start during the courtship phase. Couples need to say to each other, "I want to be honest with you; and I want you to be honest with me. I can take it, and I will give it back with tact."

※

**Lay down
your deadly
weapons.**

Lay down your deadly weapons. There's anger, and then there's anger. A temper that slips out of control is sinful. So is anger expressed in profanity. Anger that means to hurt is sin. One man bitterly told me that his father-in-law once announced, "I never did have much use for you!" He will never forget that statement. Never. That man used a deadly weapon on his son-in-law. So did the mate who cracked, "No wonder you have a brother in a mental hospital." A mate may later say, "I forgive you," but deep inside such words will not be forgotten. Deadly weapons crush the inner spirit that is so much a part of marriage.

Agree that the time is right. Couples should be sure that both partners sense when to talk. There are times to disagree, and there are times not to disagree. If we have the first rule down, we can be honest enough to say, "Let's talk a little later when the children are down." And when you say that, keep your appointment.

Frequently, couples have battle flags they wave when they need to talk. A husband may become very quiet. A wife may talk rapidly on the phone to her spouse and hang up almost before he's through. Learn to recognize these flags; don't let them pass unheeded.

After you take a verbal swing, be ready with a solution. An elder in a church I pastored used to say, "I won't listen to any criticism in this church if a person doesn't offer, along with the criticism, a suggestion on how we might correct the problem." Not a bad idea! When you come to your mate with justified criticism, be quick with a suggested solution. Criticism hurts. A positive, supportive comment will help take some of the sting out of the wound. Remember: condemnation without hope crushes.

Watch your words and guard your tone. In brief, use tact. The louder our voices, the less our mate will hear; the uglier the words, the less we will communicate. Paul says in Ephesians 4:29, "No rotten talk should come from your mouth." Tact is the bond that undergirds a relationship of mutual respect and it does wonders when it comes to removing a defensive spirit.

※

**Watch your
words and
guard your tone.**

Don't bring things up in public. There are at least two ways you can do this in a marriage: boldly embarrassing your spouse, or using subtle sarcasm. In a church I served many years ago, a husband was having a great deal of difficulty with his strong-willed wife. As a result, he became increasingly strong-willed as well, and their home turned into a powder keg. One Sunday morning I spoke on living the Christian life at home, and he came up to me after church. The vestibule was jammed with people, but he shared privately the overflow of his hurt. Quietly he admitted to me, "I have caused havoc in our home this week. I confess that in my rage I swore at her the other day. I'm embarrassed to admit our home is a wreck. Why, just last Tuesday I was ready to walk..."

About that time his wife came up. She hadn't heard his contrite confession, only the last part. She said, "It's because of your *black heart* that our home is a wreck!" The vestibule hushed; she sliced away at him for all to hear. He was devastated. Publicly proclaiming resentment only drives the resentment deeper.

When it's all over, help clean up the mess. Paul again: "And be kind and compassionate to one another, forgiving one another, just as God also forgave you in Christ" (Eph. 4:32). At the heart of the word "kindness" is grace. Be gracious enough to wipe it off the mental slate. At the heart of tenderness is compassion. Be compassionate enough to weep with the one who's hurt from the fight. And at the heart of forgiveness is the very person of Jesus Christ who forgave you.

Charles R. Swindoll

2.2 A SPOUSE WHO YELLS

My wife is a loud person. Even though I love her dearly, I wish she'd find a different way to express her anger. When she gets mad, the entire neighborhood must know and that's embarrassing. Should I adjust to her style or encourage her to change?

We've all seen it. Disorderly people marry neatniks and larks marry night owls. But a more common, and potentially more troublesome, union is the loud and the laid back.

> *Disorderly people marry neatniks and larks marry night owls.*

I'm talking about spouses who inflict noise on their soft-spoken counterparts. While yelling doesn't necessarily mean a marriage is on the rocks, it does require a high level of understanding on the part of both spouses. I asked several couples how they deal with the volume difference in their communication styles, and here's what they told me.

Remember that loudness is not a sin. In most cases, it's a cultural or ethnic trait. Some families relate to each other at high volume. A 75-year-old husband, married 55 years, told me, "The biggest adjustment I had to make in marriage was learning to tolerate how loud she gets when she's upset. I come from a very low-key family. When her folks got together, everyone shouted at each other."

When asked why he was initially attracted to his wife, this elderly gentleman beamed and said, "She's so vivacious. I'm shy and was always ill at ease socially. She can be standing in a line of strangers and will start chatting." He came to understand that the vivacity he loved had its volatile side.

Don't try to change your screamer. The screamers agreed that when their mates show disapproval by flight ("I'll come back when you are in control of yourself") or by telling them to "take it easy," it only makes things worse, which brings us to the corollary:

Work on yourself, not on your spouse. A 50-year-old wife said it well: "The first ten years of our marriage, I tried to change him. I learned that I had to change my reactions to his yelling instead. I can't worry about what other people think."

Keep your sense of humor. Realize that some of these outbursts will become the stuff of family legend. A 35-year-old woman and her husband laughed while telling me about a loud argument that they got into when they were getting their marriage license.

Acknowledge your spouse's anger—and his or her right to it. "Once my wife was on a tirade about a lot of things that ruined her day," said a 24-year-old husband. "One of the big things was I forgot to pick up the cleaning. I was defensive and began interrupting her to explain myself. Finally, totally exasperated, she yelled, 'Will you quit? I'm not asking you to make it right. I just want you to sympathize.' "

Surprise the
screamer.

Surprise the screamer. When one woman yelled in anger, her husband responded, "I love you."

"It totally disarmed me," she said. "I know that to him, I was at my most unlovable then. That he could muster his love, and verbalize it, stunned me."

Finally, the couples agreed on the most important advice in coping with screaming: *Refuse to let it shut you down.* "Even screaming is communication," said one spouse, "and without communication your marriage is dead."

Carol DeChant

2.3 HIDING FROM CONFLICT

We seemed so compatible during our courtship and yet now we're married and having arguments. I want to avoid conflict if at all possible but my husband says a fight every now and then is normal. Who is right?

When we were first married, I was frightened by discord. It was easier for me to try to work things out internally, instead of expressing my feelings. But it wasn't long before I realized that disagreements often erupted before I had time to bite my tongue.

One early argument my husband and I had began with a seemingly innocent question: "Why do these barbecued hamburgers look like briquettes?" Other quarrels erupted over dirty clothes hung on doorknobs or differing tastes in furniture.

I have found that my early marriage experience was not unusual. Newly married couples often try to avoid conflict, thinking it will damage their relationship. But the truth is, not dealing effectively with conflict can damage a marriage. The good news: Dealing properly with conflict will make your marriage stronger.

Most of us, through experience, eventually learn what works and what doesn't. But when a couple relies on the trial-and-error method, it might take years before they hit upon an approach that works well most or all of the time.

"Arguing is a normal reaction while trying to get into sync with a spouse," says Sherod Miller, president of Interpersonal Communication Programs, Inc., in Littleton, Colorado. "Early in marriage, a couple typically shifts from a visionary to an adversarial stage of their relationship. During the visionary phase, partners optimistically focus on their dreams and possibilities. In general, they view their answer in life as resting in the other person, and disregard their fiancée's or new mate's shortcomings, assuming things will change. Or the differences in character may be viewed as a complement to one's own weaknesses.

"But typically after the wedding, a couple finds that traits or habits they once ignored are no longer easy to overlook. Thus the partnership leaves the visionary stage and enters a stage where those shortcomings cause friction. If the differences aren't confronted, they create an unhealthy adversarial atmosphere.

"To avoid dormancy or marriage failure, the friction issues must be confront-ed, communicated and resolved," Miller says. "Couples need to embrace their differences and use them constructively to strengthen their relationships."

Marriages go downhill after too many compromises where neither partner feels satisfied.

David Augsburger, author of *Sustaining Love: Healing and Growth in the Passages of Marriage* (Regal), warns against settling for mere compromise as a solution to a couple's differences. He says that too many arguments are ended without really being resolved. Augsburger offers a different perspective on compromise:

"Couples need to prize each other's point of view—to see it as mutually important," he suggests. "Typically our western culture approaches conflict resolution from a thought pattern of compromise. But marriages go downhill after too many compromises where neither partner feels satisfied.

"The correct solution is to assemble a creative alternative together. Thus both partners come out winning."

Paige Jaeger

2.4 MAKING WISE DECISIONS

In the coming month we have to make two significant decisions about career choices. We've danced around the matter a few times but haven't had any real heart-to-heart discussions about the pros and cons of the options. I think what stops us is the fear that we'll disagree on some points. The deadline for a decision is fast approaching! What are some good guidelines to keep in mind when we struggle with decision making?

Making decisions as a team is a difficult but necessary part of married life. Here are some suggested ways you can successfully work through the decision-making process and come out on the other side confident you made the right choice.

Be willing to listen to your spouse. I can speak from experience. I'm much more willing to consider my husband's point of view when I feel he's "heard" mine.

Be direct about what you want. "Sometimes you may have to go along with a decision you don't like," says family counselor Nancy Lenz, "because that's the way life is. But at least you'll have had an opportunity to express your feelings." If one partner suppresses his or her feelings, he or she is more likely to unconsciously sabotage the decision later on.

Learn to brainstorm. "It's important to get away from black-and-white thinking," says Lenz. "Sometimes there's more than one way to solve a problem. Generate a list of possible solutions, no matter how off the wall, without evaluating them initially."

Learn to brainstorm.

My husband and I followed this principle and eliminated a weekly decision/argument over whose turn it was to clean the house. We hired a cleaning service.

Define the decision. "Decide what you want to accomplish with the decision, gather the information you need, identify the alternatives and figure out what the outcome of each alternative might be," suggests Lenz.

I would add: *Make a list of pros and cons.* In one marriage I know the husband and wife each write down a separate list of pros and cons and weigh them before discussing them jointly. That way they each get a chance to get their own thoughts on the table before being influenced by the other person.

Understand your own decision-making style, and accept your spouse's. Before you and your spouse can make changes in the way you make decisions, you need to understand your respective decision-making styles. Individually ask yourselves: Do you like to sit down with all the facts and make a decision without any dillydallying? Do you prefer to float a trial balloon and then let a decision percolate for a few weeks? Are your decisions colored more by feelings or "logic"? Are you a researcher or an on-the-spot decision-maker? If your style differs from your spouse's, try to recognize that one way isn't better than another.

Be willing to use outside resources if necessary. The resources you need may differ according to the decision at hand. It could be a consumer magazine, a plumber, a pastor, or a parent who can offer you the benefit of his or her experience. For one couple, who shares similar values and rarely have serious disagreements, their frustration over an extremely bright child who was having problems in school made them realize they needed to consult a counselor. The decisions they had to make were still difficult, but less so because they didn't have to go it alone.

Treat your spouse with respect. "My wife and I have noticed that in many families, acquaintances often get better treatment than family members," observes one husband. "We don't like that and try not to do it. You have to respect each other's expertise, just as you would with a business consultant."

> *Treat your spouse with respect.*

Learn from the example of others. My husband and I prevented a lot of arguments over money by following the example of another couple. Because the husband was a spendthrift and the wife was a miser, they decided that after paying their bills they would divide whatever was left over into "his" and "her" money—to spend or save as each decided individually. It worked for them and, so far, it's working for us.

Wait for the right moment to discuss decisions. "Sometimes there are things I know need to be talked about with my husband," says one wife, "but I wait for the right time and place. When our son was in college, it was an eight-hour drive to visit him. We used the time to talk about things. It worked very well because we both felt relaxed and without pressure."

Celebrate the decisions that have good outcomes. One of the benefits of making joint decisions is the fact that no one person has to take the blame when the outcome isn't good. And you both get to celebrate when it is!

Remember the power of prayer. My husband and I don't pray over every decision. But there have been some memorable ones when we've received real guidance. Moreover, we've found it difficult to be mad at each other over decisions we've prayed about together.

> *Remember the power of prayer.*

However, most helpful is the example of an older married couple whose advice about the right attitude is critical to joint decision-making. "In business, you negotiate with the attitude, 'How do I get what I want?' " says the husband, an executive at a major national firm. "I don't think that belongs in a family situation. I really care a lot about my wife and I want her to be happy. She wants me to be happy. Neither of us is trying to win. That's the basis for going into these things."

Janis Long Harris

2.5 WEEKEND BICKERING

We often feel so crunched for time that we jam-pack our weekends with activities and chores. The final result isn't a checked off "to do" list but instead two stressed out, quarrelsome people. I'm beginning to dread the weekends. What can we do to prevent these weekend blow-ups?

Experience has taught my wife and me how to prevent weekend grumpiness from setting in.

First, hold a pre-Saturday summit conference. Almost every Friday now, my wife and I sit down and say, "What are your expectations for tomorrow?" (Yes, we actually use the E-word.) At a recent meeting, my wife's list went something like this: make dessert for Sunday's company, move the patio furniture into the shed, write the family newsletter, shop, spend time with the kids, stuff the visitors' brochures for church.

Then it was my turn. I wanted to say, "Sleep in and live the life of a Roman emperor (all grapes peeled, please)," but instead I offered, "Relax, spend time together, make the new sign for the Sunday school classes, and, gulp, rake some leaves."

With that on the table, we can start negotiating the list down to a manageable size.

Next, don't promise the moon and stars. Promises set expectations in cement. So we've learned to say, "This is what I hope to do," or "I'll try to work on that."

When, for example, my wife asks, "Will you have time to fix the swing set?" I offer only, "It's on my list." I don't mention that it's Project #369. Likewise, I never give an estimated completion time for a weekend chore. The "easy, ten-minute job" is a myth fostered by hardware store commercials.

Finally, make time for pampering each other. I have overheard more than one wife say, "Men are such babies when they get sick." Hey, if the diaper fits, wear it. Some weekends I am sick of having rushed all week, and I could use some pampering. Of course, my wife could likewise use some TLC after serving as full-time mom, caretaker, and referee all week. So we have learned to try to give each person some relaxing time.

For my wife, this means browsing around at garage sales. My role is to watch the kids and then praise her for finding the bargain of the modern era. I rejuvenate through reading without interruption.

Also, make romance a priority. It's tough, during the week, to find time to really talk, linger and look in each other's eyes. So on Saturday's list, if something's cut, it isn't that. This means that some springs we still have leaves in our yard from the previous fall. But at least we're not as grumpy about it.

Kevin A. Miller

2.6 HANDLING ANGER SENSIBLY

I'll admit it—I'm lousy when it comes to expressing anger. More often than not, I allow my emotions to be ruled by what I'm feeling and I know that's not good for my marriage. What are some constructive ways to handle my anger?

Many couples think conflict *creates* trouble in marriage. But that's not true. Husbands and wives may find conflict to be a source of creative change that brings them closer together, or it may lead to the destruction of their love and commitment. One of the deciding factors is the way they handle their anger toward each other.

Solving problems in marriage requires energy and creativity. And nothing blocks our ability to be creative like the stress that comes from anger. The angrier we get, the less chance we have for coming out with a workable solution for the issue we face. How then can we deal constructively with anger in marriage?

See anger as a powerful tool for truth. When Jesus overturned the tables and drove the money changers out of the temple, his goal was not to get the anger out of his system so he would feel better. Instead, he was using his righteous anger to communicate to the temple authorities a message from God. When anger is used to confront the problems in a relationship, it can be a constructive force. When it is used to exalt oneself and humiliate the other, it destroys.

> *See anger as a powerful tool for truth.*

Learn to accept grace from each other. Spouses troubled with anger need to ask themselves: "Am I trying to work things out with my spouse, or am I trying to prove that I am a wonderful (right, long-suffering, mistreated) husband or wife?" If you are trying to prove something, anger is being used to bolster your self-esteem rather than to restore the relationship.

> *Learn to accept grace from each other.*

When anger is tied to self-esteem, we have not taken to heart the good news of the gospel. I don't have to be perfect to be loved by God. (Just check out Romans 5:8.) This is also true in marriage. If our spouse loves us, he or she will love us when we are wrong and imperfect. We need to learn to accept this love.

Learn new skills for handling angry feelings. The ability to share ourselves and listen to one another could very well be the most important skills we can use in handling anger. They are also the most difficult.

It is hard to risk sharing thoughts and feelings when we are angry. It is much easier to lash out at or blame the other. It is hard to say, "I am angry because I was running late this morning and you left me the car without any gas. I just filled it up the day before yesterday, and I was counting my time to the last second."

Another skill that can be useful in handling anger, particularly if couples struggle with wanting to win, is postponing talking about it. This does not mean long, cold silences; it means deciding together to talk about it when we have both calmed down. We need to think about what the problem really is and think through ways we can talk about it.

In preparing to express our anger, we also need to go back through the source of our anger. First, what is the actual event that set off our anger? Let's say it was the fact that our spouse was *talking* with a certain person. It was not that he or she was *flirting* with a certain person. "Flirting" is the *interpretation* one gives to the actual event.

Second, look at our interpretation of the event. What other possible interpretations could be given? It helps to keep in mind that we are angry not only because something has happened, but also because of what we thought about what happened. We should remember that our thoughts are not foolproof.

Third, we need to reflect on what is going on in our *own bodies*. Are we under stress from other relationships? Are we tired? Are we worried about something else? Are we hungry? Are we using anger toward our spouse as a channel for other tension?

We should pray continually about our anger. We need to ask God's help in taking seriously the problems that face us as couples. We also should ask for help in being loving and mindful of our partner's needs.

Diana and David Garland

2.7 PEACEFULLY WORKING THROUGH DIFFERENCES

Even when I want to peacefully work through a disagreement, I seem to come unglued. Despite my best intentions, I usually make a mess of things and we both end up angry and frustrated. What prevents us from peacefully working through a disagreement?

Consider each factor individually. At least four factors get in the way of a couple calmly working on creative changes that will make their lives easier. Those factors include power issues, the feeling of being unloved, conflicting values, and differing levels of willingness to express deeply held feelings. Let's consider each factor individually.

Playing the power game. When a couple discusses clean kitchens and where to store unfinished projects, they are often talking about how much power each has over the other. For example, a spouse who says, "If you cook, I'll clean the kitchen later" may be giving the message, "I'll clean the kitchen when I feel like it. I will not give you the power to make me feel bad for not helping with dinner." The spouse with the unfinished project may be saying, "You are in control of most of our life together, but there are still corners of my life over which you have no power."

We often feel angry when a spouse's actions make us feel robbed of control over our own lives. By spending too long in the shower, for instance, one spouse can keep the other from having enough hot water for a bath. Or by leaving the scissors in a strange place, one spouse can keep the other hunting in exasperation for 30 minutes.

Do you really love me? When my spouse leaves the car with an empty gas tank, I not only feel a loss of power over my life—I had planned just enough time to get to work and now I'll be late—I may also feel unloved. As marriages become more troubled, spouses don't allow each other to make mistakes without thinking it says something about the marriage: "If you really cared about me, you wouldn't leave your clothes on the bathroom floor for me to pick up." Husbands and wives then get confused about what the issue is. Do we need to talk about picking up clothes in the bathroom, or whether we love each other?

Your values conflict with mine. Sometimes conflict derives from differences in a couple's basic values. One spouse believes in living each day to the fullest; the other wants to plan for tomorrow and save for a rainy day. Unless one simply gives in, they will have to face their conflict.

Sometimes conflict derives from differences in a couple's basic values.

These value differences often get wrapped up in how we coordinate our daily lives. Consequently, we can't seem to tackle one issue without pulling in all the rest. A simple disagreement about whether we should try to paint the house ourselves or hire a professional may involve: (1) our values about how money and time should be spent; (2) how we each think decisions ought to be made; (3) who "wins"; and (4) the degree to which we feel our spouse understands our feelings.

Verbal versus nonverbal partner. One spouse may want to share every thought and feeling every waking moment. The other may want to protect his or her privacy and search for ways to be alone. Unfortunately, it's sometimes hard for husbands and wives to see they are simply different from each other. Instead, they may think their conflict says something about whether they love each other. The sharing spouse feels unloved and shut out. The private spouse feels smothered. As the sharing spouse tries to move closer, the private spouse pulls away. Both may become increasingly frustrated and angry, which often leads to conflict.

Diana and David Garland

2.8 INTERFERING IN-LAWS

Sometimes I feel my in-laws are interfering with our family's affairs. I don't feel as if my wife supports me or gives my views priority when they conflict with her parents' views. Is there anything in the Bible dealing with in-laws?

Aside from the relationships between Ruth and Naomi (Ru. 1) and Moses and Jethro (Ex. 18), I don't know of a passage that directly advises us on in-law relationships. However, the Bible does provide a lot of principles regarding interpersonal relationships, which include contact with our in-laws.

There is a biblical admonition often included in the wedding ceremony: "For this cause a man shall leave his father and mother and cleave to his own wife." The implicit message is that the two people getting married need to become

"For this cause a man shall leave his father and mother and cleave to his own wife."

independent and develop their own lives. To the degree that parents interfere with that process, there is going to be conflict.

Despite the conflict, let me caution you to be careful about drawing too many lines on this issue or about jumping to conclusions about your wife's motivations. What is happening may be as much due to the difference in your families as to your wife's reluctance to be supportive of you. Many factors such as birth order and family style shape a person's relationship to his or her parents. Some people grow up never feeling as if they have to fight their parents to gain their own sense of identity and independence, while others, sometimes with good reason, spend their entire adolescence pushing to achieve their own sense of adulthood. While it could be that your in-laws are too interfering, it could also just seem that way to you because your wife has a different kind of relationship with her parents than you do with yours.

I've seen too many married men who have fallen into the trap of trying to make a loyalty test of this issue. Sometimes a guy will start making arbitrary (sometimes even wrong or stupid) decisions just to see if his wife will decide to be loyal to her parents. I've known other men who develop an antiphonal view of their in-laws—they do everything opposite, even if it goes against common sense.

I think the most practical thing you can do is keep a close watch on your attitude. Be willing to carefully evaluate your in-laws' feelings and opinions. Try to find the compelling logic, the sensible answer. That will do more to alter your wife's behavior than anything you say to her.

Jay Kesler

2.9 VOICING OPINIONS WITH DISCRETION

Last weekend my husband and I got into a heated disagreement over something as trivial as who would run to the hardware store. We both behaved in a less-than-Christian manner. We really want to resolve our differences and limit the number of angry words we exchange, but we don't seem to be getting anywhere. How can we express our frustrations and concerns in a way that doesn't tear the other person down?

While all couples argue from time to time, the tactics you use will make a significant difference in the outcome of working through a conflict. Below are several tips on how to voice your opinion, work through a disagreement, and still keep your marriage healthy.

While all couples argue from time to time, the tactics you use will make a significant difference in the outcome of working through a conflict.

State your perception of the problem in a non-accusatory manner. For instance, if your spouse forgets to call when he's planning to work late you might say, "When you don't call I feel worried and upset because I imagine how terrible it would be if something happened to you." Statements like these are less likely to put your mate on the defensive, and they get at the heart of why you're bothered.

Determine whether the problem is an offense or only a misunderstanding. Try to give the other the benefit of the doubt. In the example above, the tardy spouse might have a perfectly good explanation. Before you assume the worst and lay into your partner with accusations, hear him out. If he was stuck in traffic or had a flat tire, apologize for misreading the reason why he didn't call. On the other hand, if he was merely negligent, he should apologize.

Be open-minded to the possibility that you are wrong. Defensiveness is always destructive. Let your attitude be "Well, I may be wrong in this area. Let me tell you why I said what I did."

Don't dredge up past, forgiven offenses. Part of helping each other grow is to allow the other the freedom to make mistakes. If past offenses were forgiven, they must be forgotten.

Try to remain calm. Angry voices will only exacerbate the problem. Try to make it a point to say, "We've got a problem here. Let's take a moment to gather our thoughts, then sit down and talk it through." Likewise, if things get too hot, stop for a breather by saying, "I need a few minutes to get my thoughts together. I don't want to say something hurtful in anger."

Bring closure to the issue. To be honest, sometimes couples would rather stay mad for a while. That's okay. But don't leave the issue hanging, only to have it build up inside one or both of you. After a cooling-off period, make sure all is discussed until an agreement or a compromise is reached. Then ask yourselves, "What have we learned from all this? What can we do to prevent this from being a problem again?"

Dan Benson

2.10 ENDING RECURRING ARGUMENTS

We've been married nine years and there are certain problems that we still can't fully resolve. We sure try, but we never get anywhere and end up having the same old arguments. The cycle is extremely frustrating because we truly want to work through our differences. What is causing these stalemates in our marriage?

What is causing these stalemates in our marriage?

If you're hitting a roadblock when it comes to working through certain disagreements, there are several ways you can break through the barricade.

Learn to recognize the cycle that leads to recurring arguments. Some friends of ours call their familiar battle pattern "The Death Spiral." Psychologist and marriage counselor Beverly Grall recommends that couples identify the telltale signs of their own "death spirals." Common pre-argument warning signals: obsessive thoughts about your spouse's offending behavior, a sense of building tension, and heightened irritability.

"If you can observe yourselves going into the cycle," says Grall, "you can sometimes prevent an argument that you know from experience isn't going to get you anywhere."

Slow down the process. "Once an argument has started," says Grall, "try to take a break in the middle to give yourselves time to think about what the underlying issue is. Acknowledge to each other that it doesn't have to be solved all at once. It's okay to work on one piece at a time. If you decide to postpone the argument, tell your spouse, 'I really want to come back to this.' That shows your commitment to the process of resolving the problem."

Deal with problems as they occur. One husband I know has a tendency to present his wife with a written list of several weeks' worth of grievances, a technique, which although efficient, unfailingly triggers one of their recurring arguments. One likely reason for this behavior: he doesn't recognize his own resentment in time to deal with an issue before it escalates to recurring-argument status.

"It's important to pay attention to your feelings," advises Grall, "because the earlier you realize something is bothering you, the more likely you're going to be able to head off a conflict."

Try to figure out what you're really arguing about. Let's say you and your spouse tend to argue about a very specific, concrete issue—where to take vacations. Chances are there are some bigger issues underlying that conflict. As Grall observes, "It isn't that hard to figure out where to go for a vacation. You take turns choosing or you blend choices. So if you find yourselves clashing over and over again on the subject, stop and ask yourselves, 'Why is this such a big deal?' If your wife says, 'Well, you always decide everything else,' you've identified an underlying power issue. If your husband says, 'Its a big deal because it's important to me,' you've uncovered another underlying issue—he doesn't feel that what's important to him is valued."

Once you've identified all the separate issues that contribute to the recurring argument, she adds, *try to focus on one piece at a time.* If you can't agree on one, at least let each person choose one.

Don't throw stones. In the biblical story of the woman taken in adultery, Jesus told the hypocritical onlookers who wanted to condemn her, "Whoever among you has never sinned should throw the first stone."

Don't throw stones.

"That's what we're called to do in marriage," Grall says. "Often the things that bother us in others are the dark sides of ourselves. So we need to examine our own sinfulness—'What's my part in this?'—before we start figuratively casting stones."

Seek a "third way." Once a clash has become chronic, it's rare for one of the combatants to suddenly see the other person's point of view. So it's generally pointless to rehash the same old issues. Rather, says Grall, "When two people solve a recurring problem, it's usually because they were able to come up with an alternative to the old pattern of arguing."

Reassure your spouse of your commitment. The chances of resolving long-standing, highly charged issues are greatly enhanced when both partners are convinced of each other's unwavering commitment. "Reminding your spouse of your commitment, even when loving feelings aren't present," Grall explains, "can reduce feelings of anxiety and fear."

Janis Long Harris

2.11 TOO MUCH TIME WITH RELATIVES

I get along well with my wife's family, and during our first few years of marriage I went with her every time she wanted to visit them. (They live 300 miles away.) My wife also likes to use our vacations to visit out-of-state relatives. Finally, I started resenting the number of weekends taken up with trips to see in-laws. I told my wife she should feel free to go visit as often as she wanted to, but that I wouldn't go with her on every trip. She acted hurt and disappointed. Am I being selfish?

If I had a day of vacation for every couple I've known who struggled with this issue, I could take a leisurely trip to view all the wonders of the world and have plenty of time to visit every long-lost cousin I could find along the way. What it sounds like you've done is uncovered a basic difference in family values between your family upbringing and your wife's.

In some families (I suspect your wife's family falls into this category), the focus of socialization and the most important, meaningful relationships are with family—parents, siblings, sometimes even extended family like cousins, aunts and uncles. There's nothing wrong with this. People growing up in other kinds of families develop the most meaningful ongoing friendships with neighbors, people at work or church, and so on. There's nothing wrong with that either. The problem comes when you're in one camp and your spouse is in the other.

What can you do about it? To start with, you need to talk about the issues involved so that you can understand each other's perspectives. If you think it would help, ask a mutual friend to sit in and moderate the discussion. Begin by talking about your two families' values and the focus of relationship issues I've mentioned.

☀

You and your wife need to talk about and understand the differences in your personality types.

But I suspect that's only part of the problem. My guess is you also have a difference in basic personality type. Some people are very relational; they find it relaxing to spend time relating with other people. Other personality types feel that time spent with other people, especially people they don't know that well or see only occasionally, requires more hard work than their job does. For them, time spent with a spouse's relatives doesn't serve very well as a restful vacation.

You and your wife need to talk about and understand the differences in your personality types. You have as much right to expect her to understand the quirks in your personality as she does to expect you to understand her needs.

Understanding is the first step toward the only solution I know for situations like yours: compromise. Once you understand the issues between you, you need to look for creative ways to find loving compromises that allow for her needs to be addressed. It sounds like you've taken some steps toward that end, but your wife needs to better understand why you're doing what you're doing and the feelings behind it.

One practical compromise that has worked for many couples is that they set aside vacation time just for themselves and their own children. Then, through-out the year, they try to nurture extended-family relationships with weekend trips and holiday visits. If that doesn't seem like enough for your wife, there may be other possible creative compromises. For example, if she's concerned about a significant relationship with a sister, you might encourage a weekly long-distance phone call and just accept that the larger phone bill is part of the price you're willing to pay for compromise.

As long as you're willing to take on the hard work of understanding and compromise, both your needs and hers can be met with neither of you feeling the other is being selfish.

Jay Kesler

2.12 OVERLY DEPENDENT ON PARENTS

My husband and I have a good marriage and two beautiful children. Our only real problem is that he constantly changes our plans to accommodate his parents' needs and desires. He also checks with them regularly before making decisions that affect our family. When I confront him about this, he denies that there's anything wrong in what he's doing. I resent the fact that my husband is still so involved with his parents, and that he depends on them so much. How can I make him understand that, to me, it seems like he's neglecting his duties as a husband and father?

Be encouraged: *most couples find that one family becomes a sort of dominant family*—sometimes simply because they are so loving and so full of activity and resources, and not because they want to exercise control. But your marriage needs its own foundation. You can't build on your in-laws' foundation.

I suggest you try to change the focus of your discussion with your husband. The issue really is not that you resent his parents. You're not asking him to deny his family—you love them, too. The real issue is the quality of your married life. The biblical "leave and cleave" principle says a man shall leave his parents and cleave to his wife (Gn. 2:24). Focus your discussion on your relationship together.

Tell your husband you feel left out because he goes to his family instead of to you to make decisions. Be assertive in offering to help him make decisions and then to live with the decisions you make together. Instead of making your husband agree to a negative goal like "from now on, we won't spend so many weekends with your family," help him create a positive goal of time spent and decisions shared with his own family.

Jay Kesler

2.13 DIFFERENT STYLES OF COPING WITH CONFLICT

The longer we're married, the more apparent it is that my husband and I have opposite ways of coping with disagreements. Are some ways better than others? And how can we identify our own style of confronting conflict?

Conflict is a fact of married life, but most of us haven't learned effective ways of dealing with it. James Fairfield, author of *When You Don't Agree: A Guide to Resolving Marriage and Family Conflict* (Herald Press), has noted five styles of coping with disagreements:

Withdrawing. If you view conflict as a hopeless inevitability that you can do little to control, you may not even try to work through it. You may withdraw physically by walking out of the room, or you may leave psychologically.

This is the least effective way to deal with conflict because it means giving up on meeting goals and developing your marriage relationship. This style can be beneficial, however, if it is used only temporarily as a cooling-off step toward solving a disagreement. There may be times when an argument gets so heated that withdrawing is best. But it's important to make a specific commitment to resolve the issue later on.

Winning. If you feel you must always look after your own interests, or if your self-concept is threatened in a conflict, you may be one who tries to win, no matter what the cost. Feeling the need to win every battle might achieve your immediate goal, but it can sacrifice your relationship. And in a marriage, your personal relationship is more important than the goal of winning.

Yielding. "Giving in to get along" is a third way people react to conflict. Rather than risk a confrontation, they give in to the other person's wishes. A spouse who always gives in maintains the relationship but sacrifices his or her goals. And the conflict is never resolved.

> *Feeling the need to win every battle might achieve your immediate goal, but it can sacrifice your relationship.*

Compromising. Working toward a compromise attempts to address some of each person's needs, but the bargaining involved may mean that you compromise some of your values. If you have some basic convictions about the type of young men that your daughter dates, for instance, and you begin to compromise your standards in order to have greater harmony in your family, what does that do to you? And your daughter?

Resolving. When a couple adopts this style, open and direct communication results in changing a situation, attitude or behavior. Naturally this is the most effective style because, in the final analysis, relationships are strengthened as you seek to meet each other's personal needs.

To determine your style, discuss the following with your spouse as they apply to your marriage.

1. Select your usual style of dealing with conflict: withdrawing, winning, yielding, compromising or resolving.
2. Select your partner's typical style.
3. Describe a situation in which you withdrew from a conflict.
4. Describe a situation in which you won a conflict.
5. Describe a situation in which you yielded.
6. Describe a situation in which you compromised.
7. Describe a situation in which you resolved a disagreement.

Wes and Judy Roberts and H. Norman Wright

2.14 A SCRUFFY SPOUSE

My husband has started taking less care with his manners and personal habits when we're home together. I know he needs to relax after work and on the weekends. But I still feel that he should try to keep his teeth brushed, his hair combed, and his face shaved on the weekends. He doesn't seem to care about making himself look good—or watching his manners—when he's around me. While I'm not a perfect specimen, I at least try not to be a slob around the house. What can I do to help my husband see this situation from my perspective?

Rather than confronting the problem directly, by waiting until your husband has his worst Saturday in the world and picking a fight about it, try a more indirect, positive approach. Find a time when he does fix himself up and looks good (which may be during the week). Tell him how much you appreciate it when he shaves, brushes his teeth, and so on. Romance him at those times—cook his favorite meal, plan something special for him, make it clear how much you enjoy being with him.

You might also say something like, "It's reassuring to me when you look nice for me as well as for others. You know how to look good for others; when you make an effort to look good for me, too, it makes me feel special. When you don't make an effort, I begin to feel inferior, unappreciated, and unloved." If you make the most of the times when he does look good for you, he will begin to see that it pays off.

You already understand that home is a place to relax. As someone who must shave twice a day and who wears a tie most days, I understand your husband wanting to take a break from the routine. One way my wife has helped me in this area is by buying me some fun leisure clothes. You might want to try this too. Rather than having only sloppy, worn-out work clothes to wear on weekends, it might help if your husband owned some clothes that are fun to relax in, that look good, but also make him feel comfortable. You might suggest going shopping together to pick some out.

After you've tried these positive approaches, you may have to bring up your feelings about his manners gently.

After you've tried these positive approaches, you may have to bring up your feelings about his manners gently.

For instance, "It really irritates me when you belch. Please try not to do that anymore." If he says that no one's around, remind him that you're there and it makes you feel like you're nothing when he acts like you're not around. But the more you can concentrate on the positive approach, the more likely he is to feel it's worth it to make the effort.

Jay Kesler

2.15 RESORTING TO PHYSICAL VIOLENCE

A few nights ago I did something I thought I'd never do. I slapped my wife. I was stunned and she was very upset, naturally. I don't know if she will ever forgive me, although I have apologized. I've never done anything like this before, and I'm going to try my best not to resort to physical action again. But right now, how do I begin to repair the damage I've caused?

First, make sure your apology is real. And don't just apologize, but ask your wife for her forgiveness—that is, after you've sought God's forgiveness (1 Jn. 1:9). It's not enough that she hear your apology; for this wound to heal there needs to be forgiveness. Whether or not she's ready to forgive you, there are some additional steps I'll suggest.

But before I do, I want to make it clear that I consider any kind of physical violence against another person a very serious matter. Violence is the weakest and most primitive human response. We resort to it when we're frustrated, or afraid, or feeling powerless, or when we're hurt. When it crops up in our personal relationships it is always wrong and often (as you have discovered) scary. You are right to be concerned, and your wife is right to feel upset and hurt.

I would suggest you get counseling. Though you say this is the first time you've ever hit your wife, my guess is it isn't the first time you've reacted to a problem situation with a physical response. You may be the kind of guy who pounds angrily on the steering wheel when someone cuts you off in traffic. Or maybe you kick the garage door when the lawn mower won't start. Counseling might help you break this pattern of resorting to physical responses to anger—a pattern that may someday trigger

Counseling might help you break this pattern of resorting to physical responses to anger.

another violent reaction to your wife. You may need to replace that physical reaction pattern with better communication skills. Counseling can help there, too.

Even if this was just an isolated event, counseling may help you and your wife figure out what triggered the reaction this time and in that way help reassure you both that it won't happen again. Your seeking counseling would be another way for you to show your wife you're serious about making sure it doesn't happen again. That will make it easier for her to forgive and trust you again. It may take time, but I feel confident it can happen—and trust will return.

Jay Kesler

2.16 AT ODDS OVER CAREER DREAMS

I have been married for several years, and from the very beginning I've been honest with my wife about my goal of going to Bible college. My current job allows for relocation and even part-time work. We recently had our first child and my wife is now saying, "You can't decide that this will be our next step, just because you want to go into the ministry." I've been praying that God will change her attitude. Am I being unrealistic?

Many couples face decisions regarding one spouse's vocational or educational goals and dreams. Here are some ways you can determine if your career decision is realistic.

Start by going to some people whose intelligence and spiritual judgment you and your wife trust. Talk to them about your dream, the reasons you feel you should pursue your goal and the skills you think you have to bring to the task. Insist that you want them to be brutally honest in telling you whether you're being realistic about your goals.

Sometimes one spouse is reluctant to go along with the other's dream because she understands limitations he doesn't want to accept. If your wife doesn't think you're cut out for the ministry, some outside opinions could either confirm her judgment and help you readjust your thinking, or they could allay some of her concerns.

Any change of career, especially when you have a family to provide for, can seem pretty scary. It sounds to me as if your wife has some understandable fear about your family's financial security. If that's the basic problem, or even just a part of it, you should talk to several couples who have done what you're considering doing. Find out how they did it, and maybe even what they wish they had done differently. In talking to others who have faced the same unknowns, you and your wife may find that the idea seems more and more doable.

You should talk to several couples who have done what you're considering doing.

I'd also suggest talking with an admissions officer from one or more of the schools you might attend. He or she can look at your individual case and explain what kind of financial assistance is available. Knowing a few solid facts can reduce a lot of.uncertainty and fear.

Having said that, I would caution against charging ahead if your wife continues to disagree with your plans. The ministry presents many difficult challenges. Without the support and backing of your marriage partner, I'm not sure how effective a ministry you can have.

Jay Kesler

2.17 RESISTANT TO COUNSELING

My wife adamantly wants us to try marriage counseling to work through some difficulties that we've been experiencing now that the kids are grown. I'm not convinced counseling is the way to go just yet, but how can I persuade my wife to at least give us some time to work it out on our own?

Before you reach for the Yellow Pages to call a marriage counselor, consider a couple of points. The first is that most marriages go through phases of closeness and distancing. These rhythms may last several months and are at the mercy of outside stresses, such as illness, demands from aging parents, problems with your children, career pressures or major financial problems.

Certain life stages may also pull spouses apart. For instance, childbirth, deaths of family members or friends, midlife transition, the emptying of the nest and menopause all tend to draw energy away from the marriage relationship. If you're at one of these stages, talk with your spouse about your concerns. It's

Reading a good book on marriage together may be the turning point you need.

possible that you may need patience more than psychology.

You may also need to take a step less drastic than professional counseling. If you both share the desire to improve your marriage, consider alternatives to therapy. Marriage-enrichment seminars can work wonders to help you learn better skills in communication, conflict resolution, mutual understanding and sexuality. Even reading a good book on marriage together may be the turning point you need.

Finally, before you call in the cavalry, think about timing and attitude. If your spouse is desperate for both of you to enter counseling, but you think it's a waste of time, it probably will be. Better for your wife to seek counseling alone and explore how *she* needs to change. Then later, perhaps, you can agree to go together.

Louis McBurney, M.D.

2.18 FAIRLY DIVIDING HOUSEHOLD DUTIES

We both work outside the home and the household chores aren't getting done. If we're out of milk or have no clean laundry, we both end up blaming each other. The traditional division of labor we grew up with (wife does the cooking and cleaning; husband does the cars and yard work) is failing us miserably. How can we come up with an equitable way to divide the chores?

With most of today's marriage partners holding down two careers, the challenge of establishing ground rules for household chores is often a source of heated conflict. If arguments over who cooks, who cleans, and who handles the finances are plaguing your relationship, take some time to sort out your assumptions and expectations about the home and how it should be maintained.

First, make a list of all the chores that need to get done, including the more infrequent ones such as maintaining the car and preparing your taxes. Discussing the way your parents handled these tasks may help you understand what's behind some of your arguments.

Next, divide up the tasks each of you prefers to do, and then decide how to handle the less-enjoyable chores. I encourage couples who have a little extra income to consider hiring out the jobs they either detest or are unqualified to perform, like home repairs or financial planning. Often young people in the church are happy to earn a few extra dollars by cleaning house or doing yard work.

Sure, household chores are mundane and tedious, but they can also serve as an important way to show your mate you love him or her. Among the couples I've counseled, many of the husbands are amazed at how responsive their wives become when they pitch in around the house. Like one man said, "Putting forth extra effort at home is one way to say, 'Because this matters to you, I will do it. I want you to know I care.'" One woman used to think her husband spent hours working on the car as a self-indulgent pastime. It was several years before she realized that he checked the brakes and changed the oil with her safety and convenience in mind.

As you negotiate the housework, remember to take into account whose standards of cleanliness you observe. When I went back to school and my husband took on more of the domestic work, I quickly discovered a disparity in our understanding of "clean." He felt vacuuming once a month was plenty. Now he understands the need to vacuum every week "whether the carpet needs it or not."

For many couples, agreeing to share the housework is easy. But following through on that decision is another story altogether. Studies show that 59 percent of wives do more than 10 hours of housework a week, while only 22 percent of husbands put in that much time.

What can a spouse do when his or her mate is either unwilling to help or reneges on their agreed-upon responsibilities? Nothing. That's the best advice I can give. Let the natural consequences run their course. Eventually he or she will run out of clean underwear and be forced to run a load of whites.

Let the natural consequences run their course.

Parceling out household chores carries much more meaning than merely keeping the house clean, the grass cut and the car running. It actually represents an attitude of the heart. Our willingness—or unwillingness—to help out around the house speaks volumes about the value we place on our spouse.

Judith Balswick

2.19 UNACCEPTING IN-LAWS

I'm married to a beautiful Japanese-American woman, but my parents refuse to accept her. They only invite us over on major holidays, and they don't encourage my wife to call them Mom and Dad although they extend that courtesy to my brothers' wives. My wife continues to act with love and kindness toward them, but the situation constantly makes me angry. What can I do?

There are few things that would make a husband angrier than his parents not accepting his wife. Yet you can probably understand the source of their difficulty. Racism runs deeper than intellectual knowledge, and your parents might be influenced by memories of the Second World War. The propaganda of that era was rife with harsh and unfair overstatement. It was considered patriotic to depersonalize the Japanese by treating them with disrespect and suspicion.

If you haven't already talked to your parents about this problem, you should do so immediately. It's possible that, on the strength of your own relationship with them, you can make your parents understand how their behavior breaks your heart. Also, remind them that their grandchildren will be a combination of your two lives, and that you don't want your children to endure the pain of their negative reaction to your wife.

In the meantime, keep on loving and affirming your wife, and encourage her to continue acting with love and kindness toward your parents. Jesus told his followers who were being treated unjustly to love their enemies. Eventually, one's "enemies" begin to compare the loving actions they're receiving against their own hostile, aggressive and unfair actions—and the result is a sense of conviction or "burning coals" as the apostle Paul said in Romans 12:21. Hopefully, that's when the unjust behavior begins to change.

In this instance, your loving response is the only solution.

Your goal is to wear your parents down with love. Sometimes the process takes place over a long period of time, but in this instance, your loving response is the only solution.

Jay Kesler

2.20 CRITICAL SISTER-IN-LAW

My husband's older sister visits us regularly, and I always feel uncomfortable when she's in our home. She seems to resent me, and I'm starting to resent her proprietary attitude when it comes to my husband. Her criticisms, subtle or outright, drive me crazy. While I've put up with her because my husband enjoys her company, I can't take many more of these visits. How can I express my discomfort to my husband without hurting his feelings?

This type of situation between a man's sister and his wife is fairly common. During childhood, older sisters often fall into the role of baby-sitter, and the sister-brother relationship develops with her taking a controlling, proprietary role. She changes his diapers; she looks out for him on the playground or baby-sits after school. These duties become a pattern for her relationship with her brother, even after they become adults.

In contrast, you entered his life more recently. And while you don't have the same knowledge of your husband's early life and all the things that make him tick, the reality is he married *you*. He may see his sister intermittently, but you have the inside track, relating to him day after day. So even though you sense a spirit of competition when you're with your sister-in-law, the competition does not actually exist. Your husband has chosen *you*.

At this point, you need to deal with your feelings. Perhaps your sister-in-law makes you feel inadequate because she relates to your husband in a controlling way—a way you don't choose to. Or you may resent your husband if you see him involuntarily following his sister's lead. Sometimes a wife will resent the sister's "henpecking" and her husband's apparent compliance.

It is important for you to tell him how these visits make you feel, being careful not to assign blame. Acknowledge that your sister-in-law's behavior may be inadvertent; she may not know any other way to relate to her brother. You might tell him you understand where the feelings come from, but that you can't help feeling frustrated, put down or resentful. Be specific about the things that bother you: "You defer to her wishes about our schedule or where to go out to eat, without thinking of what I might like." Or "It bothers me when she corrects you or when she tells you what to do." Such specifics might help him alter his relationship with his sister, and the changes could ease the stress for you.

Feeling like a "fifth wheel" is never pleasant.

These visits may make you feel isolated. Recently a high school friend I hadn't seen for 40 years came to visit. As we laughed and talked about old times, we suddenly noticed our wives were silently watching us. It wasn't much fun for them to sit and listen to our old stories. Feeling like a "fifth wheel" is never pleasant. Perhaps it's hard for you to see your husband interact easily and closely with his sister. And maybe some of your sister-in-law's annoying behavior grew out of her own feelings that she is "left out" of your relationship as a couple.

Do your best to keep a good sense of humor about this—personally and in conversation with your husband. Tell him this is a common problem in families. For example, "Oh, your sister's coming. I guess she's going to boss you around and drive me nuts for a few days!" The "inside joke" will bring you together instead of pushing you apart during your sister-in-law's visits.

Jay Kesler

2.21 CHANGING A MATE'S ANNOYING HABITS

I love my wife dearly but she has two habits that I find completely annoying—letting her alarm ring for several minutes every morning and leaving clutter all over the bathroom counter. Should I just live with these habits that drive me nuts or encourage her to change?

While you should accept some annoyances, we all have a responsibility to make changes that will improve our marriages. The hard part is identifying which habits need to be changed and to what degree.

Certain annoyances can be so problematic that major change is needed.

In the case of an introverted spouse, for instance, behavior can be modified to only a certain point. On the other hand, certain annoyances can be so problematic that major change is needed. For example, if your spouse continually drives the car until the gas tank is dry, it won't be enough to reduce the number of times he or she is stranded on the highway in a given month. The only acceptable change is to break the annoying habit completely. To determine if a certain change is necessary, ask yourself these three questions.

1. What are the costs of continuing to accept the current behavior? Does the troublesome behavior cause you extreme unease or unnecessary work? Also consider the interpersonal costs, such as how the behavior colors your perception of one another. Finally, consider the costs to your spouse. Is the habit harmful to your mate, or does it detract from him or her as a person?

For example, after several years of marriage, Jan decided to confront her husband, Tom, about his habit of not hanging up his clothes. "For ten years I never said anything about this," she told us, "but now that I've started teaching again I don't have the time or energy to pick up after him."

While Tom's sloppiness didn't detract from him as a person, it certainly added irritation and extra work for his wife. Besides, it made Jan feel her husband wasn't considerate of her needs and didn't care about their home. If allowed to continue, Tom's sloppiness could eventually erode their relationship.

2. What are the benefits of changing a behavior? To Jan, the benefits of Tom changing his ways were obvious. But would there be any benefits to Tom? Even though hanging up his clothes would mean extra work for him, he would feel good knowing his efforts made his wife feel more appreciated. And he might even feel better about himself, knowing his actions would enhance their relationship.

3. What are the costs of changing, and is the change worth the price? If an extroverted spouse insists that her introverted husband become more like her, the cost would most likely be too high. Her efforts to achieve an impossible task—change someone's personality—would eventually result in alienating her husband.

However, for Tom and Jan, the costs of changing did not seem as high as the costs of *not* changing. If Tom refused to change, Jan's resentment of him would build. In contrast, the cost of eliminating this resentment would be some additional effort on Tom's part and patience on Jan's part as she encouraged him to change. In this instance, the cost of *not* changing outweighed the cost of eliminating the troublesome habit.

Once you answer all three questions, you have several options. First, if you determine that the cost of changing a habit would outweigh the benefits, you might make it one of the annoyances that you "allow" your spouse—recognizing that neither of you is perfect.

Second, if you determine that the benefits of changing outweigh the costs, you can tell your spouse how the offensive behavior affects you and offer to help him or her change. It isn't a matter of "this is your annoying habit—please change it." Rather, suggest that you work *together* to change the bothersome behavior so your relationship will benefit. If your spouse agrees, decide together how you can help with the change.

Third, if you request a specific change and your mate refuses to change, you can go back to the three preceding questions and answer them together. Perhaps your spouse is aware of a cost or a benefit you haven't thought about. Or maybe your spouse disagrees with an assumption you have made.

Jeanette C. and Robert H. Lauer

2.22 WHEN TO CONSIDER COUNSELING

We've been going through some rough times lately—I've been unemployed for six months and as the financial pressures build, my wife and I seem more like enemies than teammates. Should we consider counseling to make it through this tough time in our marriage or just weather it out?

Most couples can solve moderate-level problems themselves or with the help of supportive friends and family members. However, you might feel overwhelmed by the weight of the difficulties in your marriage. In general, you should seek professional help when you encounter serious, persistent problems that seem to have no solution. The following list gives 14 indications that a couple should consider seeing a counselor.

1. Someone in your family is being hurt physically or is suffering such damage to self-esteem that he or she is seriously depressed or troubled.
2. Alcohol or drug dependency is part of the problem.
3. Marital problems have existed for a long time and seem to be getting worse.
4. You have tried almost everything you know to help your marriage, and nothing has worked.

5. Sexual difficulties such as premature ejaculation, impotence, failure to achieve orgasms or painful intercourse have become a serious strain in your relationship.

6. You or your mate have serious emotional or personal problems that seem to be caused by marital difficulties, or are causing marital difficulties.

7. Your children are frequently caught in the midst of your arguments.

8. You (or your spouse) have become distressed enough to think marriage counseling is needed.

9. One of you has contacted a lawyer.

10. One of you is having or has recently had an extramarital affair.

11. You appear locked in a power struggle, or you have several differences that you've been unable to resolve through persistent effort.

12. Either of you feels unable to forgive the other for some past transgression.

13. Either of you is allowing outside activities to reduce family time to near zero, and this absence of commitment seriously distresses the other spouse.

14. Personal or marital tensions are increasing rapidly.

Everett L. Worthington, Jr.

2.23 WHAT TO EXPECT IN COUNSELING

Our pastor has encouraged us to seek marriage counseling and our first appointment is in two weeks. While we're glad to be taking a proactive step in addressing our problems, we're also a little nervous. What should we expect once we're seated before a counselor?

Many couples are uncomfortable with the idea of counseling. Since it is unfamiliar territory to most people, a little background information might help.

Marriage counselors usually prefer to see both partners rather than only one, and your chances of improving your marriage are greatly enhanced when both of you participate. Most therapists like to meet with a couple weekly for six or more sessions over a period of two to six months. Regular meetings help

Marriage counselors usually prefer to see both partners rather than only one.

a couple change their relationship because they must report their efforts to the counselor.

Therapists try to help couples communicate better; they also intervene to prevent destructive arguments as the spouses discuss their differences. Most counselors are more interested in helping couples learn *how* to resolve differences than in helping them arrive at specific solutions to a few current problems.

Goals for marital therapy differ from one therapist to the next. Some challenge a couple to make specific changes, while others are more general, hoping the couple will improve their communication or simply feel more satisfied. In my experience, major improvements in a marriage relationship almost always require a couple to make specific changes. It's good to have a goal of changed attitudes, but in a situation where both partners have experienced extended conflict or unhappiness, it's important to change behaviors first. Behavioral changes can then become the springboard for changes in feelings and attitudes.

Everett L. Worthington, Jr.

2.24 SELECTING A COUNSELOR

We've decided that it's time to see a counselor but we have no idea how to pick one. What are some criteria we should use in selecting a professional?

In the process of selecting a counselor, the following questions may help you decide which type of counselor to see.

> *Christian counselors differ substantially in how they counsel.*

Is the counselor a Christian? A committed Christian couple may feel more comfortable with a Christian counselor. It's important to remember, however, that Christian counselors differ substantially in how they counsel. For example, clients shouldn't expect the counselor to pray aloud at the beginning of each session, quote Scripture, give sermonettes or use Christian terminology. While some counselors may do some or all of these things, there are no "Christian counseling techniques" that all Christian therapists use.

What are the counselor's beliefs and values? A potential counselor's theological positions and use of Scripture may be important to know. If particular religious beliefs might make you more receptive—or more resistant—to counseling, ask about them.

How competent is the counselor? A therapist's experience and reputation are more important than his or her degree. I know excellent marital therapists who are clinical psychologists, counseling psychologists, psychiatrists, social workers, licensed professional counselors, pastors, pastoral counselors, rehabilitation counselors and psychiatric nurses.

Another important criterion is how competently the therapist conducts therapy. *Can he or she control hostilities between you?* Does the therapist grasp the essence of your problem? Does he feel compelled to impose his values on you?

After meeting several times, do you sense the therapist is obviously biased toward one of you? No therapist can or should be *totally* unbiased. There are times when a good therapist should side with each of you. Generally, you should have the impression that he or she is not on either side of your marital conflict but is on the side of your marriage.

What is the counselor's attitude toward divorce? When I do marriage counseling, I fight wholeheartedly against divorce. I want the couple to succeed at marriage, and I try my best to help them succeed. Yet counselors know that despite the hardest efforts by counselor and spouses, some marriages fail. In those cases, with pain and tears, I will help the divorcing partners manage their trauma and hurt.

Everett L. Worthington, Jr.

CHAPTER 3

SEX:
THE WAY GOD
DESIGNED IT

SEX:
THE WAY GOD
DESIGNED IT

Australian pastor Phillip Jensen says, "The biblical path to pure sex may be a road less traveled in these times, but it is no less attractive for being so. Only in marriage can sex do successfully what it is meant to do" (Tony Payne and Phillip Jensen, *Pure Sex*, p. 94).

The road less traveled is the covenant of marriage. Culture today has removed sex from its sacred and secure boundary. As a result, the gift that was intended to seal and grace our marriage has become the weapon that tears and curses our relationships, bringing pain mixed with sorrow.

The opening chapters of the Bible make it clear that God invented sex, it was one of His good ideas, and that it was given to us to fulfill His purposes: first, to fill his world with children who will be godly (Mal. 3:15); second, to bless us with a union that God intended for our good (pleasure) and His glory. Lovemaking is the physical bond that unites us, and this union is to reflect the greater union of Christ and the church. The "one flesh" language of Moses corresponds to the "in Christ" language of Paul. "For this reason a man will leave his father and mother and be joined to his wife, and the two will become one flesh. This mystery is profound, but I am talking about Christ and the church" (Eph. 5:31-32).

In 1 Corinthians 7, Paul asserts that sex in marriage keeps us pure by freeing us from sexual immorality (vv. 2, 9). Next, he reminds us that lovemaking is each partner's marital duty (v. 2). He goes on to teach that our body belongs to not only ourselves but also our spouse (v. 4). This means we don't have absolute rights over our bodies. Finally, we are not to rob, deny or refuse our spouse of our body except for the purpose of prayer—and this only when both consent (v. 5).

Moses writes that Adam knew his wife and she gave birth to Cain (Gn. 4:4). Sex is fundamentally about knowing. Our word intercourse comes from that word. It is a knowing of fullest proportions—body, mind, and soul. Sex is loving. Mike Mason says, "Without love we will find as much satisfaction as a mouthful of sawdust" (*Mystery of Marriage*, p. 127). It is in Christ that we receive the capacity to love, and through him the ability to love.

> *PRAYER: Lord, thank You for this gracious gift. May our lovemaking be pure and honoring to You (Heb. 13:4). Keep us faithful. Help us to flee immorality (1 Co. 6:18). Guard us from lust (Mt. 5:28). Help us to rightly reflect Your relationship with the church. Cement our marriage as we enjoy the mysteries of our deep communion. May we share our love as we give ourselves to each other; and may we thank You for this good gift and the pleasures that come from You. Amen.*

3.1 UNDERSTANDING FIDELITY

I never thought I'd say this, but for me fidelity is a real challenge. I love my wife and I want to remain true to her. I thought marital fidelity would be a natural, easy thing. But that sure isn't the case. How can I see the choice of fidelity in a positive light and not the "prison" that some joke it is?

Truth be told, true fidelity is tough stuff. It's impossible outside of Christ. But it is in Christ that we can begin to experience the freedom that this radical mind, body, and soul fidelity was designed to bring into the marriage relationship. A oneness that is not a ball-and-chain commitment, but a oneness that is truly liberating.

Truth be told, true fidelity is tough stuff.

"Not everyone can accept this saying," said Christ, as He taught the scope and magnitude of marital fidelity, "but only those to whom it has been given" (Mt. 19:11). As one who "accepted this word" 20 years ago, it would appear that I am divinely mandated (as all husbands and wives are) not to content myself with "measurable fidelity" or the mere appearance of faithfulness. But rather to seek, by God's grace and power, the fuller measure of marital faithfulness that Christ challenged his disillusioned listeners with.

To be sure, this "fuller measure" is no easy matter. It takes forgiveness, patience and time (lots of it). But happily, Christian marriage offers the construct of a permanent, lifelong commitment in which mind, body, and soul fidelity can be created and experienced. Not overnight. Not in six easy steps. But eventually, over a lifetime.

How should this all-encompassing fidelity work itself out? What does this "fuller measure of fidelity" mean for the next 30 or 40 years of marriage?

First, it means I must see my wife as God sees her (and, indeed, as God has made her): ever changing, ever being refined by the day-to-day pains and pleasures of life. A "new" creation. Someone whose wisdom and insights, opinions and observations, challenge, encourage and strengthen my own insights, opinions, and observations. My wife is *not* the same yesterday, today and tomorrow. Nor, for that matter, is any man or woman—for which we should all be grateful. Such dynamism gives little time for one to be bored with his or her spouse, gives little opportunity for one's mind to wander onto someone else who supposedly is "more exciting, more interesting."

Second, God's mandate for total fidelity means I must be ever diligent in my efforts to keep the erotic voices of our culture from undermining my marriage. So myriad are these voices that we hardly acknowledge them. But we can identify their influence in the taunting disappointment and discontent we may feel toward our spouse's body. Or the unrealistic expectations we bring to our sexual relationship.

Total fidelity also commands us to withstand the clarion cries of self-centeredness.

Countering these voices takes more than canceling the subscription to a "questionable" magazine or turning off the TV—although these are certainly places to start. Combating sensualism demands the unified front of a husband and wife equally committed to looking out for the other. For gently rebuking and redirecting each other, and for lovingly opening up for one another's enjoyment the full measure of sexual love.

In addition to jointly blockading the subversive, erotic voices, total fidelity also commands us to withstand the clarion cries of self-centeredness. The persuasive arguments that would have me put the pursuit of my "rights," my pleasures, above everything—and everyone else, including my wife.

Marital oneness can only exist in the context of mutual submission (Eph. 5:21), and with an understanding of love that puts the well being of the one loved predominant in the mind and actions of the lover (1 Co. 13).

Finally and most importantly, this mind, body, and soul fidelity means I must wholly rely upon God—not by my might, but His alone can I successfully withstand the forces that would rob me of the pleasure of experiencing the mystery of oneness with my mate. If God demands total fidelity—and He does—then He will provide the means whereby that fidelity can truly characterize my marital relationship and yours.

Indeed, after 20 years I'm beginning to catch more than periodic glimpses of what it means to "find yourself" by losing yourself in another. The acceptance, the influence, the model, the commitment of my wife has forced me not only to see myself as I really am, but challenged me to become the husband God would have me be. This is the real payoff of fidelity: a oneness of two people that reflects the One who saw fit to create marriage in the first place.

Harold B. Smith

3.2 GREAT SEX AFTER A FIGHT

Last weekend we had a huge argument about our family finances. Later we cooled off, apologized, and worked out a reasonable compromise. Later that night, it seemed impossible that we could have been so upset with each other because we had such great sex. Why is it that we end up having the best sex after we've made up from some of our worst fights?

One commonly overlooked aphrodisiac is the difficult, but necessary, act of forgiveness. When offered and accepted, forgiveness can be positively magnetic.

Think back to some of the worst fights between you and your spouse. If you were able to resolve those arguments by offering and receiving genuine forgiveness, do you remember where that led?

When offered and accepted, forgiveness can be positively magnetic.

Chances are, you soon were enjoying the most enjoyable, and intimate, sex you had experienced in a long time.

Why this sudden burst of sexual attraction? It's because your essential oneness as a couple had been restored, and you wanted to express that in a physical way. When we offer—or are granted—forgiveness, we achieve a greater depth of intimacy with each other. We feel more understood, more appreciated, more accepted for who we are, and that fuels passion and ignites sexual desire.

But how do you forgive a person you don't feel like forgiving? How can you offer forgiveness to a mate who hasn't even asked for it? To forgive, you have to override any desire for punishment and repayment and instead release your spouse from any further moral debt.

Drawing from God's resources is a great help. He is by nature forgiving (1 Jn. 1:9), and he offers us the strength and ability to forgive our mate when everything within us screams "No!" It may come with difficulty, it may come slowly, and it may even come in stages. But if we truly want to forgive, it will happen.

Robert L. Moeller

3.3 ADAPTING TO AN ALTERED BODY IMAGE

My wife recently had a mastectomy due to breast cancer. I'm overjoyed that she will recover, and I want her to know how much I still desire and appreciate her body. But I'm not sure how to handle the loss of one of her breasts. For example, is that area still sensitive, or will it bother her if I try to stimulate her there?

Any bodily disfigurement can interrupt or impair our ability to open us to each other sexually. When we feel bad about our bodies, we may feel unworthy to give and receive sexual pleasure. If your wife suffers negative feelings about her body since her mastectomy, she may need a great deal of affirmation from you before she can risk sexual intimacy. Your and your wife's ability to genuinely accept her physical change and maintain a sense of security in your relationship will be essential to ongoing sexual intimacy.

Sexuality involves body, soul, spirit, and emotions.

Thus your reconnecting process following your wife's surgery can be a time to establish an even more satisfying sexual relationship. Our society often associates a woman's sexuality with her breasts, and there are some valid reasons for this connection. The breasts are receptors of and responders to sexual stimulation. Nevertheless, it's extremely limiting to focus exclusively on the breasts and genitals for sexual enjoyment. Sexuality involves body, soul, spirit, and emotions. All of our skin is responsive to touch. When we limit ourselves to certain parts of the body, we shortchange ourselves of all the potential for sexual pleasure that is available to us.

Clifford L. and Joyce J. Penner

3.4 POSITIONS FOR MAXIMUM PLEASURE

My wife and I have experimented with different positions during sex, and it's important to me that she receives maximum pleasure from our times of intimacy. Is there one position that provides the best stimulation for women?

Sixty percent or more of women do not experience orgasm during intercourse. If your wife desires orgasm during intercourse, experimenting with positions can help enhance that possibility as long as that goal does not distract the two of you from the pleasure of just enjoying each other's bodies.

It's more important for you to develop an attitude of openness and freedom that is mutually comfortable. Don't push your wife into a goal of trying new positions to enhance her pleasure. If she's happy, let *her* be the authority on what she desires for her own sexual pleasure.

Ultimately, your wife will be the best authority on what is most pleasurable for her. You might begin by doing some further experimentation to gather data about where your wife experiences the most genital sensation. (For diagrams and specific instructions, see chapter 6 of our book *The Gift of Sex* [Word]). After discovering where your wife feels the most sensation, you can then adjust positions during intercourse to maximize pressure on those areas.

Ultimately, your wife will be the best authority on what is most pleasurable for her.

Clifford L. and Joyce J. Penner

3.5 INHIBITED ABOUT APPEARANCE

My wife is extremely private about her body. Even though we've been married for several years, she still won't change clothes in front of me. What can I do to help her feel more relaxed about her body?

There are several things you can do to help. First, plan a time to talk with your wife about her feelings regarding her body and her reluctance to share herself with you. This discussion should take place apart from a time of sexual involvement or nudity. Let your wife know your reason for bringing up the subject is not to pressure her to change, but to help you understand her and to meet her needs better.

Sometimes when a woman is hesitant to share her body, the husband himself is the problem. A wife may discover early in her marriage that exposing her body will inevitably lead to intercourse. If you responded to your wife this way, she may have felt like a sexual object, rather than feeling valued as a person. For her to feel safe enough to share her body with you, she will need to experience ongoing emotional closeness with you.

Another factor that affects a woman's modesty is how nudity was handled in her family. If your wife's family was either extremely modest or inappropriate in exposure, she may have learned that it is not safe to share herself, even with her husband. Children tend to grow up knowing their bodies are God's beautiful and perfect design, and their privacy should be respected at all times. When we have been raised with a high view of our bodies and with clear boundaries to protect them, we can freely give our bodies to our spouses. But if your wife didn't grow up in such an atmosphere, your demands on her to share her body will only cause more violation and decreased openness. Instead of making demands on her, provide safety in your relationship so your wife can gradually learn to share her body with you—at her pace and on her terms. The two of you may need professional guidance with this opening-up process.

How a woman perceives and accepts her body will also affect her sense of freedom to share her body with her husband. The view we have of our bodies—our body image—was formulated during our growing up years by the way we were held as infants and children, the messages we received from significant others about our bodies, and the models we looked up to and now measure ourselves against. The wider the gap between how we view ourselves and our image of the ideal body, the bigger our body-image problem. The goal is to narrow that gap by enhancing our view of ourselves and/or changing our ideal.

If you discover your wife struggles with her body image, you can help her by conveying your positive view of her through your touch and through verbal affirmation. In addition, there may be efforts she could take to improve her view of her body. Sometimes exercise or weight-loss programs make a difference, but these must be her ideas, not your agenda for her.

It may also be important for your wife to adjust her image of the ideal body. Many women try to measure up to TV and movie personalities. To define beauty on that basis is unrealistic. When struggling with body image, it is important to remember God's message: He looks on the heart; man looks on the outward appearance (1 Sm. 16:7). Both are important, but since God accepts her as the beautiful woman he made her to be and you are the man looking on the outside, you can help affirm that perspective.

When struggling with body image, it is important to remember God's message.

Clifford L. and Joyce J. Penner

3.6 SEXUALLY NAIVE SPOUSE

We were both virgins when we married, and I don't regret that for a minute. However, I thought my husband would know a lot more about sex than he does. How is it possible that he can be so clueless at times about what brings me pleasure?

In our sexually explicit society, it seems almost inconceivable that anyone could be uninformed about sex. Yet it happens all the time. Married adults have a basic knowledge of the "plumbing" (the anatomy and physiology of the reproductive system), but that's about as far as their knowledge goes. Wives and husbands know they react differently to sexual drive and stimulation, but they don't understand the intricacies of their two very different systems.

Most women don't realize that testosterone creates a physiological drive in their husbands that demands expression every few days. Without that insistent testosterone, women experience little physical drive for sexual release. Rather, they desire the relational closeness that leads to sexual intimacy.

Married adults have a basic knowledge of the "plumbing."

Many husbands assume their wives will get aroused and reach a climax as quickly as they do. But most women are only in the early arousal stage when their husbands have their orgasm. This discrepancy often leaves a woman feeling cheated when her husband falls asleep just when she's getting interested. And her husband ends up feeling inadequate as a lover since he has failed to bring his wife to orgasm.

Ignorance about technique is only one kind of ignorance, though. Another has to do with expectations. Where did you get your ideas about a "normal" sex life? Probably by picking it up here and there—from movies, romance novels, secrets from a college roommate or the pages of a sex manual. But did you ever talk about your beliefs with your spouse?

For many couples, sexual expression has narrow boundaries. They feel intercourse should take place only in bed, in the dark, under a sheet. A couple can certainly find intense pleasure and oneness with this routine, but a few variations could enhance their feeling of romance. Experimenting with different positions and different methods of stimulation are not "abnormal" or "sick." Experimentation is fine when both partners agree, when it doesn't cause emotional or physical pain, and when it isn't always a substitute for genital union (unless genital union is not possible).

Another good rule is, "If it ain't broke, don't fix it." If the two of you are satisfied and enjoying a great sense of joy and freedom in your current range of sexual experiences together, don't feel that you have to change or do something different.

Louis McBurney, M.D.

Another good rule is, "If it ain't broke, don't fix it."

3.7 HESITANT TO ENJOY SEX FULLY

Whenever we make love I feel like I'm not fully involved. It's almost as if some invisible force is preventing me from completely enjoying our times of intimacy. What is holding me back?

Fear prevents many couples from full sexual expression. Where vulnerability is required, there is often fear, and a couple's sex life involves a remarkable degree of vulnerability.

One source of fear is the anticipation of pain, either physical or emotional. This is particularly true when there has been a history of sexual abuse. All the old images may threaten to emerge, creating intense anxiety. Old coping devices like physically hiding or becoming emotionally absent may also come into play.

On her honeymoon, one wife leaped from the bed, crying, "Get away from me!" Her brand-new husband found himself listening to her sobbing from the outside of a locked bathroom door. When they told me about this, I immediately considered the possibility of an earlier traumatic sexual experience. The boundaries of their courtship protected the wife's old scar, but the prospect of intercourse peeled away the bandage to expose the wound.

Sexual receptivity also can be blocked by fear of failure. The prospect of performing to the level the media portrays as "normal" could scare your pants on. When sexual intimacy is equated with bedroom Olympics, the possibilities for failure are frightening. This anxiety inhibits sexual freedom and function.

Sexual promiscuity also generates the fear of failure. Where there have been premarital or extramarital affairs, comparisons are difficult to avoid. Am I as good as he was? Does he find me as exciting as she was? Derail questions like these as soon as they come up.

Loss of control is another scary aspect of sexual vulnerability. Let's admit it: the intense feelings that come with erotic stimulation erode one's sense of control. One woman I know had never experienced orgasm because she feared what might happen when she lost control.

Then there's the vulnerability that comes with relational loss of control. Totally giving yourself to your spouse makes you extremely vulnerable. Any kind of power struggles in a marriage can make that vulnerability seem too risky. Making sure you resolve control or power issues between you can relieve sexual tension because it turns your "competitor" into your trusted lover.

None of these barriers to sexual joy is so complicated or troublesome that it can't be overcome. And it's well worth the effort. The sexual love story that unfolds over the years of your marriage will reflect your personal passage beyond problems to fulfilling passion.

Louis McBurney, M.D.

3.8 HARMFUL SEXUAL FANTASIES

From time to time, I've entertained a few sexual fantasies in my mind. Then a few weeks ago, I found myself wishing my wife would act out those fantasies with me. I was disturbed that my daydreaming seemed to be taking such a hold on the reality of my love life and I'm beginning to wonder, "Are fantasies really as harmless as they seem?"

In both popular and professional circles, the use of fantasy is viewed at worst as harmless and at best as the answer to a boring sex life. The conventional wisdom goes something like this: if unbridled fantasy results in fantastic sex, everyone wins. Therefore, if I fantasize about an old friend, a co-worker or my neighbor's spouse, and these fantasies enrich my sex life with my own spouse, then no one is harmed. In fact, my spouse may even feel more desired as I act out my sexual fantasies with him or her. But is all this really harmless?

Uncontrolled fantasy shortchanges reality.

Uncontrolled fantasy shortchanges reality. When we continue to fantasize about an ideal "other person," we create an unrealistic standard by which we then evaluate our lovemaking, our partner and his or her sexual responsiveness. Our sex life is left wanting, and over time our spouse becomes less desirable because he or she can't measure up. We tell ourselves that sex will never be the way we want it to be, so why put forth the effort?

Retreating into a fantasy world results in an increasing emotional withdrawal and isolation. Further, it deters ongoing, healthy communication. This kills the possibility for deepening intimacy.

Marriage doesn't kill an active imagination any more than it dampens our appreciation for members of the opposite sex. And yet, just as marriage calls us to redirect our passions exclusively toward our partner, so too it calls us to redirect our mental passions.

This is admittedly easier said than done. The place to begin, however, is with the well-known—if widely ignored—biblical injunction in Philippians to think on things that are true, honorable, just, pure and lovely (Php. 4:8). This doesn't just happen. It calls for discernment: the ability to sort out the wholesome from the unsavory, the godly from the evil, the lovely from the stained. More specifically, we need to be alert to those influences and those messages that promote unhealthy fantasies—not only explicit films, magazines, and TV shows, but the more subtle poison of media words and images pushing "contemporary" sexual attitudes.

Such "culture avoidance" may seem like excessive, legalistic reaction; but the fact is that these influences are potentially addictive and some men and women are quite vulnerable to these addictions. Some people are able to control their weaknesses without asking others for help; others rely on their spouses or a close friend to help them become more discerning. For example, a friend of mine who travels extensively keeps his wife regularly informed of the activities of his days—and nights.

Open communication with your spouse is essential in keeping your fantasy life in check. Share and explore your fantasies with your spouse. But do so under the guidance of the biblical declaration to think "pure and good thoughts." Don't think or do anything that degrades or attacks the character and respect of yourself and your mate.

> *Open communication with your spouse is essential in keeping your fantasy life in check.*

Specifically, talk to your mate about your lovemaking. If it has become routine, what can be done to liven things up? And to help heighten the pleasure of these physical times, focus your thoughts on your spouse. Fantasizing about his or her touch, intimate moments together and physical closeness provides new energy and a greater desire to be together both emotionally and sexually.

In contrast, using your spouse's body to help you live out sexual fantasies with another person can hardly be considered lovemaking. I want my wife to be making love to me both physically and mentally, not to her old boyfriend.

Fantasy should be used to heighten and enrich the sex life in your bed, not the sex life in your head. But if I am not guarding my fantasy life for my spouse, then I am leaving the door open to whoever may enter—to the detriment of my marriage.

Douglas B. DeMerchant

3.9 RE-ESTABLISHING A LOVE LIFE AFTER AN AFFAIR

My husband was involved in an affair. We have worked through some of our problems, and I believe he now intends to be faithful. But the memory of his affair freezes me up whenever we try to make love. I can't help but wonder if he's thinking about this other woman, and if he would secretly rather be with her. What can we do to get our love life back on track?

What you are struggling with is the long-term process of forgiveness.

It sounds like you have worked through the initial shock and feelings of betrayal, rejection, and anger. You also seem to trust your husband to be faithful. What you are struggling with is the long-term process of forgiveness—which involves dealing with the ongoing feelings of bitterness and resentment, and controlling your thoughts. We recommend Lewis Smede's book *Forgive & Forget: Healing the Hurts We Don't Deserve* (HarperSanFrancisco) as a helpful resource for guiding you through the forgiveness process. You and your husband also need to work together on effective communication as you examine your marriage and seek ways to enhance your sexual relationship.

Communicate your concerns to your husband. Approach the subject when you are well rested and free of distractions, and when you're not involved in physical intimacy. Let your husband know that you worry about his thoughts and preferences during sex. If your worries are valid, this may be difficult for him to respond to. If not, he can reassure you of his desire only for you. Work on finding ways of communicating during sex that allow you to share your concerns as they surface and allow your husband a way to let you know what he needs from you to keep his mind exclusively on you.

If you haven't already received counseling following your husband's affair, the two of you may need professional help in examining your relationship and the factors that your husband believes led to the affair. Sometimes a marriage is unhappy or unfulfilled because one spouse is disappointed in the other. Other times a spouse feels inadequate himself. These issues need to be examined, and a counselor can be a great help in that process. It could be that he sought out an affair because of low self-esteem or sexually addictive tendencies. It's possible that your husband's affair had very little to do with how he feels about you or your marriage.

Affairs can also result from not taking precautions to affair-proof your marriage. Many people think that since they are married, they will never be sexually attracted to anyone else. But the truth is that none of us is exempt from sexual temptation. When our response to someone other than our spouse suddenly shocks us and we haven't safeguarded our relationship against such temptation, we don't have the tools needed to strengthen our resistance.

Getting back on track sexually will require a rebuilding process. Our book *Restoring the Pleasure* (Word) contains a self-help section designed for this very purpose. Once the two of you have worked through the forgiveness issues, the communication process and the relationship factors, then begin the sexual retraining process. Make a fresh commitment to each other, and start your sexual relationship as if it were new.

Getting back on track sexually will require a rebuilding process.

As part of that process, your husband should be tested for sexually transmitted diseases. In addition to your sexual retraining assignments, plan ways for the two of you to give each other nonverbal signals when you are being distracted by thoughts related to the affair. At that point get active in enjoying each other's body and talking to each other about your enjoyment. This will help keep the two of you feeling connected.

Clifford L. and Joyce J. Penner

3.10 A HUM-DRUM SEX LIFE

Years ago our sex life was filled with a sense of adventure and fun. Now it's predictable and, for lack of a better word, dull. I'm disappointed we've let sex become such a low priority and settled for the humdrum. What can we do to bring back the excitement?

A good place to begin is to change the location and the setting or atmosphere of your sexual encounters. The location is the room or area of the house (or the place outside the house) where you get together sexually. The setting or atmosphere

Change the location and the setting or atmosphere of your sexual encounters.

involves what you do with the location. For example, you can vary the lighting; you can reverse your position in bed, putting your feet at the "head" end; you can put a comforter on the floor or by the fireplace, instead of having your sexual experience in bed. It will add spark to your relationship if you and your spouse take turns choosing the place and creating the atmosphere. This provides newness and an element of surprise.

Sometimes it takes some struggling together to come up with alternative locations that will provide the privacy both of you need. One couple, with six children ranging from two to seventeen years of age, found a unique solution. The little ones awakened early in the morning, while the teenagers stayed up later than their parents did at night. The couple found that they were rarely getting together sexually. And when they did, they were under pressure to hurry in the morning or be quiet in the evening. Without a conscious awareness of it, they had developed a routine that took about three minutes. Sexual intrigue had left their relationship soon after their second child was born sixteen years before.

Finding new locations and creating a new atmosphere took some creativity. They organized the wife's craft and sewing room so they could add a hide-a-bed and keep the room tidy. This provided an alternate location to the bedroom. The teenagers were enlisted as part of the plan. The parents told them that Mom and Dad needed some "special nights together." From the little smiles on the kids' faces, you could tell they had caught on. There's an example of a great job of modeling by parents!

The plan they worked out was as follows: after nine o'clock two nights a week, the teenagers were limited to the family room, the kitchen and their own bedrooms. In exchange for some favors, they were asked to be responsible to get up with the younger children on Saturday mornings. This gave the couple three blocks of time each week free of interruption, thus assuring privacy. They now had two possible locations that alleviated the need to be quiet, and provided the framework they needed to experience some new life sexually. It worked!

When there are no children or other people in the home 24 hours a day, any location in the house that is comfortable, free of distraction, and private is an option for creating a new setting. A van or camper could serve the same purpose.

Changes in lighting can vary the atmosphere for sex. The variations might include no light, candlelight, dim light, or bright light. You might find varying the placement of a candle or lamp enhances the visual enjoyment of each other's bodies. Some couples' sex life is so routine and predictable that even a change in the bedclothes—a new bedspread, for instance—is a refreshing change. Some couples enjoy the smell of incense burning. Others enjoy the use of perfumes or colognes.

In addition to having fun experimenting with the setting, you can exercise your creativity in many other areas. Clothing can be varied. If you have tended to begin with your nightclothes on, crawl into bed some night and let your spouse discover you *without* clothes on. On the other hand, if you are a couple who are in the nude during most of your getting-ready time, you may find it much more arousing to use clothes to add new intrigue.

Other ways to have fun and to play together include teasing each other. It's critical that the teases do not carry a jab or put-down, or pick on a sensitive issue. Rather, the tease has to be for the fun of it. Resisting your partner, in a fun way, is one type of teasing that can enhance sexual fun. This is the message that says, "Come on and try to get me," or "See if I'm available."

Whatever variation you use—however crazy it might seem—if it creates fun and laughter and does not always have to lead to intercourse, you have a good start on keeping alive your total sexual expression with each other.

Clifford L. and Joyce J. Penner

Other ways to have fun and to play together include teasing each other.

3.11 PREVENTING INFIDELITY

Last night we heard the shocking news that a couple in our Bible study group was divorcing because of the husband's continual infidelity. Needless to say we were stunned—this couple seemed to have a happy marriage. What are some ways we can affair-proof our marriage?

There are several steps you can take to reduce the possibility of infidelity. When you first become aware that another person is having an impact on you, that's the time to take action. You may still enjoy proper interaction with this person. But for the benefit of your marriage, you need to set some ground rules.

1. *Never tell the person you are attracted to her.* Talk about your spouse frequently, and tell your spouse about this person. But use your own judgment as to how fully to explain your dilemma. I have a friend who seems to delight in telling his wife about all the women upon whom he develops fleeting crushes. He encourages her to do the same. But while she admits she is susceptible to similar experiences, she prefers not to talk about them or to hear about his. My wife is aware of the precautions I take around women, and thus she isn't threatened when I extol the appropriate virtues of a business associate.

2. *Don't treat a new friend the way you treat an old, respected friend.* I'm careful about touching. While I might shake hands or squeeze an arm or a shoulder in greeting, I embrace people only when they are dear friends or relatives, and only in front of others. By doing this, I'm not even tempted to make the embrace longer or more impassioned than is appropriate. If I allowed myself to embrace anyone, including dear friends, in private, I would be less confident of my motives and my subsequent actions.

For instance, what would happen if I lingered an instant to see what kind of reaction I might get? And let's say the person's reaction was encouraging. We might both pretend it didn't happen, but what about the next time? Would we not be carefully checking each other out to see if what we thought we felt the first time was accurate? And what if it was? At what point would we overtly embrace passionately, silently declaring our feelings for each other? I don't know, and I don't want to know. That's why I keep such activity public, ensuring its appropriateness.

3. *Whenever I need to meet or dine or travel with a woman I'm not related to, I make it a threesome.* Should an unavoidable last-minute complication make this

impossible, my wife hears it from me first. My philosophy is if you take care of how things look, you take care of how they are.

Where I work we have a window in every office door. When these were installed 40 or 50 years ago, they were not intended to make immorality difficult. They were intended to eliminate suspicion and protect reputations. As long as that little eye to the outside world is uncovered, no one feels free to attempt anything untoward, and just as important, no one else is suspicious about what goes on behind closed doors.

My embargo against dining alone with an unrelated woman is also for my wife's sake. My wife is not the jealous type, but this way I don't have to keep track of every lunch partner so I can tell her about each one before someone else does.

In addition to eating out, travel can be chock full of dangerous possibilities for appearances and behavior. How does it look for a man and woman who don't belong to each other to be on a long trip together, in a car, on a plane, in a cab, at the same hotel—even if in separate rooms? The price of suspicion is high, and the price of infidelity is even higher.

4. *Avoid flirtation or suggestive conversation, even in jest.* Idle flirting gets people in trouble because the other person needs and wants attention so badly. And it's dangerous when a man hopes a woman's response to his teasing means she is interested in him, when in fact she goes along with his teasing because she never suspects the truth behind his humor. There is the opportunity for misunderstanding. Or worse, she may indeed suspect that he means it, and then there is the opportunity for real, but potentially dangerous, understanding.

Jerry B. Jenkins

3.12 OBSESSED WITH SPOUSE'S PREMARITAL SEX LIFE

My husband had sex with the girl he was dating before he met me. He says it was the biggest mistake of his life, and he has asked for my forgiveness. I know I'm harming our relationship by continuing to bring his past relationship up, but I can't get it out of my mind. He's willing to see a marriage counselor with me, but I don't think that's necessary. I just need some practical advice on how to put my husband's past out of my mind.

You've just given one of the strongest arguments I can think of against premarital sex.

You've just given one of the strongest arguments I can think of against premarital sex. The effects and implications of any sexual experience will continue into subsequent relationships. For you and many other men and women, this is an unhappy fact of life that is seldom mentioned in sex-education courses.

Yet I see several reasons for encouragement in your situation. First, you recognize the problem and the danger it presents to your marriage. Second, you seem to have a strong, healthy marriage. And third, your husband evidently is committed to solving the problem. These three factors make me think there is hope for a lasting solution.

Perhaps it would be easier to forget your husband's past behavior if you remind yourself that not doing so is actually disobedience to God, and to remember that God asks us to forgive others (Col. 3:13). Perhaps the starting point for you should be to ask God's forgiveness yourself.

Another step might be to think of the temptation to rehash the past as just that—a temptation. I believe Satan uses every little crack or entry point he can find to destroy marriages. So you might ask yourself, "What steps would I take to resist any other temptation in my life?" And take those same steps (including prayer and asking support and prayer from others) to withstand this temptation. You might also do some reading on the subject of forgiveness. The Bible, of course, has a lot to say on the subject, and I'd also recommend the book *Caring Enough to Forgive* (Regal) by David Augsburger.

"What steps would I take to resist any other temptation in my life?"

Having discussed the need for forgiveness, you should realize that often in these cases, genuine forgiveness is only part of the problem. Another factor may be your own insecurity. Perhaps you're wondering how you measure up to your husband's old girlfriend. If that's the case, I'd recommend you read a helpful book on self-image, *Healing for Damaged Emotions* (Victor) by David Seamands.

If you don't begin making significant progress in dealing with this problem soon, I'd encourage you to go to counseling together. You also need to keep in mind what you already realize: the end result of continuing to pick at this particular scab will be continued unhappiness and perhaps even serious marital strife. However, it sounds to me as if you and your husband have the kind of commitment needed to work through the problem. You just need to get started.

Jay Kesler

3.13 TURNED OFF BY WEIGHT GAIN

After my wife had our third child, she didn't lose the weight she had gained during the pregnancy. She seems to have given up the fight, and I'm having trouble seeing her as a desirable sex partner. Whenever I try to discuss this situation, she doesn't want to talk about it. What should I do?

This is a tough issue. Your wife's excess weight is something only she can change, yet you are being affected by it. Talking to her about her weight like you have in the past won't help. In fact, it could make her feel worse about herself and cause her to eat more.

Instead, the two of you might begin by deciding to see a counselor—individually at first. You and the counselor could discuss how your wife's weight affects you. The same counselor can meet with your wife to understand her feelings about her excess weight and about your reaction to her appearance. Then you can meet together with the counselor, who can facilitate your discussion. The counselor can help make sure both of you feel heard and understood, and steps toward change can be implemented.

It's possible that your wife would like to lose weight but feels helpless. A counselor could connect her with a supportive weight loss program. You can help, too. Often husbands want their wives to lose weight, but they aren't willing to stop buying and eating high-fat foods themselves. Your whole family must develop healthy eating habits if weight control is going to be an achievable long-term goal for your wife.

Whether or not your wife chooses to work on weight reduction, you must begin to focus on her positive qualities. Affirming your love for her in spite of her weight is crucial. This may not be the case for your wife, but some people

Affirming your love for her in spite of her weight is crucial.

use their weight to test the love of significant people in their lives. This especially happens to women whose parents were conditional in the way they gave and received love. It might be helpful for you to create a list of your wife's positive attributes, and keep adding to it. Then regularly mention the things you value in her.

Sexually, change your focus from a visual response to her body to focusing on the sensation of skin-to-skin contact. Enjoy kissing. Enjoy her touch of your body. Enjoy looking into her eyes. Enjoy touching parts of her body that don't trigger your reaction to her weight. Also, take over more of the household duties to give your wife additional time to take care of her appearance.

Body image is an issue that affects a person's sexuality. How we feel about our bodies determines how readily and openly we are able to share them with our spouses. How we feel about our spouse's body influences our desire for and response to them sexually. When there is a gap between how we view ourselves or our spouses and what we accept as an ideal body, we develop a body-image problem. To reverse that problem, we need to bring the actual and the ideal closer together.

Most people have unrealistic ideals about weight and beauty because television and movie personalities have become the standard. Of course, these people have the help of professional makeup artists, video enhancement, and sometimes even a plastic surgeon. So consider whether your image of the ideal body is realistic and adjust it accordingly. Other times, a person's body needs to be changed to fit more closely with a realistic view of the body. In your wife's case, that would involve a weight-loss plan. Both of you can enjoy your sexual relationship more fully as the real body and the ideal body become more similar.

Clifford L. and Joyce J. Penner

3.14 UNABLE TO ACHIEVE SIMULTANEOUS ORGASMS

We've been married three years and we've never had an orgasm at the same time. I always thought this was something most couples enjoyed, and it seems like it would be wonderful to experience it. Is it really all that important, or should we give up trying?

It really isn't all that important. The myth that simultaneous orgasm is the epitome of sexual fulfillment is based on a number of false assumptions.

First, it assumes that two people get aroused and then respond at the same pace. That is highly unlikely. Second, it assumes that goal-oriented sex is more fulfilling than pleasure-oriented sex. On the contrary, goal-oriented sex can interfere with fulfillment by introducing demand, anxiety, and often a feeling of failure, all of which hinder the body's natural response mechanism.

Goal-oriented sex requires a wife to be orgasmic during intercourse, which is not the case for more than half of all sexually active women. It often assumes that she will only have one orgasm so she has to time that orgasm to occur when her husband is about to ejaculate. Women have the capacity to have more than one orgasm, and it's more likely that a woman who pursues multiple orgasms may have one when her husband does. Even then it works best when it is simply allowed to happen rather than worked toward as a goal.

Goal-oriented sex can interfere with fulfillment.

As one woman put it, "I wouldn't want to orgasm when he does because then I would miss out on his." Many couples prefer to enjoy each other's orgasms. That way, you can double your pleasure.

Clifford L. and Joyce J. Penner

3.15 DIMINISHED SEXUAL EXCITEMENT

My husband and I got physically involved when we were dating. Although we didn't have sex, we did frequently reach a point where we felt very sexually aroused. Now that we're married and are free to enjoy each other, I find that the level of excitement is much lower for me. We try to go slow and take our time, like we did when we were dating, but I still don't feel as passionate as I did before we were married. What is going on?

Many of us associate sexual feelings with sin. Yet God beautifully designed our sexuality as part of his perfect plan. Sexual union is recorded in Scripture before the Fall. We are sexual beings; our sexuality, our sexual feelings, and our sexual urges are from God, and they're good. However, our sexual behaviors are our responsibility. We can choose to abstain from sex until we're married; and we are the ones who make sex happen in our marriages.

When our involuntary sexual feelings are associated with guilt, as they were for you in your premarital activity, there is an adrenaline rush that occurs with sexual arousal. This guilt/adrenaline connection heightens the feelings of the intensity of arousal. But that is not the type of arousal we tend to experience in marriage. Married sex, as God designed it, is deeply satisfying for both partners and is combined with fun, pleasure, and the free enjoyment of each other's body. Married sex is not likely to grab you with an intense adrenaline rush that sweeps you off your feet. Unfortunately, many couples who grew up watching the guilt/adrenaline rush on television and in movies find it hard to shake that expectation and make the shift to the warm, fulfilling sexual relationship of marriage.

Make time for your sexual relationship rather than waiting for the passionate feelings.

So relax your expectation for that adrenaline rush of excitement. Instead, focus your energies on building intimacy, pleasure, fun and fulfillment. Make time for your sexual relationship rather than waiting for the passionate feelings, and your sexual relationship will grow to be a vital and meaningful part of your shared life as a couple.

Clifford L. and Joyce J. Penner

3.16 DIFFICULTY GETTING AN ERECTION

I've never had a problem, sexually speaking, until recently. Now, all of a sudden, I seem to be having difficulty getting an erection. I really do love my wife. In fact, she's probably more attractive today than she was 23 years ago when we first got married. So what's wrong with me?

Getting an erection is an involuntary response controlled by the relaxed branch (parasympathetic) of our involuntary nervous system. So when a man is relaxed and soaking in pleasure, he is likely to get an erection. However, anxiety or physical factors can interfere with this natural bodily response.

We would recommend first that you be checked by an urologist for tumescence evaluation. A cardiac and vascular workup would also be indicated since an erection is a vascular response. You need to be sure that diabetes and certain medications can be ruled out as a possible cause of your difficulty.

Once the possible medical causes are eliminated, you should consider the emotional reasons for a man having difficulty getting an erection. First, men of all ages experience erectile difficulty at some time or another. The occasional inability to get or maintain an erection need not be an issue of concern.

Men of all ages experience erectile difficulty at some time or another.

However, once anxiety and preoccupation with getting an erection has occurred, it tends to perpetuate itself. But the good news is that erectile responsiveness can be regained. Here's how to do it:

First, you need to be distracted from the anxiety about getting an erection. To do that you need to temporarily rule out sexual intercourse and all attempts at having intercourse during your times of lovemaking.

Second, you need to focus on pleasure and enjoying each other's body, rather than concentrating on having sex. If you came to our office for counseling, we would take you through the teaching, talking, and touching exercises of our sexual therapy plan.

In addition, we suggest that spouses make a habit of regularly touching each other's genitals in an affirming manner. (Remember that sexual intercourse is not the goal here.) If preoccupation or concern about the state of your penis enters in at any time, you should tell your wife. Verbalizing your anxiety interrupts the control your concern has over your penis.

Third, it's important that your wife be freed to really enjoy your body for *her* pleasure. The more freely she can lose herself in the pleasure, the more likely it is that your natural response of erection will occur. In contrast, if she is concentrating on how your penis is doing, her evaluation will increase the performance demand on you and will likely decrease your erectile response. If following these guidelines does not solve your problem, you may want to consult a sexual therapist.

Clifford L. and Joyce J. Penner

3.17 FINDING PRIVACY FOR SEX

Our children are approaching middle-school age, which has made us begin to wonder: how can my wife and I continue an active sex life when our kids are old enough to know what's going on?

We, as parents, have the idea that our children should not know that we have an ongoing sexual relationship. Indeed, children *should* be protected from inappropriate exposure to sexual activity between their parents, as well as details about their parents' sexual experiences. However, most children are comforted to know that their mom and dad are taking time to love each other.

Most children are comforted to know that their mom and dad are taking time to love each other.

With this in mind, we recommend that parents plan private times for themselves. One of the gifts that we parents can give our children is the gift of a marital relationship that is based on love (as well as on a fulfilling sex life). This is sensed by the child and is a major source of security for the child.

But how can parents do this? Since children can be both an interruption and an intrusion in a couple's sexual relationship, here are ten guidelines that can help you keep "turned on" to each other—even after your children are old enough to know what's going on.

First, make certain your sexual experiences are satisfying. These experiences need to be free of demand and anxiety, and full of care, warmth, pleasure, fun and intimacy.

Second, take care of your bodies. This includes making sure you get adequate rest, exercise and nutrition, as well as good grooming and preparing your bodies for your sexual times together.

Third, keep your sexual feelings alive by being aware of and affirming your sexual thoughts and sensations. If those feelings get triggered in response to someone other than your spouse, then turn those thoughts to each other.

Fourth, schedule quality time to be together physically. This time must be free of interruption and free of demands. You can either schedule this time when your children are being cared for away from home, when they are sleeping, or when they are old enough to be self-sufficient and know they should not interrupt you (except for emergencies).

Fifth, learn to give and receive bodily pleasure for the sake of pleasure. Learn to delight in each other's bodies. Arousal, release, and sexual intercourse could be the result of this time, but it should not be your expectation. These times work best when you are free to connect through talking, touching, caressing and loving without a demand for response.

Sixth, each of you should take responsibility to pursue your own sexual pleasure, but not at the expense of your spouse. For example, whenever you communicate what your body hungers for and do not demand that your spouse simply *know* what you desire, the sexual experiences will flow more freely. This removes the anxiety caused by trying to read each other's minds.

Seventh, plan special treats such as music, candlelight, a "love nest" in front of the fireplace, a fun snack, or a night away at a motel. Plan for these special treats by preparing your minds, your feelings, and your spirits for each other. Think special thoughts. Thank God for your time together. Do any preparation that is likely to enhance your sexual feelings for each other.

Eighth, set aside times for experimenting with each other. Show your spouse the kind of touch you like. Teach each other about your bodies. Experiment with kissing. These are good times to work on areas of your sexual relationship that might need some enhancement.

Show your spouse the kind of touch you like.

Ninth, schedule sex-talk times that are separate from your physical times together. Use these times to communicate with each other about your sexual relationship. What things would you like to change? What are you particularly enjoying? What would you like to increase?

Tenth, go for help when your sexual relationship is not satisfying; if it has demands; or if it is filled with anxiety. Dealing early with any problems that occur is the best way for a couple to avoid developing bad sexual habits.

Clifford L. and Joyce J. Penner

3.18 GUARDING AGAINST LUST

How can I guard against sexual lust when I am traveling on business? It is at these times—when I'm alone and in an unfamiliar city—that I find myself surrounded by pornographic magazines at airport newsstands and by X-rated television movies in my hotel room. Can you give me some suggestions on ways I can resist the temptation to indulge in these readily available magazines and movies?

We are created in the image of God, so we are created to be in relationship with God and with each other. That means that the sexual relationship between a human couple is more than just the physical act that we see animals engage in.

As humans, we have the capacity to think, to verbalize, and to have mental pictures or images. These mental images may include fantasies in which we picture sexual activities. It's not the fact that we have these images, but the *content* of these mental images that can cause us to violate God's standard for us.

The Bible teaches that we are not to lust after something that is not ours.

The Bible teaches that we are not to lust after something that is not ours. It also teaches that what we put into our minds influences who we become. Jesus said that if a man even looks at a woman (other than his wife) with the intent to be with her sexually, he has committed adultery (Mt. 5:28). We do not understand that to mean that a man will never find other women attractive. Rather, we are to limit how we respond to those natural attractions by controlling both our thoughts and our actions.

Yes, it's true that our world bombards us with sexual images. But it is our choice whether to pursue these images or resist them. We can choose *not* to turn on the X-rated movie in the hotel room. And we can choose *not* to look at the pornographic magazines at the airport newsstand. If a person doesn't have control over those behaviors, then he has a sexual addiction.

So how can we keep our mental life pure? First, we fill our sexual thoughts with creative pictures of sexual activity with our spouse. Then we keep our sexual relationship with our spouse alive. Further, we avoid sexually explicit material that is pornographic in nature. Instead, we read healthy sexual material with our mate. And we make ourselves accountable to someone if we aren't able to control the situation by ourselves.

None of these things is easy. They all take discipline. But they are essential if we are to maintain a pure thought life and a healthy, fulfilling sex life with our mate.
Clifford L. and Joyce J. Penner

3.19 REDUCING VULNERABILITY TO AFFAIRS

I know that just because I'm a married Christian that doesn't mean I'm automatically exempt from the temptation of an affair. I've seen ample proof that infidelity can happen even among believers. Even though I've only been married two years, what warning signs in my marriage might indicate I could be headed toward an affair?

Newly married couples are not immune to extramarital affairs. I have counseled many couples whose marriages have been violated by adultery—sometimes in the first six months of marriage. But the more common problem for newly married couples is overlooking the warning signals that indicate potential trouble. When I perform a wedding, I list five words—each beginning with "C"—that represent critical areas that, if left untended, will open the door to sexual vulnerability.

Newly married couples are not immune to extramarital affairs.

The first "C" is *calendar*. Early-years couples need to block out time for each other—no friends, no family. I'm counseling a husband and wife who are both professionals. He travels constantly on business, and she is handling the job of parenting their young children while maintaining a part-time career. Their too-busy lives robbed them of time for intimacy with each other. And in this instance, the husband had an affair. Fatigue, whether it be from the demands of work or children, places the greatest strain on relationships today.

The second "C" is *communication*, and that means sharing both feelings and thoughts. I can't tell you how many times I've heard spouses, especially women, admit that they had an affair because they found someone else who would talk and listen to them.

The third "C" is *caring*—developing a sensitivity to the fact that you have married a person who has very different needs from your own. The more effort you put into meeting each other's needs, the less likely either of you will be to go outside the marriage to get needs met.

Courtship, the fourth critical area, is closely related to caring. Couples often stop courting after the honeymoon. Time and again I see new husbands stop being affectionate and sensitive to their wives. Invariably, the wife gets angry and begins to shut down emotionally. Then, instead of approaching life as a team, they turn into adversaries.

To help couples break this cycle, I have them work on "courtship assignments." The man has to do one thing every day that shows his wife she is special to him, but he can't tell her what those special things are. The following week, I ask the woman what her husband did to express his love. Then she gets the same assignment for the following week. Whenever I can get couples courting again, the tone in the marriage changes immediately.

The last "C," *commitment,* is the most important factor in protecting your marriage from an affair. It's important to remember that all relationships ebb and flow. The flow takes care of itself. It's the ebb that requires commitment, especially during those times when you begin to feel disillusioned with marriage. And of course, in a Christian marriage the couple is committed to Christ, as well as to each other.

Couples need to establish boundaries for behavior and relationships with members of the opposite sex.

No list of reminders can completely ward off the possibility of an affair. That's why couples need to establish boundaries for behavior and relationships with members of the opposite sex. In any male/female friendship outside marriage, a person needs to ask: "What deep need in my life is being met by this friendship?" If the answer is a need that only your spouse should be fulfilling, you should re-evaluate that friendship.

Many times when men and women work closely together or serve on the same committee, they find they have more in common with each other than they do with their spouse. Any time you enjoy another person's company more than your mate's, and you continue to cultivate that relationship, you are a prime candidate for an affair.

Jim Smith

3.20 CONFLICTING EXPECTATIONS ABOUT SEX

I don't understand my wife. We have sex several times a week and she still wonders out loud if I really love her. Or she laments that we don't seem "very close." To me, the answers are an obvious "yes." Why are we having this misunderstanding?

Couples often have trouble understanding that they behave in ways that are foreign to each other simply because they are members of the opposite sex.

For instance, men and women bring two different sets of expectations to the way that they view sex. Frequency of sexual activity is often one of the first areas where differences begin to surface. Studies indicate that a woman's libido rises and falls according to her 28-day ovulation cycle. The typical male, on the other hand, has sexual thoughts every few minutes. While it is true that some women say they want more sexual activity than their husbands, more often the man is the one who feels he's not having enough sex. I tell couples, women especially, that sometimes they will need to offer the gift of availability to their spouse out of love and sensitivity to their partner's needs (1 Co. 7:5).

Most women place a higher priority on romance and affection than men do. Not that men don't want these things too, it's just that they don't usually rank them at the top of their needs list. And both approaches are valid. The senior pastor of our church used to describe sex like eating: sometimes you sit down to a gourmet feast with candlelight, soft music, seven courses. Other times it's a snack on the run. Neither would be healthy all the time. So spouses need to be realistic about their sex life and willing to accommodate each other's desires.

Most women place a higher priority on romance and affection than men do.

If couples can work on developing their communication, they will be more likely to bridge another gap—the different levels of intensity or emotional involvement that each spouse brings to their encounters. Men and women have opposing fears of intimacy, the woman's being a fear of distance, the man's a fear of closeness. Often, when this fear manifests itself in a couple's sex life, the wife will complain that intercourse has become nothing more than a physical release for her husband. Yet from the husband's point of view, sex is his primary way of expressing intimacy, both emotionally and physically.

One of the ways I help couples learn to move beyond their individual need for emotional intensity is by getting them to stretch out of their own comfort zone. For a man that might mean being willing to show a variety of expressions of affection before and after sex, perhaps beginning with the way he kisses his wife goodbye in the morning.

Likewise, women need to understand that a husband's sexual advances may be the only way he is comfortable expressing intimacy. Women need to recognize this difference and try not to feel rejected when their husband appears to be shutting down emotionally after making love.

If we focus on serving one another and developing a deeper understanding of our mate, problems over sexual frequency, variety and intensity often take care of themselves. Whether husbands and wives are unique by virtue of hormones, social programming, or divine design, we need to see each other as whole persons. That is, to realize that all people—male or female—have the same needs for love, affection and intimacy.

Jim Smith

3.21 A HUSBAND WITH A LOW LIBIDO

My husband and I are newlyweds, but we only have sex about three times a month. He just says he is unwilling to become more affectionate toward me. Sometimes when I bring up the subject, he pushes me away or gets sarcastic. Am I doing something wrong?

Begin by sorting out with your husband the source of his resistance to sexual intimacy.

Eventually, you might need to see a counselor, but you can start with self-help. Begin by sorting out with your husband the source of his resistance to sexual intimacy. It will be important for him to feel that you genuinely care for him as you attempt to understand what is causing him to avoid sex. Review the following possibilities, and encourage him to identify which category best describes his resistance to sex.

Childhood experiences. Men who were raised without intimacy end up resisting sex. They have a sexual drive but no capacity for closeness and warmth with a woman. The sexual retraining process of gradually learning to give and receive pleasure can help a man gain the capacity and desire for intimacy. However, he has to be willing. The decision to pursue sexual closeness may require the help of a therapist.

Sexual addiction. If your husband is uncomfortable with intimacy, he is probably finding sexual release through self-stimulation. A sexual addiction may lead him to get sexual release by looking at pornography or engaging in some other sexual preoccupation. If so, he probably feels conflict and guilt about his secret life. Your sexual approaches then only irritate him because they remind him of his sexually destructive behavior. If addiction is the problem, you will get the most help from one of the 12-step programs. Call one of these numbers to get information on programs available in your community: Sexaholics Anonymous; Sex and Love Addicts Anonymous; Codependents of Sex Addicts COSA (763) 537-6904.

Personal issues. Some men avoid sex because of a personal issue, such as their wife's bad breath or an aversion to vaginal secretions. If that is the case, your husband may not feel comfortable telling you. You will need to free him to express whatever he is feeling, even if it hurts you. A personal issue can usually be resolved by changing the habit.

Sexual inexperience. Your husband might feel sexually inept. The good news is that a sexually inexperienced male responds quickly and positively to education about sex and to sexual retraining. If you feel competent, teach him by talking him through a sexual experience as you would enjoy it.

Past influences. Perhaps your husband grew up with a dominant, controlling mother who denigrated men; or he might have received rigid anti-sexual teaching as a boy. If he came to marriage with deeper emotional blocks caused by destructive influences such as these, you should see a counselor.

Feeling crowded. If your husband senses neediness from you instead of sexual desire, his sarcasm and pushing away may be a reaction to your approach. A turned-on woman is a turn-on for a man, but a needy woman is a turn-off. If this is the source of the problem, get help with understanding the gap in your life that you are trying to fill with sex. In addition, allow your husband to initiate all sexual experiences and work on ways to connect with him nonsexually to fulfill your longing to feel desired.

Overwork. If your husband puts all his energy into his career, he may have no energy left for you. This is clearly an issue of priorities. You will have to schedule

The solution you pursue will depend on the source of your husband's resistance to sex.

time for just the two of you—even if you become an appointment on his crowded calendar.

As you can see, the solution you pursue will depend on the source of your husband's resistance to sex. If the steps you take don't achieve the results you desire, find a counselor who specializes in treating sexual problems. You can't make your husband want you; you can only eliminate the issues that interfere with his desire for you.

Clifford L. and Joyce J. Penner

3.22 REDUCED SEX DRIVE AFTER HAVING CHILDREN

My wife and I have been married for 19 years. We have a solid Christian marriage, but our sex life began to deteriorate after our second child was born. My wife has lost virtually all interest in sex and refuses to talk about it. Is it usual for a woman to lose interest in sex as she gets older?

No, it is not "usual" for women to lose interest in sex as they get older. Loss of interest is usually related to issues other than age. If, for example, your wife's interest in sex had begun to diminish after your first child was born, we would suspect the effects of pregnancy and childbirth. Fatigue, body changes, 24-hour responsibility for a totally dependent infant and changes in self-image ("now I'm a mother, not a sexual partner") could affect her interest level.

However, since the loss of desire started after the *second* child was born, we wonder whether your wife experiences pain during intercourse (caused by the effects of childbirth) or if she struggles with emotional/psychological issues that make sex less enjoyable or fulfilling for her.

We also wonder if *your* response to her waning sexual desire has, in any way, exacerbated the problem. We find that when a husband is anxiously preoccupied with his wife's lack of interest or seems to need sex to feel good about himself, then the normal ebb and flow of sexual desire will be interrupted. It may be very difficult to rekindle the fires of passion when one's attention is fixed on what may be a normal "dip." This fixation may have the effect of further dampening your wife's desire.

If this is the case with you and your wife, you need to back away from any expectation for sex and, instead, focus on other critical dimensions of your relationship. Take time to communicate, to get to know your wife's heartbeat. Take walks; enjoy being together. Slowly, over time (and yes, it may take a long time), the building of this nonsexual intimacy will lay the groundwork for a more fulfilling, less frustrating sex life for both of you.

Clifford L. and Joyce J. Penner

Take time to communicate, to get to know your wife's heartbeat.

3.23 HAUNTED BY CHILDHOOD SEXUAL ABUSE

Before we were married, we could hardly wait to be together. But no sooner had the honeymoon ended than our sex life began to cool. By our six-month anniversary, it was as if a wall would go up between us every time I even mentioned to my wife the possibility of making love. Needless to say, I'm feeling frustrated and rejected. What is happening to us?

When a woman's sexual desire changes so early in a marriage and is accompanied by an aversion to specific sexual activities, that usually indicates that she was sexually abused as a child. For a woman who was so abused, her sexuality has been aroused prematurely, and it has been associated with shame, demand, immobilization, and lack of power. It may also have been the girl's only way to get "love." Therefore, as an adult before marriage, when sex is not expected (no demand) or when she can choose how far to go (not immobilized), sex can be pursued and enjoyed. Once the commitment of marriage occurs, however, when sex becomes expected (demand), the feeling of lack of choice and immobilization during sex sets in quickly. She resumes the feelings and flashbacks of the abused and used victim. Consequently, her resistance to you is her protection against repeating what her emotions perceive as victimization.

Her resistance to you is her protection against repeating what her emotions perceive as victimization.

This association between her childhood sexual abuse and post-marital sex can change, but professional help is usually necessary. Being part of a support group of other women who were sexually abused is most important. Your wife will need to talk about what happened to her as a child. She will have to relive those painful details and grieve the losses she experienced during those acts of violation. Keeping a journal of any memories, thoughts, feelings, or flashbacks will help relieve the power that the past has over her current sexual life.

When the two of you are ready and willing to rebuild your sexual life together, it will be important for you to allow her to be the active and dominant partner sexually, so that sex is not something "done to her," but something she chooses to do.

Second, it will be important for the two of you to discuss the specific violations that happened to her and avoid those behaviors as much as possible.

Third, she will need to let you know when—during your sexual times—she has flashbacks of past abuse. At that time, stop what you are doing—just hold and affirm her.

Clifford L. and Joyce J. Penner

3.24 PLAGUED BY EARLY EJACULATION

This is probably a typically early-married question, but I'll ask it anyway: How does a guy control early ejaculation?

There are four basic principles and guidelines for learning to control ejaculation.

The single most common problem men report is premature ejaculation—not having control of when ejaculation occurs or ejaculating before he and his wife are ready for him to respond. The seriousness of the problem varies. A man may have so little control that he ejaculates before entry or when his wife touches his penis. More commonly, the man is unable to last more than a minute or two after entry. This seems to be a learned reflex response that can be effectively reconditioned when husband and wife actively pursue learning ejaculation control together.

There are four basic principles and guidelines for learning to control ejaculation. *First,* the husband needs to shift his focus away from ejaculation onto pleasure. He needs to savor the sensations of touch and arousal rather than being anxious about or eager for release.

Second, the man must allow himself to be passive and "soak in" pleasure rather than actively pursuing arousal and release. The active branch of the involuntary nervous system controls ejaculation, so passivity helps delay that automatic active response.

Third, the man needs to increase his awareness of the sensations of arousal building so that he can identify, on a scale of zero to ten, if he is experiencing no arousal (0) or if he is approaching orgasm (10).

Fourth, awareness of sensations of arousal and ejaculatory control can be learned on your own by a step-by-step process. We teach couples the use of the squeeze technique, as adapted from Masters and Johnson. Helen Singer Kaplan teaches the stop-start technique, which is basically the same as the squeeze, except instead of applying the squeeze, all genital stimulation is stopped. To learn this process, be very deliberate in mastering each step we have outlined in *The Gift of Sex* (Word), or the technique described in Kaplan's book *PE: How to Overcome Premature Ejaculation* (Brunner/Mazel). To prevent failure, be sure the squeeze is applied or the stimulation is stopped as soon as the husband reaches full erection rather than waiting until he is approaching ejaculation (when he is identifying his arousal in the lower numbers rather than when he is approaching level 10). Take a break by moving away from genital touching to general body caressing. The man's thoughts and focus must move with the touch. With careful attention to the step-by-step process, pleasure can be enhanced as control is learned.

Clifford L. and Joyce J. Penner

3.25 SEX IN THE LATER YEARS

What kind of changes in our physical relationship can my husband and I expect as we get older? We're in our thirties and have sex an average of two to three times a week. Will that frequency change? Does passion lessen? What can we do now to ensure that our sex lives will always be fun and fulfilling?

Procreation may be for the young, but sexual pleasure is for the young and old.

Procreation may be for the young, but sexual pleasure is for the young and old. God designed us as sexual beings from the moment of birth until the moment of death. Our sexuality does not die until we die.

Yes, there are some changes as we age that will affect sexual functioning. For most women, estrogen and progesterone levels drop in their fifties (sometimes as early as their thirties or as late as their sixties); and with that drop, women stop menstruating and reach menopause. Unless a woman undergoes hormonal replacement therapy, she is likely at this time to have vaginal dryness and some irritation, which may make sexual intercourse uncomfortable for her. This can be lessened, however, by using a vaginal lubricant and exercising the P.C. muscle.

For men, the male hormone testosterone begins to decrease at age 40 and decreases significantly from age 60 on, and its effectiveness in the body also decreases. Because of this, there are five changes that men experience as they age. However, none of these need to affect the frequency or pleasure of the sexual experience.

1. A man will require direct penile stimulation to get an erection, rather than responding to visual stimuli or thought stimulus. This may actually enhance lovemaking for the older couple, because the man and the woman will become more similar in their arousal response pattern.

2. After a man reaches 60, his erections may not be as firm as they were when he was younger. He still will be able to enter and have total fulfillment, unless he becomes anxious about his decrease in firmness. It's the lack of awareness that this is a normal result of aging that triggers anxiety and then impotence. Impotence is not the result of the aging process; it is a result of anxiety about the aging process.

3. The man's ejaculations become less intense as he ages. Yet the experience is equally satisfying.

4. After age 40, a man may not need to ejaculate with each sexual experience. He may feel totally satisfied without any ejaculation.

5. As he ages, a man will need a longer rest after ejaculation before he can be restimulated to another erection.

All of these changes need to be recognized and adjusted for, but they need not lead to a decrease in frequency or passion. Keep your sexual relationship alive as you progress through the next stages of life. Make certain your time together is a priority, that you both are satisfied, that you keep reading and talking about your sexual relationship, and that you bring something new to your sexual experience every now and then. By doing these things, you will find new joy as you continue the pleasure of your marital bed—even into your old age.

Clifford L. and Joyce J. Penner

> *Make certain your time together is a priority.*

3.26 PAINFUL INTERCOURSE

My husband and I have been married six years and have a good sex life. But I always experience pain at the moment of penetration. We take things slowly, and after the initial pain things go well. But what can I do about that early discomfort?

God intended sex in marriage to bring pleasure. When that pleasure is interrupted because of pain, the entire process of "becoming one" is affected.

Unfortunately, pain is often difficult to relieve because the reason for it can't be identified. To help you and your doctor determine why you are having discomfort, for the next four or five times you have intercourse, write down a description of the pain. Describe exactly when you feel the pain begin and when it lessens, the exact location of the pain, and the type of pain (stinging, burning, jabbing, or a feeling of pressure).

It's also helpful to write down information from a vaginal self-examination. In a comfortable position, and using a vaginal lubricant and holding a mirror, examine the opening of your vagina for redness, irritation, rash or sores. Is there tightness or pain when you insert a finger? Note any sensations you feel when tightening or relaxing your vaginal muscle around your finger or when pressing your finger against your vaginal wall. Write down what you discover.

Once you have recorded the data, schedule an appointment with your physician. If he or she still can't help, try to locate a medical doctor who is both a gynecologist and urologist who specializes in treating painful intercourse

Once you have recorded the data, schedule an appointment with your physician.

(dyspareunia). Inflammation or irritation of any of the structures of the genital area will cause pain and will require medical attention. Chronic infections such as genital warts or herpes also can cause pain upon entry.

As sexual therapists, we treat a common cause of painful intercourse called *vaginismus,* the involuntary spastic tightening of the muscle controlling the entrance to the vagina. To relieve vaginismus, the woman uses a series of graduated dilators to stretch and relax the muscles that control the opening of the vagina. She begins by inserting the smallest dilator that she can comfortably insert—several times a week—using the same process as recommended for vaginal self-examination. She leaves the dilator in place for 15 to 30 minutes while tightening and relaxing the vaginal muscle. When she feels ready, she tries the next largest dilator. She continues to graduate to large dilators until she is able to comfortably insert a dilator of the same or larger circumference as the head of her husband's erect penis. You are fortunate to have a good sex life in spite of your initial discomfort. But you need to pursue a solution that will enable you to have entry without any pain.

Clifford L. and Joyce J. Penner

3.27 WHEN PMS INTERRUPTS SEX

For two weeks every month I'm on an emotional rollercoaster due to premenstrual syndrome (PMS), and it has done real damage to our sex life. My husband is reluctant to suggest that we have sex because he's afraid I'll shoot him down. Since he doesn't have a similar hormonal civil war going on in his body, he doesn't understand what I'm facing. What should I do about this?

PMS is real! It affects the quality of life for millions of women, yet too many couples do not realize there are ways to battle this problem.

Begin by identifying the specific symptoms you experience. Typical symptoms include fatigue, depression, irritability, angry outbursts, cravings for sweet and/or salty foods, headache, abdominal bloating, anxiety, confusion, difficulty with concentration and/or memory, swollen hands or feet, tender breasts and tearfulness.

Next, keep a log of the dates you experience certain symptoms. On your monthly chart, mark your symptoms with a number from 0 to 10, indicating the severity of the symptom on a given day.

These charts will enable you to predict the onset of your internal warfare and plan ahead for its effects. Plan positive sexual times for you and your husband for the two weeks leading up to your symptoms. Then, depending on the severity of your PMS, plan for the type of sexual encounter that would meet your needs and help relieve your stress during that difficult time. For example, you might enjoy being caressed everywhere except your breasts and genitals. Or you may not want to be touched anywhere, but would enjoy caressing your husband.

During those difficult two weeks, make time in your schedule for extra rest. Schedule a "walk-and-talk" time together to occur before your sexual time. Begin your actual physical time with a relaxing bubble bath or a warm shower. Planning for your PMS will reduce the damage to your sex life and increase your husband's understanding.

It might also be possible to treat your PMS. Nutritionists and medical researchers recommend avoiding fat, sodium, alcohol and caffeine, increasing fresh fruits and vegetables, legumes and whole grains, and drinking eight to ten glasses of water a day. Some nutritionists recommend avoiding red meats and dairy products and including a daily intake of safflower oil and Evening Primrose Oil (a nutritional supplement).

In addition, aerobic exercise is a must. Exercise is thought to stimulate the release of ankephalins and endorphins—neurotransmitters responsible for a person's sense of well being. They need to be elevated in women who have PMS, so work up a good sweat with at least a half-hour of jogging, swimming or some other aerobic exercise.

As the medical world begins to identify possible causes of PMS, treatments are becoming more effective. Some doctors encourage taking a vitamin-mineral supplement that, after a month or two, relieves mid to moderate symptoms in many women. Consult with your physician or nutritionist for a recommendation.

Ankephalins and endorphins need to be elevated in women who have PMS.

Two supplements that we have found to be effective are Optivite and Theraids; one of these may work for you.

If these measures don't relieve your symptoms enough to boost your sexual relationship, seek further medical help.

Clifford L. and Joyce J. Penner

3.28 FACING A HYSTERECTOMY

My wife, who is only 43, just learned that she needs a hysterectomy. What can I do to be supportive of her and reaffirm her sexuality? I'm also wondering if a hysterectomy will adversely affect our sex life. I'm not sure what to expect.

We recommend you take several steps to prepare yourselves before your wife's hysterectomy.

A hysterectomy is a major surgical procedure as well as a life change for your wife and, indirectly, for you. It is one of the safer surgeries, and many women find the quality of their lives improve afterward. We recommend you take several steps to prepare yourselves before your wife's hysterectomy.

First, make certain the hysterectomy is necessary. Some medical authorities believe that some of the hysterectomies performed are unnecessary, so seek a second medical opinion. Also, get as much information as you can—from other women who have had hysterectomies and from reading. One source would be Dr. Joe S. McIlhaney's book *1250 Health Care Questions Women Ask* (Baker). McIlhaney addresses the issues of necessary and unnecessary hysterectomies.

Second, take charge of other factors that will affect your wife's recovery and sex life after her hysterectomy. Before the surgery, she should get herself in as good physical condition as possible. Afterward, she should explicitly follow her doctor's instructions for recovery. Support her in taking time to get back on her feet, and be certain she does no lifting and does not have sexual intercourse until her doctor approves these activities.

Third, the two of you should discuss with her physician what other surgical procedures will be involved. Will her ovaries need to be removed? Even though the ovaries decrease in their production of estrogen and progesterone as a woman goes through menopause, they excrete small amounts of testosterone until a woman is into her eighties. Since testosterone stimulates sexual desire, some women's sex drive may lessen noticeably when the ovaries are removed. Even so, if there is a history of ovarian cancer in your wife's family, keeping her ovaries may not be recommended.

Will she need a cystocele repair for a sagging bladder? If your wife is responsive sexually to G-spot stimulation (stimulation of the front wall of the vagina just beyond the inner ridge of the P.C. muscle—the muscle that controls the opening and closing of the vagina), surgery for a cystocele repair may interfere with that source of stimulation.

Another question to ask is if your wife will be on hormonal replacement therapy after her surgery. If she has not started menopause and will be keeping her ovaries, hormonal replacement therapy is unlikely. However, if she has started menopause or her ovaries will be removed, hormonal replacement therapy started immediately will greatly decrease the loss of sexual desire and enhance your wife's sexual experiences after surgery.

Fourth, know your wife's sexual response now. Some women are very aware of the sensations of the uterine contractions that occur when they experience orgasm. These women have to shift the focus of their sexual sensations after a hysterectomy from the uterine contractions to the vaginal contractions. The vagina is not affected by a hysterectomy so the sensations of the penis in the vagina will not be disturbed, nor will vaginal lubrication be affected.

All these issues must be addressed to ascertain how your wife's sexual experience will be affected and what your role needs to be as you support her. In general, more women find their sexual experience is improved after a hysterectomy than those who find it is negatively affected because they simply feel so much better. You can be supportive in gathering data, making decisions, giving your wife time to recover adequately, and positively participating in any new sexual discoveries and adjustments that become necessary.

Clifford L. and Joyce J. Penner

CHAPTER 4

INTIMACY:
GROWING CLOSER
TOGETHER

INTIMACY:
GROWING CLOSER
TOGETHER

"For this reason a man will leave his father and mother and be united to his wife and they will become one flesh. The man and his wife were both naked and they felt no shame" (Gn. 2:24-25, NIV).

We were created to have an intimate relationship with God. And thus our relationship in marriage is to reflect the intimate relationship that God has with His people (Eph. 5:32). The marriage relationship is so close that the Bible's word for it is one flesh. Genesis 2:18 says it was not good for Adam to be alone, so Adam was given a wife. Eve was created to be a helpmate, someone who was bone of Adam's bone and flesh of his flesh. The words "naked and not ashamed" are not so much a physical description as a description of their intimacy. Indeed, intimacy is a gift from God, which comes through Christ, and is similar to the spiritual intimacy we have with Christ. Malachi 2:15 says it is God who makes us one. Just as God brought Eve to Adam, He brings us together as husband and wife (Mt. 19:6).

Genesis 2:24 gives two prerequisites for becoming one: leaving and cleaving. We are commanded to leave our parents so we can cling to our spouse. Although this command is directed toward the husband, the principle applies to wives as well. No leaving equals no cleaving. This does not mean we abandon our parents, but that after Christ, our spouse is now our number one priority. Moreover, the leaving is more than physical. It involves our emotions and finances as well. A marriage committed to leaving is prepared for a life of cleaving.

Cleaving is like a super glue adhesive. We stick to each other. A beautiful description of this is found in the life and words of Ruth 1:14: "Ruth clung to Naomi."

This loyal "stick-to-it-ness" keeps us together through thick and thin, like Naomi and Ruth. Cleaving makes oneness a possibility, but demands time spent together where we regularly share what is on our hearts and minds. In cleaving there is an emotional, spiritual nakedness which uncovers our souls like Adam and Eve.

But let us also remember that when Adam and Eve sinned, shame entered the picture. They hid from God and covered up their nakedness. They blamed each other for what had happened. Consequently, the greatest threat to our intimacy is our own sinfulness! Because our nakedness uncovers our shame, we need to exercise unconditional love and forgiveness. These, along with trust, become the glue that binds us together.

> *PRAYER: Lord, help our marriage to rightly reflect the mysterious union that You have with Your bride, the church. Remove anything in our marriage that is keeping us from cleaving. May we hold on to Your grace and the truth that you alone can make us one flesh. Amen.*

4.1 FOSTERING AN ATTITUDE OF LIFE-LONG COMMITMENT

Having seen so many short-term marriages and the damage divorce creates, my husband and I are even more determined to make our marriage a long-term deal. But in a practical sense, how do you live out the idea of a life-long commitment—especially in a world where the word "commitment" has so little meaning?

Lifetime commitment is not primarily about length of time. I don't, for example, think along these lines: "If I live for another 20 years, I will have to live with my wife for 240 months, or 1,040 weeks. Can I stick with her that long?" I don't think about the calendar when I think about my commitment. Nor do people I know. It's when we are *not* committed that we worry about the number of years ahead of us.

Committed people don't hunker down before the terrors and tedium of time to come. In fact, many of us make our commitments by the day. We choose each day to put someone else's needs ahead of our wishes. We choose each day to care for someone.

Committed people don't hunker down before the terrors and tedium of time to come.

Then what does the "lifetime" in commitment mean? It means "unconditional." A lifetime commitment is about not having exit routes along the way, just in case things don't work out the way we had expected. A lifetime commitment would never sound like this: "I'll stay with you unless you get stomach cancer." Or "I'll be with you as long as you remain thin." Or "I'll stick with you until somebody better comes along." A lifetime commitment doesn't have escape clauses in the fine print. Lifetime commitments are simply commitments we intend to keep, no matter what.

Most of us seem to believe that marriage entails this sort of commitment because of the sort of thing marriage is. For instance, we still get married only when we are ready for commitment. Isn't this why we need ceremonies? A ceremony, whether in a church or a civil chamber, is an occasion on which we make vows for everyone to hear, vows to live together until the sharp blade of death slices us apart, vows spoken in a festive setting, vows we celebrate afterward with our friends and family.

There is probably no other person in the world we need to trust more than the person we marry.

We all share the deep human need to trust in another person. There is probably no other person in the world we need to trust more than the person we marry. And nothing creates trust like knowing that the other person is unconditionally committed. Legalities don't help much. Would it help, when we felt especially insecure, if our spouse said, "You've got a marriage license, isn't that enough for you?" Would it help if our partner offered us a contract that guaranteed us a fair share of things in the event that he—or she—should leave us? Not really.

It takes a personal commitment to create trust. Not just a vow spoken a year, ten years, a lifetime ago, but a commitment reborn every day by our reliable presence, renewed by acts of care, resurrected by generous forgiving. Our commitment to someone in caring love is the only guarantee we can give, the only basis for trust.

Lewis B. Smedes

4.2 FINDING COUPLE TIME

We keep hoping our schedules will open up and we'll finally have more time to go out to the movies and dinner like we did before we were married. But once again, as we studied our calendar, we realized it's been at least four months since we've had a "date night." We really do want to do things as a couple, but time always escapes from us. What are we doing wrong?

Wayne Rickerson, author of *We Never Have Time Just for Us*, feels that recognition of neglect is crucial to any remedy in a suffering relationship. "We do not go into marriage thinking, 'Our plan is to have fun and excitement, share goals and interests for the first two years, and then neglect these areas.' But we invite neglect into our marriage when we do not *plan* ways to have fun and excitement, share interests and set common goals," he explains.

Planning is fundamental to establishing ongoing quality couple time together. Couples who really desire more time together make more time available to be together. They meet for lunch. They call each other during the day or leave notes to touch base on both important and unimportant matters. They set aside a time of day "just for us." Sometimes it's a jog at 6 A.M. or a walk at 10 P.M. They guard weekend time and often turn down invitations because they value time alone together.

Couples who really desire more time together make more time available to be together.

They develop mutual interests, like the couple I met who make a day of cooking together on Sunday. Or they get excited about a sport and enjoy playing it or watching it together. Or they take up a hobby together. Or they take off on unplanned camping trips, just the two of them. (I found spontaneity to be a hallmark for these couples. When they find themselves with a bonus of extra time due to a blizzard, plant shutdown, or appointment cancellation, they grab the opportunity to do something together.)

Other couples work creative solutions into the fabric of everyday routine. A man wrote to *Woman's Day* magazine, "As my wife works in the morning and I in the evening, I've found that a little extra something I can do for her is drive her to and from work. It saves parking costs and she appreciates my effort. The drive to work gives us precious extra time for sharing, and during the drive home, I am glad to serve as a sympathetic listener for the events of her day. It spares her the bother of fighting traffic and allows her to unwind with the man who was lucky enough to marry her."

Dolores Curran

4.3 WANING ATTRACTION

I hate to admit this, but after 17 years of marriage, I can sometimes look at my husband and wonder "What ever attracted me to you in the first place?" I'm concerned that I'm falling out of love. What can I do to keep these feelings at bay and build on the love I do have for my husband?

The following principles can help you restore love to your marriage or enrich the love affair you now have with your mate.

Love is rational. I can understand love and grow in my understanding of it throughout my lifetime. The Bible contains the story of God's unfailing love for an often-unlovable human race. We find God wooing, nurturing, caring, and doing the best for those he loves, always seeking to draw people to himself.

Love is always doing the very best for the object of one's love.

If we were to sum up all we can learn about love through a study of God's dealings with mankind, it might be stated as simply as this: love is always doing the very best for the object of one's love. And there's nothing mysterious about that.

What is it that makes us want to do the best for the one we love? The answer, again based on biblical principle, is that love recognizes a unique value in the beloved and chooses to affirm that value. Real love is a choice backed up by action.

Love is not easy or simple. It is an art that I must want to learn and pour my life into. This principle corrects a common misconception, that it is easy to love, requiring neither thought nor effort. In other words, that it's just a matter of doing what comes naturally!

The fact is that *love is costly.* It requires much from the lover even when the giving is pure joy. If you do what comes naturally you will be wrong almost every time. Again, the Bible has the information we need on how to love. The most concentrated lessons on the art of loving your mate can be found in the Song of Solomon.

Love is an active power that I control by my own will. I am not the helpless slave of love. We are barraged by propaganda suggesting that love is an uncontrollable feeling that comes and goes like a wayward sparrow. Most of the boy-meets-girl plots of films and television are based on the premise that love is a feeling that just happens. Or else it doesn't happen.

The truth is that love is an active power that you were meant to control by your own will. You can choose to love; you can do what is necessary to restore love to your marriage; and you can refuse to be enslaved by passing emotions.

Love is the power that will produce love as I learn to give it rather than strain to attract it. Advertising tells us we must learn how to be lovable in order to be loved. But the Bible shows the real secret of being lovable and desirable to your marriage partner. It involves learning to give love rather than striving to attract it—a powerful secret that relatively few people know (1 Jn. 3:11). One word of caution: many mistakes are made in the name of love. You need to give love in ways that truly meet your partner's needs and desires.

Most people consider feeling to be of supreme importance. But the truth is that reason—what you think about love—is what controls your behavior. The desired feelings come as a result of right thinking and right actions. This points the way to a genuine love affair for you and your mate that should provide enough thrills and satisfaction to suit even the most romantic individual. When reason is excluded from love's excitements, what results is not love but lust, infatuation or empty sentimentality. And who wants that in marriage?

Ed Wheat, M.D., with Gloria Okes Perkins

4.4 NEEDING MORE SPACE

While our marriage is good and I enjoy my spouse's company there are times I'd like a little solitude. However, when I go off on my own to do an errand or watch a TV show, I have a feeling my wife is hurt by my actions. Am I being unreasonable to want some time to myself?

A recent Louis Harris poll found that 63 percent of working women and 40 percent of working men say they don't have enough time for themselves. Solitude may not seem like a priority, but it's an indispensable aspect of a healthy marriage. Just an hour alone in a library or a leisurely 30-minute walk can provide time to reflect, time to dream, even time to grow emotionally and spiritually. Offer me a choice between a vacation in the Bahamas or a day in a mausoleum without interruption, and you might find me heading for the cemetery.

> *Without time alone, marriage relationships become entangled.*

Without time alone, marriage relationships become entangled, according to marriage and family expert Donald M. Joy. "A good marriage," Joy says, "enhances the opportunity for both spouses to develop as individuals." In other words, good marriages do not restrict the husband or wife from continuing to grow. And often that growth requires time away from each other. Joy says extroverts especially need alone time.

His analysis finds credibility in my own marriage. As the introvert, I find it quite natural to be alone. My personality predisposes me to making sure I find regular periods of solitude. My wife, on the other hand, enjoys being with people. She genuinely likes "mothering" our children, she loves the interaction of teaching, and for relaxation she enjoys having friends over. But because she's with people so much, she has an even greater need for the emotional refueling that comes from moments alone.

If it were as simple as finding time to be alone, the goal of solitude in marriage could be approached by plugging in an evening here or a weekend there. But there are valid reasons why it's not that easy.

For one thing, the very nature of marriage is togetherness. Remember your courtship? For us it seemed we could never spend enough time with each other. I envied my married friends not only because they slept together, but also because they got dressed together, ate breakfast together, even cleaned house together. At the age of 21, nothing seemed more appealing. We chose marriage because, among other things, we didn't want to spend the rest of our lives alone.

In healthy marriages, it is sometimes difficult to balance this yearning to experience life together with that basic need for privacy and solitude. How many times have you been away on a business trip only to wish your spouse could join you? The last thing most of us want out of marriage is to be alone. It just doesn't seem right, so we seldom go out of our way to do it.

There is another reason we deprive ourselves of time alone: we care too much for each other's feelings. After all, I got married because I wanted a companion.

If I spend too many evenings at the library or at ballgames, what message do I communicate to my wife?

I'll never forget how I felt the first time my wife drove off by herself after politely, yet firmly, telling me she needed to get away. I could not deny that she needed and deserved some time by herself, but I struggled with feelings of rejection. The kids were in bed, the work was done, and *I* was available. So why was she going off by herself?

The last thing most of us want out of marriage is to be alone.

You may say (accurately) that my feelings were selfish and insecure, but they were real. And they work both ways. How do I tell my wife I want to spend a weekend camping by myself, when I know she was hoping to go to a movie with me? Couples who care a great deal for each other would rather not cause such feelings, so they seldom ask for personal time.

At this point, says Joy, the relationship becomes destructively dependent. Like the adolescent couple who hangs onto each other in the hallway between classes, these marriages cross over from a legitimate desire to share life's experiences to an unhealthy need to manipulate and control each other. The need for solitude remains, but is manifest in resentment and frustration.

Lewis B. Smedes writes of the need for couples to allow each other to be who they are—to trust each other enough to let go. That is what we do when we protect each other's private moments. We relinquish control in favor of allowing our most loved one to retain those characteristics that attracted us in the first place.

Lyn Cryderman

4.5 STUCK IN THE MARRIAGE DOLDRUMS

We celebrated our eleventh anniversary last month and to be perfectly honest it was a non-event. Rather than dine at a special restaurant we ate at home. The cards we exchanged weren't sentimental but instead the rudimentary "I love you" type. At first I wasn't too concerned, but the more I thought about it, I realized I didn't want to settle for a sense of comfortable complacency about our relationship. How can we get out of the doldrums we seem to be in?

Your experience is common among couples who have been married for several years. When a "love recession" hits, there are things you can do to turn it into a time for strengthening your marriage.

Accept what you are experiencing as something that is normal. Don't deny your feelings. Instead, write them down—both positive and negative. Then set up an appointment to talk to your spouse. Lovingly share the entire range of your thoughts and feelings, not as an ultimatum but as a point of information signaling your interest in making your marriage stronger.

Evaluate your recent thought life toward yourself and your partner. Also, evaluate your behavior and your partner's behavior. Be sure to give yourselves credit for the positives.

Try some new loving behaviors toward your partner. Make a special effort to act out your love even if the feelings are not as strong as they once were. Consider the following ways of expressing love:

Touching. I'm not talking about erotic caressing that leads to the bedroom. I'm referring to daily acts of physical contact that are ends of romance, love and communication in themselves.

Hugging. It's both a preventative and a cure for a love recession.

Blessing your spouse. The word "blessing" in the New Testament is based on two Greek words that mean "well" and "word." Blessing your spouse means to speak well of that person. You can build up your spouse by becoming his/her greatest fan. You are in the front row of the grandstands, cheering "Go for it! You can do it! I believe in you!"

> *Blessing your spouse means to speak well of that person.*

Your verbal response to your partner's words is important. Saying thank you, expressing appreciation and offering requested information or opinions with kindness will bless your mate. And the ultimate way of verbally blessing your partner is to lift that person to the Lord in prayer and intercede on his/her behalf.

As you build up your spouse you will increase his or her sense of self-worth. The result will be an increase in your spouse's capacity to give of himself or herself to you. I like what Ed Wheat suggests for building up your spouse:

1. Decide to never again be critical of your partner in thought, word or deed. This decision should be backed up by action until it becomes a habit.

2. Study your spouse so you can develop sensitivity to the areas in which he or she feels a lack. Discover creative ways to build your spouse up in those areas.

3. Spend time every day thinking of positive qualities and behavior patterns you admire and appreciate in your spouse. Make a list and thank God for them.

4. Consistently verbalize praise and appreciation.

5. Recognize what your spouse does, but also who your spouse is.

6. Husbands, publicly and privately show your wife how special she is. Keep your attention focused on your wife—not on other women.

7. Wives, show your husband how important he is in your life. Ask his opinion and value his judgments.

8. Respond to each other physically and with facial expressions. Your spouse needs to receive more of your smiles than others.

9. Be courteous to each other in public and in private. Each of you should be a VIP in your home.

H. Norman Wright

4.6 WHAT "FAITHFUL" REALLY MEANS

We promised to be faithful to one another, but besides mutual fidelity, what more is there to faithfulness?

There is great comfort when you can count on each other to be faithful, no matter what. The ways you demonstrate your faithfulness will build bridges of trust for a lifetime. Here are seven ways to do that.

1. Consistently behave in faithful ways. Support and encourage your partner by helping out whenever and wherever possible. When you see a job that needs to be done, do it without being asked. Be consistently honest in all your dealings, showing yourself trustworthy in even the smallest detail. As a troubled wife once said, "It takes a lot of energy to love someone you can't trust." Being trustworthy means keeping your word. If you say you will meet your mate at a certain place and

When you see a job that needs to be done, do it without being asked.

time, make sure you are there. Most of all, show kindness in your actions, not just your words.

2. Avoid doing things to offend or disappoint your mate, and don't do anything to create suspicion in your partner's mind. Consider these two cases of couples who came for counseling. One husband had a habit of casually putting his arm around other women in social situations. It meant nothing to him, but it disturbed his wife and consequently affected their relationship. In another case, the wife sometimes praised other men she admired and respected. Her husband felt threatened, believing his wife found him inadequate. If you are unsure whether some action may offend your mate, ask yourself this: "Will this seem like faithfulness or unfaithfulness to my mate?"

3. Let your partner know that being faithful brings you joy; you are not faithful out of a sense of duty. Your happiness is the greatest compliment you can give your loved one, and expressing joy gives marriage vitality. But sometimes one partner will go through times of sadness, brooding, worry or depression. And the other will experience some anguish, wondering: "Have I done something wrong? Doesn't my mate love me anymore? If my spouse is not happy, it must be my fault." Be open with each other during these times, reassure each other and pray together about all your concerns.

4. Consistently show appreciation for all the ways your husband or wife blesses your life. Thank him or her for even the smallest things. Speak positively about your partner to other people, and give thanks to God. Showing appreciation not only demonstrates faithfulness to your partner, it builds more loving faithfulness in your own heart. We tend to believe our own spoken words. So be careful what you say, and always speak positively.

5. Learn to be sensitive to your spouse in even the smallest details. A faithful lover goes to a great deal of trouble to understand the beloved. If birthday celebrations are important to your wife, don't casually postpone the celebration to a more convenient time but instead work on special ways to remember her on her exact birthday.

6. Pray that you will be faithful. It's not always easy to be what your partner needs, and we can use all the help we can get. Keep the goal of faithfulness uppermost in your mind, and pray about it regularly.

7. Look to God. What you can't do in your own strength, He can empower you to do.
Ed Wheat, M.D., with Gloria Okes Perkins

4.7 RENEWING A FRIENDSHIP WITH A PAST FLAME

Recently an old girlfriend I haven't seen since college contacted me. After talking to her, I learned that she and her husband have moved to our area, and she is interested in renewing our friendship—with our spouses included, of course. I understand my wife's reluctance to become friends with this couple, even though I have assured her that my old girlfriend poses no threat to our marriage. Is it wrong for me to want to rekindle an old friendship?

I believe it should be possible for mature Christian men and women to enjoy friendships with the opposite sex that don't have sexual overtones. But it takes open communication between spouses at all times, and a solid commitment to the marriage and to having no secrets. It means acknowledging that there might be some attraction there, but you are going to close the door firmly on any form of flirtation or clandestine activity.

In your case, if your wife is reluctant to get together with your old friend and her husband, you should honor her feelings and simply not cultivate the relationship in any way. And don't put her down for feeling threatened.

But if she is open to at least seeing if all four of you could enjoy socializing together, then you might try getting together and seeing what happens. It's important that you all feel comfortable with each other. If the only connection between you two couples is you and your friend, there's bound to be jealousy.

Almost everyone at some point deals with this issue of what to do about old relationships. Should they resume old friendships with members of the opposite sex? They then feel guilty at the thoughts that may quite naturally run through their minds. For instance, thoughts of "What if I had married this person instead of my spouse? How would my life look now?" are quite common.

We don't have to feel guilty about such speculations. But sometimes thoughts like this can lead to realizing certain weaknesses in your marriage. For instance, you might realize that you have a better intellectual relationship with your old friend than you do with your wife. In this case, the responsible thing to do is to work on that area in your marriage. Remind yourself of what attracted you to your spouse in the first place, and let the situation become a diagnostic tool for improving your marriage.

Jay Kesler

4.8 WE NO LONGER SHARE THE SAME INTERESTS

When my wife and I first got married we had many common interests. But now that we've been married a few years, it's obvious we're quite different. Our hobbies and reading preferences are different, and we don't agree on things like music, what car to buy, or our level of church involvement. I feel that our changing tastes and preferences are a result of healthy growth and maturation, and that doing things separately is not always bad. My wife, on the other hand, thinks we're drifting apart and wonders why we can't find more things to do together. Who's right and who's wrong?

I doubt you were ever as much alike as you thought you were before you got married. Human beings have a marvelous capacity for overlooking things we can't or don't want to deal with. And nowhere is this capacity more in evidence than in our dating experiences.

There seems to be no end to the differences between our spouses and us.

What so many of us discover as we work on our marriages is that there seems to be no end to the differences between our spouses and us. But I also believe the success we have in dealing with those differences is primarily one of attitude and focus. If we can appreciate our differences and see how we complement each other, instead of viewing our differences as problems to overcome, we'll find our marriages much happier and our spouses more compatible.

I don't think either you or your wife is all right or all wrong. The real issue is how a couple defines "too much togetherness." Any two people will have different needs along these lines. In your case, your wife seems to feel the need for more time together than you do. So my first suggestion is that together you talk about your feelings as calmly and unemotionally as possible, listening to and trying to accept each other's feelings.

Suggestion number two: each of you should write down things you'd be willing to do, in an attitude of love, to try to meet each other's needs for togetherness or time alone. When you've got a list you can agree on, try putting those ideas into practice for one week. Then sit down again and talk about any needed adjustments to your lists. This focus on the other person—as opposed to dwelling on one's own unmet needs—will make it easier to compromise and even sacrifice for the sake of the other.

Suggestion number three: there's nothing wrong with you and your wife enjoying separate pursuits. But you ought also to have some interests that you can share. I don't think any couple is so different they can't find *some* area or areas of interest they can enjoy together. When a husband does this on a regular basis, when his wife knows she can count on that time together, the kind of ongoing tension you're facing is greatly reduced.

Suggestion number four: remember that God made us all individuals. On top of that, He made half of us male and the other half female. And then He created marriage. Unless you think this was just a cosmic practical joke, He must have had a good reason.

One explanation is that God wanted to challenge us to change and grow to our fullest potential as human beings. And there's no better laboratory than marriage to help us do that. But it takes unselfish compromise.

Jay Kesler

4.9 LIVING WITH A KILLJOY

There are times my wife is the ultimate killjoy. For instance, when we were making plans for a vacation she kept pointing out the possible negatives of the trip. By the end of the evening my sense of enthusiasm for the trip was nil. Why is my wife so inconsiderate when it comes to my happiness? Is it too much to expect her to consider my feelings?

When people believe the key to a happy marriage is choosing or having the "right mate," they relegate the responsibility for their happiness to someone else. But the truth is you are responsible for your own happiness. While being careful in selecting a marriage partner is important, being the right kind of mate yourself is far more critical to achieving a healthy marriage.

In all marriages each mate will do and say things that displease the other. Constructive actions to negotiate some changes are in order. But when you expect your marriage partner to make you happy, you tend to be passive as though waiting for him or her to serve you generous portions of happiness. This mentality frequently leads to disenchantment and disappointment.

Failure to assume responsibility for oneself may result in scapegoating—blaming others when they fail to make you happy. You might blame your parents, your brothers or sisters, your birth order or the fact that you are an only child. You can blame your friends—or your lack of friends. You can blame your childhood circumstances, or your current circumstances.

But the scapegoat most frequently put on the block is your marriage partner. People blame their spouses for their own obesity, alcoholism, career failure, and other ineffectual ways of coping with life. If we can point the finger at someone else, then we don't have to assume the painful responsibility ourselves. Scapegoating does its damage when wives and husbands refuse to take responsibility for becoming all that God intended them to be and resort to excuses in defense of "what might have been."

Instead, if you place the emphasis on being the right kind of person yourself, it puts the responsibility for the relationship where it belongs—on you. After all, you have much more control over yourself than over your mate.

People can't give what they don't have.

People can't give what they don't have. You must love yourself before you can give it to another. The Bible says, "You shall love your neighbor as yourself" (Mk. 12:31). We are to love others as much as ourselves—not instead of ourselves and not more than ourselves.

Self-love and the ability to love someone else are closely tied to self-respect and the ability to treat others with respect. Respect has two sides. One is respect for your own individuality; the other is respect for your marriage partner's individuality. Before you can love or respect another, you must have a certain measure of love and respect for yourself.

Marriage is probably the most demanding challenge any mortal ever encounters. In *On the Contrary*, columnist Sydney J. Harris offered his analysis of the basic key to marital happiness and success: "A marriage will flourish when it is composed of two persons who will nurse each other; it may even survive when one is a nurse and the other an invalid; but it is sure to collapse when it consists of two invalids, each needing a nurse."

Barbara Russell Chesser

4.10 WHY SERVING ONE ANOTHER DOESN'T COME EASY

At our wedding ceremony our pastor challenged us to serve one another. We know a "servant's heart" is essential to a godly marriage, but being selfless isn't easy. In fact, it seems that the longer we're married, the harder it is for us to put one another first. Have we missed the meaning of serving one another?

Serving each other includes the following actions:

Giving affirmation. We need each other. We were born dependent upon others for our survival. As we mature, we are better able to provide for ourselves, but we will always need others if we are to flourish emotionally. Since we need others in our life and they need us, we should let them know we're glad they're in our world. We certainly like to know they enjoy having us on earth. We appreciate their affirmation of our being, talents, and efforts, and we need to reciprocate.

Recognizing equality. Serving each other can be demonstrated by the consideration we give to each other. If a husband and wife look down on each other, treat each other with contempt, or even use the Bible as a club to beat the other one down, they have lost the sense of serving each other.

Some modern writers and speakers who tell women how to get along with their husbands make subtle—and sometimes not so subtle—suggestions that men are fools. "You just have to know how to get around them in order to get your own way," they say. That's actually a putdown to men, and it is certainly not equality. Sometimes husbands do the same to their wives. Men laugh and say, "The only thing she can do is shop till she drops."

Equality is a two-way street. It's a way of thinking of your mate, and it's also a way of thinking of yourself in relationship to your mate. It means that you consider your mate and yourself to be peers. It also means that both mates commit themselves to helping each other grow. Family time and money are used for the growth of both spouses.

Encouraging your mate's unique gifts. Helping may mean arranging your schedule to care for the kids while she attends classes or living on less income while he changes jobs. When you say, "Go for it!" you must include all the physical and emotional support you can give.

By helping your mate use his or her gifts, you are building your mate's self-image and reinforcing the fact that you value him or her. In addition, the world is enriched because of the talents you have helped to unleash.

Focusing on commitment. Dr. Urie Bronfenbrenner says that the family is "a group which possesses and implements an irrational commitment to the well-being of its members." Sometimes you best serve your mate by having an "irrational commitment" to him or her and your marriage. Commitment provides a stability that frees the two of you within your marriage to grow and to develop all of your potential. You're not wasting your energies looking over your shoulder, wondering if the rug is going to be pulled out from underneath you because you're afraid your mate is going to leave.

Respecting your mate. Isn't it strange that a husband will open the car door for a woman guest who is riding with the couple, but he won't normally open the door for his wife? It's sad that we withhold common courtesy and respect from each other. We interrupt, badger, put down, ignore or condemn our mates, when we would never think of doing that to another person.

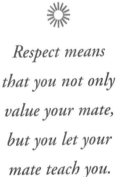

Respect means that you not only value your mate, but you let your mate teach you.

Respect means that you not only value your mate, but you let your mate teach you. If your mate has important God-given abilities that you don't have, his or her contribution to your life is essential.

Jim and Sally Conway

4.11 DOUBTING A PARTNER'S LOVE

Every day my husband says that he loves me and yet I still have my doubts. He's a wonderful, thoughtful man and has never given me any reason to truly question his feelings for me, so I'm perplexed as to why I sometimes feel so unloved. What's my problem?

Several years ago I met a man who told me how much he enjoyed being with his wife, and how easy it was to tell her he loved her. It was refreshing to meet a man so enthusiastic about his marriage.

A short time later, this man's wife came to me for counseling. Her problem: she was convinced her husband didn't love her. I found out that this man had been expressing his love, but not in terms his wife could understand.

Just as we have inborn preferences regarding problem solving and decision-making, so we have preferences in regard to giving and receiving love. We prefer a certain "language" to express and accept appreciation and affection. Here are some of the common ones.

Touching. If touchers want to tell someone they love them, they kiss their cheek, hold their hand or gather them up in a bear hug.

Stating. When these folks feel love welling up inside, their only comfortable outlet is to verbalize it: "I love you. I love you." While some people find it hard to express their love in words, these people can't stop.

Serving. For "servers," love isn't love unless it's demonstrated in practical terms—wallpapering the kitchen, washing the car, preparing favorite meals.

Providing. Providers consider their breadwinning to be their greatest expression of love.

Presenting. These folks buy gifts, wrap them beautifully, and present them with childlike glee to the ones they love.

Challenging. Some spouses express their love primarily by challenging and inspiring their loved ones to greatness. Their goal is to open up opportunities that will offer stimulation and fulfillment.

Giving time. People in this category are primarily concerned with spending time with or giving time to others. They're willing to rearrange their schedules so they can offer large blocks of time to the significant people in their lives.

When it comes to expressing love, do you and your spouse both speak the same language? If you're like my wife and me, you don't. For years we expressed love differently and didn't know it. My wife decided she needed to speak the language of the Galloping Gourmet. She knocked herself out to prepare lovely meals she thought would make me feel loved. But they didn't. A gourmet meal says the same thing to me as a tuna sandwich.

I finally told her, "Don't spend all this time on fancy meals. Just sit down and talk to me. Call me a super-husband. Cheer me on. That'll make me feel loved."

Being an introvert, she isn't naturally free with words. But when she learned I needed to hear them, she disciplined herself to tell me what I needed to hear.

Another way I enjoy receiving love is through having people open doors of opportunity for me and I assumed my wife would, too. For years I urged her to take flying lessons, or go helicopter skiing in the Rockies. Finally she said, "I feel like you're never satisfied with what I'm doing. I wish that once in a while you would just put your arms around me and let me feel loved and accepted just the way I am." What she needed was a loving embrace, but that never crossed my mind—because I thought she needed what I needed.

Most of us mistakenly assume our spouses want to receive love the same way we do. So we use whatever language comes most naturally to us. And that usually doesn't work. We must tell one another which love language communicates most clearly to us. It's not hard to learn new ways of communicating love. And it can transform a marriage where spouses hope they're loved into a marriage where they know they are.

Bill Hybels

4.12 AN OVERLY DEPENDENT SPOUSE

My wife is so dependent on me that I'm feeling suffocated. She grew up in a home where her father made all the decisions, managed the finances, planned the vacations and disciplined the kids. My parents worked at things more as a team, and I expected the same for our marriage. After seven years of marriage, I'm worn out by having to do it all. My wife's a great mother and homemaker, but that's where she thinks her responsibilities end. What should I do?

Could there be some level of perfection-ism in your life that causes your wife to relinquish responsibility?

My first word of advice is to check your own life. Could there be some level of perfectionism in your life that causes your wife to relinquish responsibility or that has robbed her of a sense of competence? I have a friend whose father is a master mechanic, yet my friend can hardly change a tire on his car. When, as a boy, he tried to tackle mechanical problems, his dad would grab the wrench and say, "Let me do it. You're not doing it right." Without intending to, this father destroyed his son's sense of competence in that area. Sometimes a spouse's reluctance to take on responsibility is related to the fact that her husband does things so much better, or maintains overly high standards.

I can understand your sense of exhaustion and your wife's hesitancy isn't good for either of you. It's a hard truth, but most men will die before their wives. And if a husband doesn't help his wife gain confidence and competence in all areas of life before he goes, he runs the risk of leaving her virtually helpless. I constantly meet women who don't understand their own family finances. The husbands of these women need to get started right away in turning over some decision-making and financial tasks to their wives. You can help your wife by providing opportunities for her to develop these skills. And as she learns, be patient: don't intimidate her when she makes mistakes. The checkbook is an excellent place to start. Let her begin to do the bookkeeping. Add other responsibilities one at a time over the course of the coming months and years.

Part of equipping your spouse with these skills may mean making yourself less available. If you feel sure your wife can handle a certain decision, just tell her, "Honey, I know you can make this decision on your own." And when she makes it, right or wrong, affirm her choice. Sometimes husbands put down their wives inadvertently with comments such as "Don't you think that cost too much?" or "Were you really thinking practically?" Live with your wife's decisions.

As she is encouraged by seeing her own successes, your wife will gain a sense of personal competency and be more apt to tackle bigger responsibilities in the future. And you'll begin to gain a sense of which decisions need to be shared ones and which can be delegated to you or your wife.

Jay Kesler

4.13 WHY EMOTIONAL INTIMACY IS DIFFICULT

My husband and I talk a lot and I consider us close, but there are times I feel a wall between us—a hesitancy to share the real "us." Why is emotional intimacy so difficult?

The dilemma is, how can I be an individual, yet not be left alone in life? We cry out, "hold me!" and "not too tight" in the same breath. This tightrope-walking act especially comes into play when husbands and wives try to communicate. Sometimes our attempts at oneness are awkward—or even painful—as we risk vulnerability. At times we retreat into silence or isolation, just because it seems safer. Our fears can prevent us from pursuing the intimacy and oneness we all desire. Here are five major fears that sabotage our efforts to communicate.

Fear of failure. Husbands primarily are hesitant to share with their wives, mostly because they don't feel practiced or well equipped in this type of communication. Men, especially, are more motivated to act when they feel capable, so they tend to avoid anything that might leave them feeling like a failure. When the level of conversation feels uncomfortably close, or the intimacy level seems dangerously unfamiliar, a man might clam up to avoid failure. A woman, on the other hand, needs emotional closeness, and she may try for years to find ways to get her husband to talk before the frustration of going away with her needs unmet—again—forces her to stop trying. That leads to the second greatest fear.

Fear of rejection. It's easy to think, "If my spouse *really* knew what I was like inside, he or she would run away." It feels very risky to let our mate, who may be our only anchor to some intimacy, see the doubt, pain or unacceptable impulses that inhabit the stagnant swamps of our lives.

Sometimes we respond to each other in ways that communicate rejection, even though we don't mean to shut down our spouses' attempts to share. In one recent couples group, a woman told her husband, "I always feel inadequate." His response was, "But that is so stupid! I never see you as inadequate. I always tell you that it's dumb for you to think that way!" This husband thought he was helping, and it had never occurred to him that his answer reinforced her negative feelings about herself. His comments about "stupidity" felt like rejection to her, so she just quit sharing her feelings.

Marriage is one of the instruments God uses to make those rough edges smooth.

Fear of starting a fight. Because a couple won't agree on every subject every time they discuss something, marriage inevitably spawns conflict. Many couples fear conflict, and this becomes a third barrier to intimacy. My wife and I are individuals with lots to learn, with rough edges that need to be polished; and marriage is one of the instruments God uses to make those rough edges smooth. When that process gets painful and one of us withdraws into a shell, we both become more isolated. And isolation is part of that fear of rejection. But if my wife and I can face our conflicts openly by talking them out together, we end up with a stronger connection—and we overcome the isolation.

Fear of losing control. It's natural to want to remain in control of your life, but marital intimacy challenges that control. With increased vulnerability, one person might fear that his spouse may use confidential information against him or exploit his closeness as a way to control him.

Not wanting to lose control is a particularly subtle fear. Most people aren't even aware of it. But they do sense a vague inner warning that prevents them from risking vulnerability. People who grew up with dominating parents may especially resist honest, transparent communication. A woman might remember too well how confining her father was, or a man might remember how strongly his mother forced his dependency on her. A wife feels, "What if he tries to control me, like Dad used to do?" And a husband is thinking, "What if she tries to run my life, like Mom always did?"

The good news is that persistent, honest communication can break down this barrier. As trust grows between a husband and wife, these fears can finally be put to rest.

Fear of getting too close. The fear of intimacy itself is part of that balancing act between maintaining one's individuality and developing greater closeness with one's mate. The give and take involved in "becoming one" in marriage is a tricky business, and there is always the danger that one spouse's personality will overpower and dominate the relationship.

The fear of intimacy has no gender bias—it's an equal opportunity barrier. Women feel worried about being swallowed up by their husbands' lives, and men feel worried about losing themselves to their wives. Unfortunately, our society emphasizes individual "rights" above mutual giving up of self, and few good models of marital intimacy remain. Couples are left to forge their own way, continuing to communicate even when it's tough, and even when they are afraid.

Clearly, fear takes the lead as the most dangerous enemy of good communication in marriage. But God's Word says in 1 John 4:18 that perfect love banishes fear. As you and your spouse pursue better communication in spite of your fears, your heightened level of trust can banish the fears that have been getting in your way.

Louis McBurney, M.D.

4.14 OUR CAREERS ARE DRIVING US APART

It's not uncommon for my wife and I to each put in 50 hours a week at work. We're starting to notice that when we are together we're so tired from the day that we have very little energy for our marriage. How can we make sure our marriage doesn't become a casualty of our careers?

Years ago my husband and I were busy building our careers. And though our work placed heavy demands on each of us, it didn't detract from our relationship. If anything, it revitalized it. That's one of the benefits of a dual-career marriage. Couples who derive a sense of satisfaction from their work often have more energy to invest in their marriage.

Those were exciting years for us as we shared our successes and setbacks with each other at the end of every day. But I wouldn't be honest if I didn't admit this lifestyle presented its own set of pressures. With both of us going full-tilt at work, we were faced with the serious challenge of how to maintain a vital marriage in the midst of intense career demands. My advice is always the same— your marriage *must* take priority if you hope to survive more than a few years as a couple.

People make the mistake of thinking their marriage will somehow take care of itself. But the reality is unless you are intentional about building your relationship you will not end up with a functional marriage.

When I counsel dual-career couples, I ask them to define their marriage with as much passion as they do their careers. What skills do you need to develop over the next two or three years to become a more effective husband or wife? What habits are you willing to establish now to protect your relationship against overwork and other outside interference? The old adage "If you don't know where you're going, you'll never get there" applies as much in marriage as it does to life in general.

Next, it's important to reserve plenty of energy for the process of shaping your identity as a couple. It takes time to sort through decisions such as how often you'll visit each other's family or what activities you'll pursue together. For dual-career couples it's critical that you have a clear understanding of each other's professional goals as well. For example, if I want to become a doctor and my husband wants to be a lawyer, how will we achieve these goals and what effect will they have on our home life?

Husbands and wives who both have strong career drives face any number of complicated choices. How will you support each other in working out your professional aspirations? Are you willing to sidetrack your own goals for your partner's sake or for your children? Unless you make these tough choices together, you will undoubtedly end up in a power struggle over whose career is more important.

Husbands and wives who both have strong career drives face any number of complicated choices.

Friends are a critical source of support. While I advocate exclusive "couple time" for spouses, I think it's equally important to develop mutual friendships with other married people and same-sex friends outside the relationship. For working spouses especially, it's common to make friends at the office that your spouse only meets at company functions. One of the best ways to let your mate experience your work world is to give him or her opportunities to interact with your co-workers socially.

While work can energize you and add another dimension to your marriage, it can also leave you tired and depleted. But still the tension remains: how do you devote energy to your marriage when your job takes all you've got? One way my husband and I used to unwind after work was to meet at a restaurant that had free appetizers. Home sometimes represents the routine of life. And for us, meeting on neutral ground in a relaxed environment gave us a chance to share our day without the distraction of dirty dishes or unpaid bills.

If you have to head straight home after work, try to build in some individual respite time, like listening to music or drinking a cup of tea in quiet—whatever activities tend to revive you. By giving each other a chance to shift gears, you will be better prepared to interact with each other, to share some of the events of your day or talk about your relationship.

Judith Balswick

4.15 DOES PREDICTABLE MEAN BORING?

After ten years of marriage, our life together has fallen into a predictable, routine pattern. I look at younger couples and I'm almost jealous when I see the sense of excitement and wonder they exhibit. I long for those early years in our marriage. How can we prevent our marriage from becoming a victim of chronic boredom?

While even the healthiest marriages go through periodic low points, it's the cases of ongoing, chronic boredom that can seriously disrupt or even destroy a marriage. But no couple needs to resign themselves to a boring marriage. God created marriage to enrich us, not to cast a yawn over our lives. Here are three important steps you can take to bring vitality back into your relationship.

1. Commit yourself to "marriage time." Keep in mind that marriage time—the time you spend together as a couple—is not the same as "family time." For instance, early in marriage a couple may spend a good deal of time with their parents or adult siblings. This is family time, not marriage time. And once children come, marriage time tends to be swallowed up by family time. It's not just that baby makes three, but that baby obliterates the notion of two.

The demands of parenthood often coincide with heavier-than-ever career involvement. So it's easy to see why marriage time gets short shrift. But we often remind couples that one of the best things they can do for their children is to rear them in a home where there is a happy and vibrant marriage.

When you spend time with each other you are providing your children with a rich gift—a portrait of a committed and loving marriage. And if you're committed to the idea, you can find a way to maintain marriage time—even during the hectic child-rearing years.

2. Keep changing, and help your partner to change. Sometimes we hear a spouse complain, "He [or she] isn't the person I married!" That should be a goal of marriage, not a sign of failure or betrayal. "Stay just the way you are" may sound romantic, but such a sentiment provides worse than useless advice, because both you and your spouse *will* change. The important thing is to use change to nurture and enrich your marriage. The lack of change contributes to boredom.

3. Find and nurture shared interests and experiences. As people pursue separate interests and involvements, they often find they have less in common than they did when they were first married. Shared interests and experiences are the soul of intimacy and are critical in avoiding marital boredom.

A number of couples have told us one of the most difficult challenges they face is finding something to do together that each spouse can pursue with vigor and passion. Our answer is to keep looking. Go to the library and browse around. In addition to various sports and hobbies—from walking to collecting something to refinishing furniture to raising plants—there are a wealth of topics to study. We know a couple in their eighties who each have a passion for politics. They read books and newspapers and watch television programs, and have many lively discussions together about political issues.

If you're having trouble finding a shared passion, commit yourselves to try one new thing each week or so. Your shared experience may be the ongoing pursuit of things to do. Or you may hit upon something you both really enjoy. In any case, it's important that each spouse give the new activity a thorough tryout. Sometimes we don't like something at first simply because it's unfamiliar and we're not very good at it. But over time, you may continue the activity simply for the pleasure of doing it together.

Commit yourselves to try one new thing each week or so.

Jeanette C. and Robert H. Lauer

4.16 KEEPING A MARRIAGE GROWING

I've been so involved with our kids and my husband has been so involved in work that we barely know one another. In fact, I'm beginning to think we don't even know ourselves that well any more. I'm so worried we'll settle for a distant, stale marriage. I want better than that! How can we get in touch again with what made us the interesting, fun people we once were years ago?

Marriages grow stale when the partners aren't growing. But this can be helped if both husband and wife are willing to grow and change. But how does that happen? Spouses often deny who they really are—in order to be liked. Growing psychologically means that you are willing to say, "God made me this way. I'm a worthwhile person."

People often ask us, "How am I supposed to appreciate myself if I don't know who I am or what my special abilities are?" Taking inventory is a good first step.

1. First list the things you like. Start with your favorite styles of music, along with the kinds of books and magazines you like to read. Make sure you don't list particular songs or books just because they are popular. You might think, "Well, I *ought* to like this artist or this author." If you fall into that trap, you won't discover who you are as a unique person.

   - Make a similar list dealing with your preferred clothing styles. Again, we're not talking about what's in style. Write down what kind of clothes make you feel "This is the real me."

   - Then list the friends you really enjoy spending time with. Identify their characteristics and qualities that nourish you. Don't think in terms of obligation: "I ought to like that person because he is my second cousin."

   - Make lists about everything you like in your life: your work, neighborhood, art, movies, and food. Don't allow other people's opinions to influence what you write down. You are looking within yourself to understand your God-given uniqueness.

2. Now make a list of all your favorite activities, whether serious or frivolous. List recreational activities you enjoy, but also things like watering the plants or watching the sun set. And forget traditional roles. If you are a man who enjoys doing needlepoint or a woman who feels good after changing the oil in the car, then write it down.

3. Also make a list of all the things you can do well, your abilities and strengths. Include your education, positive experiences and opportunities. And write down the things that your friends say you do well. These help give a total picture of yourself.

4. Follow that list with another one that includes all the things you want to do before you die. Allow yourself to "dream the impossible dream."

After you have finished writing, try to detach yourself and ask, "Who *is* this person? How would I describe him or her? What kind of things does he or she like? What does he or she really value in life?" Knowing who you are is part of developing a healthy self-esteem. The next part is to *affirm* who you are. Say to yourself, "These things are good!"

Now live out the things that are on your lists. Begin to become the person you have just defined. The more accurately you live as the person God has created you to be, the more confident and effective you will be.

Marriages that stay together over the long haul are composed of two people who are growing in all areas of their lives. Growing becomes a part of the glue that holds them together. They are not the same old people with the same old problems. They are continuing to improve and mature, and this growth gives both of them *hope*. You can keep the sparkle in your marriage as you continue to change and grow.

Jim and Sally Conway

4.17 HIS PUBLIC FACE DOESN'T MATCH HIS PRIVATE FACE

Why is it that my husband is Mr. Congeniality at work and yet at home he's a different person—one who easily and often vents his frustrations? There are times I wish I was his co-worker rather than his wife—he'd certainly treat me better and I wouldn't have to deal with his bad moods. Why is he so blind to how he behaves at home?

We use the term "two-faced" to refer to the mate who has a public face and a private face that contradict each other. In its milder form, this contradiction involves acts of graciousness toward others that a person does not extend to his or her spouse. For example, a man may show consideration and sensitivity toward a female co-worker and at the same time be insensitive to his wife. Or a woman may listen to others and express her understanding and support. Yet she may shrug off her husband's worries by telling him curtly that his concerns are groundless.

To some extent, we all observe certain social conventions in public that aren't always necessary at home which may be the case with your husband. First, ask him what is happening at work. It may be that when his boss makes up his mind, he will tolerate nothing less than full support of his decision. Your husband may disagree with his boss but knows he must keep quiet at work. His frustration with work then spills out when he gets home.

To some extent, we all observe certain social conventions in public that aren't always necessary at home.

While you would understand the frustration and irritation that such a work situation generates, you may still question whether it is fair for him to vent his frustrations at home. We suggest you try to view his behavior from a different perspective. His behavior is actually a compliment to you. He feels he can express to you what he can't express at work. He feels safe and we all need to have someone with whom we can share our vexations in life. And in a good marriage, that person is likely to be your spouse. It's one of the helpful things that spouses can do for each other.

Thus, in some cases the contradiction between a mate's public and private face is appropriate or necessary. In other cases, it is neither. What, then, can you do if your spouse has two faces that are destructive to your marriage? It will be necessary to confront him with the problem. But if the problem is very severe, as in the case of verbal or physical abuse, your spouse must have counseling. Abusive people are notoriously quick to apologize and to promise an end to the abuse, but they are also quick to fall back into the same pattern.

To help avoid becoming a living contradiction, we all need to remember that God has called us not to defend our image but to protect and develop our marriages. The more consistent our words, feelings, and behavior are, the more easily we can nurture our marriages.

Robert H. and Jeanette C. Lauer

4.18 EMOTIONALLY DRAINED BY INFERTILITY TREATMENTS

We've been trying to conceive for two years and the emotional strain of infertility is starting to show. We seldom fought before but now we bicker constantly. The sense of closeness we once felt has all but evaporated. We never imagined that infertility treatments would take such a toll on our marriage. Why are we having such a difficult time handling this setback?

Men and women tend to respond to infertility differently. When people are confronted with something they don't know how to handle, they tend to avoid it, hide it, or try to get rid of it. Men, especially, tend to intellectualize their experience. For example, a man will talk about the unfairness of the situation, whereas a woman generally will express the hurt and anger she feels. Typically, men are not as tuned into babies as they are to older kids. While a baby shower might be an intensely traumatic experience for an infertile woman, a man won't feel the equivalent of this pain until his buddies start taking their kids on camping trips or to ball games. This is often when a man will begin to grieve the emotional loss caused by his wife's or his own infertility.

Understanding and accepting each other's way of confronting infertility is a major step toward maintaining emotional intimacy. Often, men will take a problem-solving approach: we've got an infertility problem, so how do we fix it? This attitude can be maddening to a woman who is still working through the tremendous relational loss. She's thinking about the children she may never know and trying to cope with the reality of the loss. Yet her husband is failing to consider the emotional impact of their situation. At this point, there is often a disconnection between the husband and wife. He's trying to move on before his wife has had a chance to grieve.

To keep from becoming isolated from each other, it's important to recognize that each person handles pain and confusion differently. The problem-solving approach isn't wrong; it's a typical reaction to a crisis. Once partners realize this, they can both work at understanding what their spouse's response means to him or her.

Each person handles pain and confusion differently.

Daniel Green

4.19 TIRED OF LAX ATTITUDE ABOUT MARRIAGE

We're very intentional about some aspects of our life like disciplining our kids or making wise money decisions. And yet, when it comes to our marriage, we're somewhat nonchalant. The breakup of a close friend's marriage jarred us from our complacency and we'd like to set some goals but we don't know where to start. What should we do?

The four questions that follow will help you and your spouse set goals that you can both agree on. Working separately, read each question and then write out your answers.

1. If you woke up tomorrow and found your marriage had become much better than it is now, exactly what would be different?

2. How would you know your marriage had improved? Would your feelings be different? Would your actions (or your spouse's) be different?

3. How would your spouse know your marriage had improved? What changes would he or she observe?

4. Would change have been sudden, gradual, or stop-and-go? Would there have been any intermediate steps or plateaus along the way?

Your answers to these questions will help you clarify the areas in which you would like your marriage to improve. By comparing and then combining your written answers, you and your spouse can create a list of positive goals that will help bring about desired improvements in your marriage.

Everett L. Worthington, Jr.

4.20 DISCOURAGED BY NEEDS GOING UNMET

I got married because I first of all love my wife, but second, because I expected some of my needs to be met. After 18 months of marriage, I'm beginning to realize how naive I am—especially when I see some of my needs sink to the bottom of the relationship. What's going on? Should I have married someone else?

Most people get married believing a myth—that marriage is a beautiful box full of all the things they have longed for: companionship, sexual fulfillment, intimacy, and friendship. And that somehow the box mysteriously remains full of those goodies. After marriage they start to empty the box, believing their spouse will fill it again. But it won't happen, at least not for long. The box gets empty, disappointment sets in, and the relationship takes a nosedive.

The truth is that marriage, at the start, is an empty box. You must put something in before you can take anything out. There is no love in marriage; love is in people, and people put it into marriage. There is no romance in marriage; people have to infuse it into their marriages.

A couple must learn the art and form the habit of giving, loving, serving, praising—keeping the box full. If you take out more than you put in, the box will get empty. Love is something you do—an activity directed toward your mate. It takes two to keep the box full.

J. Allan Petersen

4.21 WHY HUSBANDS SHUT OUT WIVES

When I'm stressed out or feeling ill, it helps if I talk about my concerns or at least have others around—especially my husband. But when he's upset, he seems to get quieter. I don't like to be shut out. Is it his personality, or is it just the "guy" way to respond?

On our honeymoon, my husband struggled valiantly, behind a bolted bathroom door, with a severe case of 24-hour flu. I *knew* that if he really loved me, he would allow me to offer him comfort and sympathy. After all, I wanted to support him the way I expected him to support me. Instead, I was literally locked out of his suffering and feeling terribly dejected.

Then the tables turned. This time, I was the one who awoke in the middle of the night with a burning fever. I groaned with the agony of an upset stomach—desperate for comfort—only to find that my husband had tiptoed into another room, leaving me to suffer alone.

It took a dark night on our honeymoon to reveal that our differences could actually leave me feeling more confused than completed. I didn't realize that the differences I thought were strictly between my husband and me were actually shared by most other couples. There is a predictable difference between the sexes, and without this knowledge I had evaluated my husband's behavior according to my feminine standards. Research and experience generally point to this fundamental yet powerful distinction: in times of stress, men need more space while women desire closeness.

According to John Gray in *Men Are from Mars, Women Are from Venus* (HarperCollins), men, when faced with stress, become increasingly "focused and withdrawn" while women become increasingly "overwhelmed and emotionally involved." Men typically don't want to talk about their pressures or be held and comforted until they have first had time to themselves. Under pressure, they set out on a quest for space, while in similar circumstances a woman craves the reassurance of relational security.

As a man, my husband needed some space to "conquer" his illness. Once he achieved health, he

My husband gave me the gift of space not because he didn't care about me, but because he cared so much.

was free to reconnect with me. For me, however, illness in either of us was another opportunity to strengthen our emotional bond, a chance to offer tenderness and support. That night on our honeymoon, as I lay moaning, my husband gave me the gift of space not because he didn't care about me, but because he cared so much. In contrast, I interpreted his style of caring as cruelty.

Leslie Parrott

4.22 WHEN THE ROMANCE COOLS

When we were dating, my husband was "Mr. Romance." Now that we've been married several months, the romance has cooled to the point I'm wondering if he even loves me anymore. Why did the flowers and nice dinners stop?

I can identify with your experience. During our fourth or fifth month of marriage, I remember wondering why my husband wasn't as romantic as he used to be. Before we got married he planned exciting evenings, kissed me at stoplights, saved ticket stubs from our dates and even wrote tender love poems. But once we were married, his romantic side waned. It wasn't that he stopped his romantic ways altogether, but something was distinctly different. "Am I doing something wrong?" I wondered. "Is he having doubts about our marriage?"

As it turned out, I wasn't the only one who thought things had changed. From my husband's perspective, I was more happy-go-lucky before we crossed the threshold. And he was right. Back then, I felt good about our relationship and optimistic about the future. But soon after we married, I became more concerned about "our relationship." Without realizing it, I had relied on my husband's romantic gestures to serve as a love barometer. As those outward demonstrations of love diminished, I mistakenly believed his love was disappearing.

I wanted to talk about it and process our feelings together. Not so with him. My compulsion to talk about our marriage made him feel anxious, like he was failing as a husband. He just wanted to get on with living as husband and wife.

The truth is that neither of us had really changed. The goal (getting married) that made my husband especially romantic was met, so he felt that romance purely for the sake of romance—which I still valued—was no longer a priority. He had shifted his energies to building a stable home with a secure future. He couldn't have been happier with our new life together.

After 13 years of marriage and after counseling hundreds of newlywed couples, I now realize that these "changes" weren't unique to us. The turbulence we experienced stemmed from the fact that men focus on achievement while women focus on experience.

My husband, like the majority of men, focuses on future goals. He justifies a present activity by what it will accomplish in the future. He asks, "What good can this produce?" He likes words such as "progress" and "useful." He can be very patient doing romantic little things as long as they ultimately prove productive.

On the other hand, as a woman I focus on the feelings and activities of the present—for their own sake. I don't need a goal; it's enough to simply enjoy the moment. I read a book simply to experience the story, to allow it to change me. When my husband reads a book, he is constantly gathering information for future projects. I like words like "connected" and "relational." I can be very patient doing romantic little things simply because doing them has its own value.

It took some time for us to learn of our gender differences, and it has taken us even longer to value and appreciate those differences. And yet those differences, if heeded and accounted for, can become the source of greater intimacy. Recognizing that fundamental differences between men and women do exist has allowed us to avoid an ongoing battle between the sexes.

Leslie Parrott

4.23 CONCERNED ABOUT DRIFTING APART

Our lives are so busy and we have so many demands on our time that I'm worried we might be drifting apart. How can I tell if we're still really connected and keeping our marriage a priority?

Keeping marriage a priority has never been easy, and it's not getting any easier. That's why we all need to be more vigilant about not allowing other commitments and responsibilities to get top billing. The sense of unity and fulfillment that is so essential to a successful marriage isn't destroyed by a single, cataclysmic event. It erodes gradually in small, barely discernible ways. It's only after a matter of months or years that we realize how far we have drifted apart.

To get a feel for where your marriage is, take a look at these seven signs of erosion.

To get a feel for where your marriage is, take a look at these seven signs of erosion.

1. You find yourself looking for alternatives to being with your spouse. Time demands are always barriers to oneness, but when your relationship slips to a lower priority, the time demands tend to multiply. They may masquerade as legitimate demands—work, church and community activities, or children's needs. We generally do the things we find rewarding. That's why a marriage that provides minimal rewards gets minimal attention.

2. You feel increasingly irritated by your mate's behavior. Everyone has a list of pet peeves about his or her spouse, and normally we negotiate or adjust to those quirks. However, when things aren't going well, those irritating habits become even more irksome. The resulting frustration is expressed through criticism, humiliation, or avoidance.

3. You depend less and less on your spouse. A healthy marriage exhibits the comfortable balance of mutual dependency. (This is not "co-dependency," an unhealthy dynamic that squelches individuality.) When one or both partners are dissatisfied with the marriage, that dependency creates guilt or anxiety. It becomes easier to regress to independence than to ask your mate to help meet your needs.

4. You quit sharing details of your life. In the daily routines of life, information is exchanged. When the marriage is slipping, however, sharing even minor experiences and mundane schedules begins to feel threatening.

5. Your sexual interest wanes. Even with the high male drive for sexual release and the strong female need for closeness, when the magic is gone, so is the sexual desire. Spouses might purposefully avoid each other. Or they might begin to subtly increase the emotional distance between them by voicing physical complaints, arguing just prior to bedtime or simply going to bed at different times.

6. You begin to want to spend time with a member of the opposite sex—other than your spouse. Remember that spark you felt when your mate first came on the scene? Whatever that was—hormones, unresolved needs, the competitive urge or a heavenly touch—lovers light up when their beloved appears. When you find yourself lighting up for someone else, look out!

7. You withhold financial resources. Most couples have a strong sense of financial responsibility for their marriage. And that feeling of responsibility may survive long after relational oneness is gone. But when marriages begin to fail, partners often start looking out for themselves. They may open separate bank accounts, often secretly, and full disclosure about their finances diminishes. Money, like sex, is a powerful barometer of marital health, and withholding it can signal problems. *Louis McBurney, M.D.*

4.24 COMMITMENT ISN'T ENOUGH

I'm committed to sticking with my wife—I made a promise and I intend to live by it. But lately, I've felt like something was lacking in our marriage. I thought commitment was the secret to a happy, lasting marriage. Obviously, there must be more but what?

I hear it all the time: "If couples were just more committed, there'd be a lot less divorce." While that statement contains a grain of truth, it's far from the whole story. Commitment can keep couples together. But it takes a certain kind of commitment to keep a marriage growing and happy.

Mike Johnson, a sociologist at Penn State University, points out the two ways we use the word "commitment." The statement "Becky sure is committed to that project" conveys something quite different from "John committed to serve on that committee, he can't back out now." The first statement conveys a sense of dedication that produces enthusiastic involvement. The second is an example of constraint, a sense of obligation that might keep a person involved, but not necessarily with passion or enjoyment. Constraint might keep a couple married—but their heart won't be in it. In contrast, dedication means active devotion to one another and to the marriage.

Some couples are together because of constraint. They're not happy, but they believe in life-long commitment. They also feel the costs of leaving would outweigh the pain they are experiencing. In most instances, constraint is actually positive. Without it, couples would break apart over the most trivial frustrations. But a couple living like that soon discovers that commitment based on constraint alone makes for a pretty miserable marriage.

Marriages don't have to slide into a state of "committed misery." But to avoid it, spouses have to nurture dedication for a lifetime. Here are three ways to make dedication grow.

First, don't trash your future. Take a couple who start out arguing where their daughter will attend school next year and end with harsh words that threaten whether they will even be together next year. When disagreements lead a husband and wife to openly threaten the long-term view, dark clouds will gather and eventually blot out the flickering light of commitment.

For marriage to work, you have to invest time, money and your very soul. But who is going to keep investing in a marriage where one or both partners are throwing around the idea of divorce? Don't threaten your future just because you're frustrated and angry in the heat of battle.

Second, ignore greener grass. When people start losing a sense of dedication to their mates they begin thinking more about the "what ifs." "What if I weren't tied to this person? What if I were married to her (or him) instead?" Some would say that merely considering other possibilities is harmless. But the research is clear that when one or both partners seriously and regularly contemplates the alternatives, a marriage is headed for trouble. In contrast, one study showed that people who are highly dedicated to their partners are not only less likely to consider alternatives, but when aware of available alternatives they tend to look for what's not so great about this other person.

> *God says, "Guard yourself in your spirit, and do not break faith with the wife of your youth."*

In Malachi chapter 2, God makes it clear He hates divorce (not divorced people, by the way). In verse 15, God says, "Guard yourself in your spirit, and do not break faith with the wife of your youth." We can choose with God's help to take responsibility for our thoughts. Everyone is likely to be attracted to others from time to time, but it's how you handle the attraction that counts. You can pine away for the lawn next door or you can pull some weeds and care for the lawn where you live. It's your choice.

Third, think in terms of "we" rather than "me." Whenever two people are dedicated to their marriage, there is a strong sense of "us." To use the scriptural idiom, dedicated couples have a kind of oneness that unites them in life and opens the door to the great blessing of marriage.

Spouses who think in terms of "me" will increasingly make key decisions without input from the other. Couples who think in terms of "we" will consistently nurture their mutual dedication by approaching problems as a team.

Scott M. Stanley

4.25 WE'VE BECOME STRANGERS

My husband and I got married 11 years ago and immediately had four children in six years. Our kids are doing great, but we're not. I often feel overwhelmed, and I'm depressed about the distance in our relationship. Though I want to be close to my husband, I don't know where to begin. What should I do?

To begin with, let's agree that you are tired! Most couples are blindsided by fatigue and the effect it has on their relationship. But the fatigue is understandable. When couples marry, they begin the emotional, sexual, and spiritual task of making two into one. At the same time, they are trying to get established financially. Add to the mix pregnancy and child rearing—and all the nurturing and support that kids require—and it's no wonder a husband and wife have no energy left for their marriage.

And even if it seems like your relationship is hindered while everyone else is doing just fine, think again. Inside their homes, where you can't see, other couples are struggling with fatigue just as you are.

Now, what should you do? First, it's helpful to recognize the connection between fatigue and difficulties in your relationship. You're only human, after all, so lighten your load by cutting back on the stressors wherever you can. And remember that this time of life with young children is only one stage of your marriage.

Second, get a physical examination. I've known several women who felt overwhelmed and depressed, as you do. A doctor's exam showed that pregnancy and childbirth removed trace chemicals from their system that were never restored. When this chemical imbalance was corrected, their lives were changed.

Third, consider whether your marriage has fallen into resentment and resignation. Many couples find their former freedoms crowded out by a growing list of obligations—jobs, mortgage payments, their kids' needs, ministry responsibilities—and they begin to live with resentment. Sometimes a husband will react by "disengaging," getting heavily involved in golf or some other hobby. When that happens, his wife is stuck with more than her fair share of family responsibilities.

Women also struggle with resentment, but they are less likely to disengage from the family. Instead, their resentment often turns to anger and depression because they are saddled with duties night and day. After a time, resentment moves into resignation, a feeling that "being married and having children make for a miserable existence. We'll just have to accept it and put up with the drudgery."

Fourth, guard against resignation by realizing that commitment is a far better response. Commitment acknowledges the difficulties of your current stage of life, but it diligently looks for what's good about it. Commitment says, "Sure, we're exhausted and living under a lot of stress, but let's enjoy being a family in spite of our circumstances."

Tackling the problem together will build unity.

Half the battle is to deal with your challenges together. Perhaps your husband feels as overwhelmed and as low as you do. Tackling the problem together will build unity, even if the stressors in your life don't let up. Talk about fatigue, resentment and resignation. Together, search your schedule to see what can be eliminated or what can be enjoyed together instead of done separately.

Jay Kesler

4.26 MARRIAGE IS ALL WORK AND NO FUN

My wife and I have been married 15 years, and we have three great kids. We both work outside the home, so our time together is limited. But when we do have time together we just don't seem to have fun anymore. My wife does have a monthly night out with the girls and I play basketball with the guys weekly. But our "fun" times together involve visiting our parents or attending one of the kids' events. How, given the realities of our lives right now, can we find the time and energy to enjoy each other again?

Why is "fun" something each of us seems to crave, especially in marriage?

Anything that is done routinely becomes monotonous. And for many people, there is a sense in which monogamy and monotony mean the same thing, because they're both repetitious. A couple might kiss goodbye every morning before going off to work. Even if the kiss is heartfelt, there's an element of duty—and therefore monotony—present. Or maybe you have a tradition of eating pizza and watching videos every Friday night. After a while, that will get stale, no matter how good the pizza!

In the context of marriage, fun involves commitment. Each spouse has a duty to try to understand what makes an activity fun to the other person. We're called to this because Scripture tells us to love each other and to prefer one another (Rm. 12:10). Often when spouses try to explore the areas of fun that the other person enjoys, they learn to enjoy it too.

My daughter's husband is caught up in sports, and she decided that if she couldn't fight him, she should join him. Now she's somewhat of a sports addict herself. Of course, sharing interests ought to be a two-way street. Often after doing a new or unusual activity with their spouses, people say, "I didn't know this was so much fun!"

It's also imperative that they find a *third* thing you both enjoy. Often you have one person leading the other person into personal territory, for instance, a husband leading his wife into the adventure of sports. But there are women who simply cannot enjoy it; they might tolerate it, but it doesn't fulfill their need for fun. Sometimes a wife leads her husband into the adventure of antiques, an area where he feels very much the amateur beside an expert. In such cases, couples need to find alternative ways to be together. Not just the man doing his thing and the woman doing hers.

The process of finding activities that can be shared and enjoyed by both is one of the ways we deepen the marriage relationship. We create a world where we get to do things we've discovered together. Many times, this happens through travel. By going to a place new to both spouses, the couple becomes novices learning together. Often their mutual enjoyment overcomes even the fears and apprehensions connected with new experiences.

Courtship almost always involves planning and plotting. In fact, some anthropologists would say courtship is a highly socialized form of stalking. A hunter never catches anything without thinking about where the game goes, what the game likes to do, what its habits are, and how to bait a trap for game.

Often, after people get married, the stalking is discontinued because the individual has already been caught. That is the precise opposite of the way people ought to think. They ought to continue the stalking, the courting, the planning and thought and effort that were put forth in courtship.

Courtship is a demanding process. People pursue it at the risk of their well being, their rest and everything else until the capture is made. Then they somehow feel no more need; they can relax and enjoy their capture. That's when they actually do need to continue the process. It's what makes marriage fun. Who can resist the element of surprise and the fact that your spouse is plotting to make you happy? I encourage couples to have at least one night a week when they get alone to do something themselves that draws them together.

Fun is easier to pull off when you're flexible.

Plus, you get more mileage out of an anticipated activity. Having plans for a vacation, or even an evening out, can make the days or routine work seem more tolerable. But it's important not to overplan to the point of rigidity. Fun is easier to pull off when you're flexible, willing to change direction. Most people tell me the real fun stuff happened when they were carrying out a plan and then decided to try something different from that. Take a risk! It throws both of you into the unknown.

Even if money isn't a big obstacle, it still comes down to priorities. I remember a point in my marriage when I decided I no longer had time for a night out with the guys. Because I had so little time, I knew I had to give my marriage top priority. You might find you will have to trade your basketball night and your wife's night with the girls for a night together.

It's important to rekindle your early courtship behaviors, the things you did together that you now miss. And not just the date nights and the fun things you used to do, but the spontaneity and the silly things you did with each other. When we get married we tend to start buying kitchen appliances and air conditioners and alternators for the car; but occasionally we need to remember the personal touches—the flowers, the poem, the piece of jewelry or whatever—that communicate "you're special." And we need to take time to be together and discover what's new about this person we married.

Jay Kesler

4.27 MAKING COUPLE FRIENDSHIPS HAPPEN

We enjoy one another's company but would sometimes like to do things with another couple. The problem for us is finding another couple where all the friendships click. What is the secret to making couple friendship a reality?

Based on my experiences and those of others I've talked with, here are a few suggestions for building and maintaining marriage-enhancing friendships:

Actively seek out friendships—don't wait for them to just happen. After several moves and a major rift in their church, one couple realized they didn't have any really good friends any more. "We sat down with a notebook and thought about what our options were," recalls the wife. "We picked about 10 couples and invited them over one by one over a period of about six months. We served a lot of chicken breasts. It's just a trial-and-error process—a lot of the couples didn't pan out as friends, but some did."

Don't expect all your friendships to be mutual. Pat and Rick have been married 15 years. They met and dated in college and have a number of mutual friends. Pat's closet friend, however, is someone she has known since childhood. "Emily and I remained best friends despite the fact that our husbands were just socially polite," explains Pat. "There was a time when Emily had a fantasy that the four of us would be as close as the two of us, but it never happened. We finally came to the point where we said, 'Okay, this friendship doesn't work that way. It would be nice if we could be mutual friends, but you don't dump a really good friendship because you can't make a fabulous foursome from it.'"

Seek out friendships with people who share your values and interests. Shared beliefs, whether they relate to religion, child rearing, social concerns or other deeply held commitments, can draw people together in friendship as well as in marriage. I wasn't surprised when many couples I talked to told me that many of their friendships started at church. Just attending church services, however, may not be enough. Attending Sunday school class, volunteering on a committee or joining a study group can provide a niche within which deep friendships can develop.

Remain open to unexpected friendships. Friendship isn't always predictable. Although chances are you and your spouse are more likely to become friends with people with whom you share a neighborhood, age bracket, church or work situation, it doesn't always happen that way. One young couple became best friends with a couple almost 20 years their senior—despite few outward circumstances in common. Their advice to other couples: be open to serendipity. If you stick too rigidly to your categories you can miss some great friendships.

Janis Long Harris

CHAPTER 5

GROWING IN
SPIRITUAL
ONENESS

GROWING IN
SPIRITUAL
ONENESS

Spiritual togetherness is only possible through the work of the Holy Spirit. If we have been set apart by the Spirit, He resides in our life. The result is a mysterious union with Christ, and with those who know Him as Savior. So if we want to grow closer spiritually, we must make sure that each of us has a saving relationship with God through faith in Christ.

Although spiritual intimacy is primarily a work of the Spirit—that doesn't mean that we don't work at it. The disciplines that we use in our relationship with Christ are the very ones that must be pursued in our marriage.

We must, for starters, read the Bible together. We will grow in our oneness as we continue to submit to the authority of the Word in our lives (2 Tm. 3:16-17). Having the Word central in our marriage means that we are reading, meditating, and memorizing the Bible (cf. Ps. 1:2-3). It enters into our conversations, governs our thoughts, and is lived out in our lives. We cannot just be hearers of the Word, we must be doers (cf. Jms. 1:22). The husband is the spiritual leader and has been called to sanctify his wife through the washing of the water of the Word (cf. Eph. 5:26). This ministry of the Word has a cleansing effect. The life they live and the words they speak make their wives more like Christ.

We must also pray together. Spiritual intimacy grows on the seedbed of prayer. Prayer aligns our thoughts and hearts with God. For those who find it hard to pray together, use God's Word as your guide. Pray through Ephesians 5:22-33 for your marriage, or use Philippians 1:9-11 to pray for a child. Use a psalm to lift your voices in praise to God. Pray that God will continue to help you grow in this area. And keep your spouse high on your prayer list.

Finally, in pursuing spiritual oneness, we must serve together. Being involved in ministry provides a wonderful context for spiritual intimacy. Find places to serve together. Aquila and Priscilla's ministry with the Apostle Paul serves as a great example (cf. Ac. 18). When we expend ourselves for the advancement of God's kingdom, our hearts are knit together in a common purpose that is eternally big—the result is a strong spiritual bond.

> *PRAYER: Lord, help us to stimulate each other to love and good deeds (Heb. 10:24). Give us grace to weed out the selfishness in our own lives so that we might serve each other with the attitude of Christ. Help us to confess our sins to each other, being quick to forgive. Help us to encourage each other all the more as we see the day of Christ's return drawing near (cf. Heb. 10:25). And thank you that in Christ we have everything we need for life and godliness (2 Pt. 1:5). May we be disciplined for the purpose of godliness so that through us Your light might shine. Amen.*

5.1 MAKING SENSE OF SPIRITUAL LEADERSHIP

I'm a confused guy—at least when it comes to understanding my spiritual responsibilities in my marriage and family. From some I hear I'm almost to be a dictator of the home, and yet others say the truly biblical approach is an egalitarian one. I want to be a good husband and father, but just what does that mean?

Unfortunately, much of the biblical teaching about husband being the "head of the wife" has gotten tangled with emotional issues such as women's rights and changing sex roles. As a result, we've failed to focus on a disturbing societal problem: the growing disappearance of men from spiritual leadership in our churches and families. Too many men have abdicated their responsibilities.

But before I'm misunderstood, let me make clear what I'm *not* saying.

I'm not saying men are superior to women. Men and women are of equal worth before God, since both are created in God's image. Christian men and women are also equal heirs of the grace of Christ. Christian marriage is to be a picture of how God relates to His people. Husbands are commanded to love their wives as

Men and women are of equal worth before God.

Christ loved the church and gave His life for her. Christian leadership is servant leadership.

If you're serious about being a spiritual leader in your family, my advice is simple. But it's also demanding. There are some specifics you should give attention to. You can set an example for everyone in your family by getting up in the morning and having a personal time of Bible reading and prayer. You can set a regular time for your family to read Scripture together. You can offer thoughtful prayers at mealtime. You can make church involvement a priority. You can offer spiritual insights that encourage your wife and children.

Being a spiritual leader, though, is not as much what you do as what you are.

Being a spiritual leader, though, is not as much what you do as what you are. The Bible tells us the fruit of the spirit is the hallmark of the believer. And the fruit of the Spirit is love, joy, peace, patience, kindness, goodness, faith, gentleness, and self-control (Gl. 5:22-23). When a man consistently practices walking in the Spirit not just in his public life, but also when he's with his wife and children at home, he becomes a spiritual leader.

Jesus made it clear that Christian leadership isn't power. The essence of spiritual leadership is the same as the essence of Christianity; we are called to be servants. The man who best serves his family will be a true leader.

Jay Kesler

5.2 DIFFERING DEGREES OF SPIRITUAL MATURITY

I was raised in a Christian home. My husband, on the other hand, didn't become a Christian until he was in his teens. He didn't grow up seeing his parents pray and witnessing God's answers to prayer as I did. The result is that we're on different spiritual levels. Because of this, he isn't the spiritual leader that our pastor describes in his sermons. What should I do about the spiritual imbalance that exists in our marriage?

A lot of women wrestle with this question, but the truth is this same issue was a serious problem in the early church. Up until that time in history—when the new Christian religion gave women dignity and value as persons—women were primarily viewed as the property of men. Their function was to provide amusement, serve the desires and wishes of men, and raise the children. They had no real place in life other than that; it was an almost entirely male world.

But many women who followed Christ were assigned unprecedented roles in the fellowship of early Christian churches. When you think about it, who could better understand and emulate Christ's model of servanthood and sacrifice than women who had both characteristics ingrained in them by their culture? The heart of this revolutionary new religion must have come more easily to the women of that day than to the men.

As early Christian women began to show their spiritual competence—just as you feel you have spiritual competence—it seems safe to assume that it made many of the men uncomfortable. They were being forced to accept women in a whole new light.

So on the one hand, Paul seemed to be warning women to be careful about upsetting the social order of the day. (Note the 1 Corinthians references to "the head of the woman is the man" and the instruction for women to keep their heads covered, according to the Mideastern custom.) But he also was telling men to get moving and accept their spiritual responsibilities in the home.

Before we go any further, I want to give my own warning. A lot of people who ask the question you're asking are assuming a stereotyped picture of what spiritual leadership should look like in a marriage. Untold harm is being done at women's meetings by speakers who stand up and paint a picture of what a "perfect" Christian husband ought to be. Often that picture ends up looking a lot like the person doing the talking—a professional communicator with Bible training who's personally warm and spiritually articulate. And then a lot of women go home, compare that slick model with what they have in their own unexpressive, spiritually struggling husbands, and they become even more disenchanted. And thousands, maybe millions, of Christian husbands feel like spiritual losers because they don't measure up to the image they see in pastors and seminar leaders who tell them what they ought to be doing.

We need to remember that as Christian husbands or wives, we have only one model we're

As Christian husbands or wives, we have only one model we're supposed to try to look like. That's Jesus.

supposed to try to look like. That's Jesus. We get a multifaceted picture of a very complex Jesus from the stories in the New Testament. What did Jesus look like? Love, joy, peace, patience, kindness, goodness, faith, gentleness, and self-control (Gl. 5:22-23).

Your husband may be providing spiritual leadership in ways you haven't considered. It could be something as subtle as his quiet example or the consistency of his life. Even if he hasn't reached your "spiritual level," he could be leading in the amount of growth he has experienced from where he started. Maybe he's leading by his spiritual persistence in getting up and trying again every time he fails.

I'd encourage you to look for those areas where your husband is showing spiritual growth and leadership. Affirm them. Try to give him other opportunities where he can succeed. And don't force him into a preconceived image of what a Christian man or husband ought to be.

What if you can't find any areas in which your husband is providing spiritual leadership? Even if the man you married is a spiritual foot-dragger, that doesn't have to hold you back. Focus on the fruits of the Spirit (Gl. 5:22-23), which have a wonderful way of spreading from one person to another.

Actually, if we live out the fruits of the Spirit and sincerely attempt to apply Jesus' teachings to marriage, much of the discussion and debate regarding spiritual leadership and husbands' and wives' roles becomes a moot point. The simple teaching of Jesus is that the way to live, to love, and to lead is to serve. If one or both spouses lead by serving, each will come out ahead. Servanthood is the secret to marital success. And we can all be servants in our marriages.

Jay Kesler

5.3 OPPOSITE STYLES OF WORSHIP

My husband and I grew up in different denominations with different worship patterns. He was raised in a liturgical church; I grew up in a more informal church. We've just begun our family, and that is complicating our decision concerning a home church. Our little boy is six months old and we want to get involved in a church where our child can come to know Christ at an early age. I realize that the truths he learns about God at home will shape him more than what he learns at church, but

I also know that a good church will be invaluable to us as parents and to our child as he grows. Is there a compromise we can reach?

Compromise doesn't have to be a bad thing. You can't compromise absolute truth, of course, but in a situation like this, give and take may be the best solution. It's far more important to choose a church that is faithful to the Bible, where the people try to put their faith into practice, than it is to require any particular form of worship.

You need to find a community of believers that is sincerely trying to obey Christ and his Word. That can happen in a liturgical or an informal atmosphere, so don't base your decision solely on form.

It's far more important to choose a church that is faithful to the Bible.

With churches as with anything else, people tend to feel most comfortable with things that are similar to the way they were raised. While there's nothing wrong with feeling comfortable, we need to make sure those warm feelings aren't the main consideration in deciding on a church. Keep in mind the real issues—biblical fidelity, spiritual vitality and practical Christian living—and use them as your yardstick.

Now let's come back to your question about compromise. True compromise, in this situation, should start with understanding. You and your husband need to understand what each of you finds meaningful in worship styles and why. Talking about it will not only increase your own understanding of the other person's feelings, it may even give you a new appreciation for a worship form you knew nothing about. Compromise will come easier if you work on this understanding first.

Compromise will come easier if you work on this understanding first.

Finally, consider that there is probably a church that falls somewhere between extremely liturgical and extremely informal where you both can settle in. You might look for a church where the morning worship services have quite a bit of form and structure, yet where there are also informal opportunities such as small-group meetings or Bible studies.

Jay Kesler

5.4 FORGIVING REPEATED FAILURES

I know it's wrong to expect my husband to be perfect, but there are times I'd like to think he's at least tried to work at some of his shortcomings. I keep forgiving him and hoping that the situation will improve, but the cycle continues. Is there a point where I should say, "Enough is enough," and quit forgiving him?

The worst thing we can be is legalists, saying we should stop forgiving at a certain point, or that we should keep on forgiving no matter what. Jesus said forgive "seventy times seven" (Mt. 18:22), but He didn't mean to count. What He meant was, "Be the kind of person who doesn't ask the question, 'How many times should I forgive?' Just be a forgiving person."

The proper question is not, "How often?" but rather, "Under what circumstances can I forgive?" Let's take a marriage in which there is savage and persistent brutality. I don't believe a spouse can forgive while the brutality continues. The spouse must first get out of reach and *then* begin a process of forgiving.

Forgiving is not the same as being a doormat.

A second consideration is this: Repeated forgiving should not be confused with toleration of what's going on. We must be intolerant of evil—of any kind—whether it happens to us or to anyone else. We must signal that forgiving is not the same as being a fool, and forgiving is not the same as being a doormat.

You can forgive your spouse almost anything, but if you tolerate everything he does you will make matters between the two of you worse. There does come a time when one spouse will say to the other, "I cannot forgive you while this continues. It must stop or I must get out, so that I can begin to forgive."

Lewis B. Smedes, with James D. Berkely

5.5 SPIRITUALLY LAX SPOUSE

When we were first married, my wife and I both joined Bible studies, faithfully attended church, and seriously worked toward maturing in our Christian faith. Six years later, it seems like I'm the only one who is still eager to grow. I'm very concerned about my wife's spiritual indifference. Should I hold her accountable or act as if nothing is wrong? Just what is my role in encouraging her spiritual growth?

We are responsible to encourage one another in the faith (Eph. 5:25-28). We are not, however, responsible *for* our spouse's faith. That is his or her duty before God.

Consider the situation of one young woman I know. After three years, this woman is just now coming out of a period she can only describe as a "dark night of the soul." For years she had been meeting weekly with two other women, and they had been extremely close. They had talked freely about their marriages, children, hopes, and anxieties. Together they grew remarkably in their understanding of God.

Then one of the women moved hundreds of miles away. The other got cancer and died. Suddenly, this woman found herself alone, without the support system she had come to count on. During the same period, her husband had a series of job crises and their boys were struggling through adolescence.

"I didn't know what was happening to me," she explained. "What do you do when you want to pray but can't find the desire? You want to study Scripture, but you just don't care? I didn't want to go to any more meetings and be with groups."

"I could see she was starving to death spiritually," said her husband, "and I prayed for her with a passion. I was worried at moments. But I knew this was one of those things she, with God's grace, was going to have to work through."

Slowly this woman is regaining her spiritual equilibrium. She has recognized how much the death of her friend affected her. She also found some help from participating in a Bible study. But it has been a long, hard road. How was her husband able to hold back and not try to "fix" the situation for his wife?

"My wife's experience of Christ," he says, "is always going to be different from mine, as different as our personalities. I have to continually turn her over to Christ—no matter what her situation is. And she has to do the same with me.

"Once I saw that I am not responsible for her faith, it made it easier to handle. We've always prayed for one another and tried to serve one another as Christ calls us to, but we've never tried to be accountable to one another for faith. We each have others we go to for that."

Mark Galli

5.6 STRUGGLING WITH LUSTFUL THOUGHTS

My 52-year-old husband has labeled me "jealous" because I am offended when he looks at other women—not quick, fleeting glances but deliberate double takes. The women he finds attractive are 25 years younger than he is and usually dressed immodestly. When I challenge him on this point, he denies that he's staring at other women. I maintain that the problem isn't me but him, and the core issue is lustful thoughts. Who is right?

Understanding what's really going on with your husband will help you deal with this situation. First of all, many women don't realize that for a man, the eye is the "sexual trigger." Men respond to visual stimulation. Even so, a Christian is responsible for how he handles this natural condition.

You, of course, recognize that ogling young women does not honor Christ.

You, of course, recognize that ogling young women does not honor Christ. However, I doubt your husband's real problem is lust. He may, rather, be struggling with the realities of aging—coming to terms with his own lessening powers, not just sexually but socially, professionally, and physically as well.

If your husband is feeling inadequate, the answer is to help him feel good about himself. You may need to make an effort to rekindle the romantic aspects of your marriage. After many years of marriage, it's easy to take each other for granted. Your husband needs someone who will see him afresh, point out his accomplishments, praise him for his positive character qualities. It's interesting that in most cases in which a middle-aged man does have an affair with a younger woman, it's usually because the woman makes him feel wonderful about himself. Make sure you're the woman who makes him feel great about who he is as a man, and he'll be much less likely to continue looking at other women.

While you've discovered it does little good to criticize your husband while he looks at women, there is something you can do in those circumstances. I call it contextualization: you help put the woman he's looking at in the context of human relationships. She is not just a beautiful "object"; she is someone's daughter, sister, perhaps wife. I believe this is what Paul meant when he urged

Timothy to view women as "sisters and mothers" (1 Tm. 5:2). The Christian man may be attracted, but he then reminds himself that here is a person who is to be respected.

You can casually remind your husband of reality when he's doing his double takes. Remarks such as, "If our daughter dressed like that, I'd be embarrassed" or "She's about old enough to be our daughter," could bring him down to earth. Whenever you can, let the fresh breeze of humor blow into the situation as well (without being sarcastic).

Try not to feel threatened; your husband's behavior probably has little to do with you and everything to do with how he feels about himself. Pray for his adjustment to aging. Pray for wisdom for yourself as you seek to build him up in love. As he comes to grips with his own successes, failures, and unrealized dreams, it's quite likely he'll stop paying so much attention to younger women.

Jay Kesler

Your husband's behavior probably has little to do with you and everything to do with how he feels about himself.

5.7 NO TIME FOR SPIRITUAL GROWTH

Before I got married, it seemed like I had a lot more time for my spiritual life—I was involved in several Bible studies and church groups. Now I have a spouse to factor in when I manage my time, and I'm finding there is less and less time for spiritual growth. How can I continue to mature as a Christian and still have time for my marriage?

Being married can play havoc with your spiritual life.

Being married can play havoc with your spiritual life. Many people feel they were better friends in Christ before they got married.

To be married means to have our privacy invaded, to live dangerously close to another sinner, to be interfered with by someone that claims to love us but does not always know how. Yet to be married also means to celebrate a gift God has given every day, all day, through everything we share, even when we are not together. Marriage itself is a source of spiritual renewal because it offers three gifts to the spiritual life: sustenance, healing, and growth.

Sustenance is experienced in the context of a down-to-earth reality. Take my sweater, for instance. My wife knitted me a beautiful red sweater during time squeezed from her busy schedule, time stolen from other people who needed her. But I accidentally left it at a conference center. By the time I contacted the center, it had been given away to the poor. Some lucky man did not know he was wearing a "sacrament."

Without a word my wife sat down and knitted me an exact replica of the first sweater. But this one communicated "I *really* love you" with every stitch. Could God show me His love more directly than through acts like these, through my nearest and dearest neighbor? Sustenance is received from God daily in marriage through mutual provision of shelter, food, and psychological and emotional support.

Healing is received when anxieties and fears are dispelled by mutual acceptance and companionship. While daily ministries to one another can quickly be taken for granted, a period of stress often reveals they are nothing less than a means of grace. For instance, my first day on the job as a carpenter pushed me off the stress scale. I could not keep up with my younger co-laborers. I banged my thumb with the hammer and, while walking along some floor joists, slipped down with one leg on each side! But when I went home that night, my wife ministered to me with a good warm meal, words of encouragement and a listening ear.

When we collapsed into each other's arms that evening on the sofa, I was renewed by a spiritual grace through acceptance and companionship. The preacher in the Old Testament said, "Pity the man who falls and has no one to help him up" (Ec. 4:10, NIV). Could God have ministered to me in a more direct way than this? Perhaps the preacher was reflecting on the presence of God in a marriage covenant when he said, "A cord of three strands is not quickly broken" (Ec. 4:12).

Growth comes through the disciplines of adjusting your life to another from whom you can never hide. Because I know my wife loves me almost unconditionally (for only God's love is truly "unconditional"), I can trust her hardest words to me, knowing that confrontation is not rejection but an opportunity to grow.

Marriage turns out to be a school of Christian character, earthly and heavenly at the same time. It is a place to find God. The vows we took in marriage are reality statements: for better, for worse, for richer, for poorer, in sickness and in health, until death do us part.

God is especially present where the marriage is human, earthy, vulnerable, painful, troubled and just plain hard. And he is also present in moments of hilarious joy or close companionship—deepening and sanctifying these moments.

Paul Stevens

Marriage turns out to be a school of Christian character, earthly and heavenly at the same time.

5.8 CONQUERING ANGER AND RESENTMENT

My husband's company was sold and he was laid off. He wasn't able to find another job in his field, so he has been working as a cashier and night manager at a convenience store. I've taken a job to supplement our family income but frankly, I don't want to work. My sense of resentment toward my husband is growing—as if it were his fault that his company was sold and he got laid off. How can I combat my negative thoughts about him when he needs my support more than ever?

You may be misdirecting your anger and frustration at your husband, rather than at your situation. You realize your husband isn't guilty of anything, he's merely a victim of some unfortunate circumstances. But middle-class Americans aren't used to being victims. And when we don't know whom to blame, we tend to lash out at the people around us.

It won't help to simply try hard to stop your anger. But it will help to find ways to redirect your anger and then allow it to dissipate. One way is to remember a belief that is central to Christianity: the idea that God is sovereign. He made the heavens and the earth and everything in it, and He is able to cause all things to work together for good to those who love Him (Rm. 8:28). That's not to say that everything that happens to us is good. Not being able to use the gifts God gave us in our work is not good. But God can bring good out of circumstances that aren't good. If we believe that, we will ask ourselves, "How can I respond in such a way that I cooperate with God's intentions to bring good out of this situation?"

There is a certain refinement of character that comes only through weathering life's storms. You probably know people who have been through great difficulties and have amazing strength of character as a result. Is it possible that God would like to refine you through the difficulty you and your husband are experiencing? If instead of turning on your husband, you can together aim your energy toward meeting the challenge the two of you are facing, you may come out of this stronger as individuals *and* as a couple.

Another way to redirect your anger and cooperate with God's sovereignty is to relate your own suffering to that of other people who are in unfortunate or unfair circumstances. Many people were born into poverty, or have a disability, or were damaged because of the sin of others. Most of us are oblivious to their pain. But God can use your situation to make you more compassionate and attuned to the helplessness and despair that many are feeling. And perhaps that compassion will lead you to take action on their behalf.

You might also remind yourself of what you do have—your family, and two jobs that, while not ideal, nevertheless enable you to keep body and soul together. Though many people spend their lives in unfulfilling jobs, most likely in your case this will be just a chapter in your life. It can either be one in which you allow God to teach you marvelous lessons that refine your marriage and make each of you into a better person, or it can be a time of terrible anger and resentment that debilitates you for the rest of your life.

Jay Kesler

5.9 STAYING SPIRITUALLY CONNECTED

It seems that my husband and I never take time to relate to one another on a deeper spiritual level. We do go to church together, and we're raising our children in a Christian home. But I wish we'd pray together more, discuss our faith and read the Bible together. He's not big on family devotions. What are some ways we can feel more spiritually connected?

When I lead marriage seminars, I hear this question more than any other. I find that this problem often occurs when spouses have very different personalities. Some people simply find it easier to talk about intimate matters of the soul than other people.

The problem is also largely due to a basic difference between men and women. Men have been trained to be guarded in expressing their innermost thoughts and feelings. Many men feel that life is like a terribly competitive poker game in which they must never betray what they're really feeling, lest another person know what's in their hand and somehow do them in. And because men bring this way of relating to all their relationships, they are often closed and unable to share their emotions and personal thoughts, not even with their wives. Because their spiritual life is very personal, many men find it almost impossible to communicate on this level.

It sounds like you already respect your husband's boundaries by accepting that he isn't ready for regular family devotions. But you should consider a few nonthreatening ways to help him open up. One thing that has been helpful to my wife and me is to use a third element to open the way to sharing about spiritual issues. We read the same book and then discuss it, or go to a well-selected movie and afterward, over coffee, talk about the ideas in the movie in light of our Christian commitment.

Another way you might try to help him open up is by leading from your own openness and inviting—not pushing—him to respond in kind. For instance, you might say, "Last night I was thinking about this particular spiritual issue, and struggling with X. Do you ever feel this way?" Then give your husband a chance to share.

You might also suggest that your husband read from a daily devotional guide, as a sort of family ritual. You might say, "Honey, it might be a good thing for the kids if once a day we read from this devotional guide. You don't have to comment on the passage, just read it." He might feel it's hokey, but he might also feel it's the least he can do. And it may help him open up to making a comment, or to responding to a comment you make.

You are not demanding that your husband respond, but are opening the door for him to share some of his thoughts and feelings. As you offer such opportunities you may well begin to find the level of spiritual communication you seek.

Jay Kesler

5.10 THE IMPORTANCE OF SHARED PRAYER

We really want to build a strong marriage and one essential element we keep hearing about is shared prayer. We say grace together at meal times and occasionally pray out loud together before bed. We're not very comfortable with shared prayer just yet and plan to work at making it a natural part of our daily life. But we were wondering, "Why is shared prayer so important?"

There's a story about a young couple who decided to start their honeymoon by kneeling beside their bed to pray. The bride giggled when she heard her new husband's prayer: "For what we are about to receive may the Lord make us truly thankful."

Research shows that the happiest couples are those who pray together.

Humor aside, research shows that the happiest couples are those who pray together. Couples who frequently pray together are twice as likely as those who pray less often to describe their marriages as being highly romantic. And get this—married couples who pray together are 90 percent more likely to report higher satisfaction with their sex lives than couples who don't pray together. Prayer, because of the vulnerability it demands, also draws a couple closer.

No amount of being "religious" can replace the time a couple spends in shared prayer. Take the situation of one young couple who came to us for counseling. Both were extensively involved in their church and they appeared to be dedicated, vibrant spiritual leaders. But when we met them, their five-year marriage was falling apart. In spite of their spiritual fervor, overinvolvement with everything but their marriage had caused the soul of their relationship to wither.

"When was the last time the two of you prayed together?" we asked them. As they looked at each other, the answer was obvious. Prayer had taken a back seat to activities.

We gave them a simple assignment. For the next week they were to pray together briefly just before going to bed. Five days later the wife called and exclaimed, "I know this sounds crazy, but our relationship has done an about-face." She told us that spending a moment together in prayer was rejuvenating their spirits and their marriage.

If prayer is so good for a marriage, why don't more couples do it? Because it's not easy, and the price of vulnerability, even with your spouse, can seem too high. Praying together hasn't always been natural or easy for my wife and me either. At times we have fallen into the trap of preaching through our prayers and subtly jabbing each other with our "good" intentions. But through the years we have picked up some principles that have helped us pray more effectively.

Often, we say a prayer of thanksgiving to God rather than try to pray about our needs or difficulties. Occasionally we say the Lord's Prayer together. And sometimes one of us simply initiates a time of silent prayer or a time of brief sentence prayers. The point is to pray—there is no right or wrong way to do it. Every attempt we make to commune with God in shared prayer nurtures the soul of our marriage.

Every attempt we make to commune with God in shared prayer nurtures the soul of our marriage.

We are convinced the most desperate need in many marriages is not for more excitement, glitz or activity, but for depth. To avoid superficiality, which is the curse of a restless marriage, you must sojourn together toward communion with God through worship, service and prayer. Only then will that aching, burning urge you have to be connected—soul to soul—be satisfied.

Les and Leslie Parrott

5.11 IN-LAWS WHO ARE HOSTILE TO CHRISTIAN FAITH

My wife had a wonderful relationship with her mother all the years she was growing up—that is, until my wife became a Christian. Now her parents are openly hostile toward us, and communication is virtually impossible. Even though we love her family and continue to get together with them, my wife is really distressed over the fracture in this relationship. What can we do?

Most likely one of two things is going on in your fractured relationship. The first is referred to in the New Testament as "the offense of the cross" (Gl. 5:11). Your wife's parents may fear the Christian faith because of the implications it has for their own lives. They might be resisting Christianity because they don't want to change their behaviors and lifestyle.

But it's more common for people to react negatively due to a false understanding of Jesus Christ and Christianity. Your in-laws appear to be hostile to the Christian faith, but their definition of Christianity may have been twisted by unfortunate experiences with people who claimed to be Christians but whose actions were repugnant.

A man once accosted me after a church service to announce, "I don't believe in God, and I hate churches." I said, "Tell me what God you don't believe in. Maybe I don't believe in Him either." The man described his mother's family, who had all participated in a backwoods folk religion full of contradictions, legalisms and heresies. "If Christianity were presented to me on that level, I wouldn't touch it with a ten-foot pole!" I told him. "But do you have the time, the energy, and the honesty to really examine the New Testament?" We spent a couple of hours together and parted amiably. This man wasn't fighting against God, but against a caricature of Him.

When it comes to talking about Christianity with a person who is fighting against a warped idea of our faith, it's like trying to untangle a big knot by pulling on one end of the string. The more you try—especially by arguing or defending—the tighter the knot gets. The only way to untangle the knot is with authenticity. Your life will have to show the difference between genuine Christianity and your in-laws' false understanding of it. It sounds as if you and your wife are already on the right track, since you continue to love her parents and to get together with them.

There comes a time, especially in family relationships, to quit talking about one's Christianity and just live it. Then let the Holy Spirit do His work. Over time, the quality of your lives will have an effect on your in-laws. Perhaps they'll find themselves saying, "Well, I can't stand religious people. But my daughter is a Christian, and she really is a lovely person and a wonderful daughter. She's an exception to the rule." Sooner or later, they may realize there could be many such "exceptions" and that their analysis of Christianity has been unfair.

Jay Kesler

5.12 BECOMING A TRUE SERVANT

Most of the time, I do an okay job of putting my mate first. But there are times it's a real challenge to put her needs before my own. To be perfectly honest, there are times when I feel like I'm the only one doing the giving! Living sacrificially for my mate sure isn't easy. What can I do to develop a consistent attitude of genuine servanthood?

No one likes to feel they are being taken advantage of. And when you're struggling just to keep your own head above water, it's tempting to believe you can't do any more to help your mate. But couples who adopt the "every man for himself" approach end up feeling like married strangers.

We're commanded to love each other with the love of Christ. And that often means sacrificing personal comfort or convenience to help ease your mate's burden. It takes work, but by keeping a few suggestions in mind, any couple can develop a mutual, self-sacrificing love:

> *Realize that no one is too good to be a servant.*

Realize that no one is too good to be a servant. Instead, follow the example of Christ, who served others without feeling the service was "beneath him." He is the Creator and Lord of the universe, but Jesus had the humility to kneel down and wash the dirty feet of those who should have been washing *His* feet!

Don't expect blessings in return for your acts of kindness. Of course, the goal is to develop *mutual* sacrificial love, in which both spouses are serving each other. But it often takes time to reach that point.

Cultivate an attitude of service. We know a woman who serves her husband, but she hasn't developed the attitude of service. She does all the household tasks—cooking, cleaning, laundry, yard work, shopping and other errands—because her husband's heart condition keeps him from helping. She grumbles about all that she has to do, because she wants him to recognize the great sacrifice she is making. However, she fusses and complains so loudly that she destroys any "credit for sacrificing" that should be due her.

Remember that when you serve your mate, you are also serving God. It's easier to serve if you envision your loving Lord rather than your flawed spouse. If you feel you have to go too far beyond the call of duty, just picture doing it for Jesus. The imposition then becomes an honor!

Accentuate the positives when thinking of your spouse. If you focus on your mate's strong points, you'll find much to honor and more reasons to serve. Shortly after we were married, I started picking on my husband's grammar. I had been an English major, and he had to be tutored in English to make it through graduate school. Consequently, I nit-picked his every lapse in writing or speaking. Finally, God got the message to me: "Why don't you appreciate Jim's spiritual maturity or his sense of humor and creative ideas? Why not admire his good qualities instead of picking at his weak grammar skills?"

Show your appreciation when your spouse serves you. Even if it is only an imperfect, incomplete attempt, you can affirm the intention or some action of love.

Look for examples of mutual sacrificial love in other couples. As you study their ways, you can incorporate the same caring for your mate that you see in them.

If you blow it, try again. Practice won't make you perfect, but it will help establish a good habit. We are always encouraged by this reminder: "Not that I have already reached the goal, but I make every effort ... one thing I do: forgetting what is behind and reaching forward to what is ahead, I pursue ... (Php. 3:12-14).

We both have been guilty at times of blurting out our quick-fix solutions, rather than hearing each other out. We preach to others about the elements of good communication, but sometimes we rush in and violate all the principles of good listening. Instead of giving up, we ask God and each other for forgiveness again and then start over.

Jim and Sally Conway

5.13 FOSTERING AN ATTITUDE OF HUMILITY

There are times when I'm very understanding and supportive of my husband's problems at work and the stress he endures day after day. But then, at other times, I lack all compassion for his problems and say the most angry, critical things. Despite my best intentions, I can't always be the loving person I want to be. What is causing me to behave in such a contradictory way?

Surprisingly, pride has much to do with why we behave as we do. If pride is so deeply embedded in our souls, driving spouses apart through self-centered behavior, how can we ever achieve true intimacy? The antidote is found in the power of humility.

Humility isn't the process of becoming a relationship doormat, encouraging your mate to wipe his or her feet on you. Nor does it involve assuming a false frailty or sense of unimportance. It's actually as simple as asking Christ to live out in you the attitude He assumed on earth.

Humility isn't the process of becoming a relationship doormat.

In Philippians 2:3-7, the apostle Paul gives us an idea of what motivated Jesus' actions: "Do nothing out of rivalry or conceit, but in humility consider others as more important than yourselves. Everyone should look out not only for his own interests, but also for the interests of others. Make your own attitude that of Christ Jesus, who, existing in the form of God, did not consider equality with God as something to be used for His own advantage. Instead He emptied Himself by assuming the form of a slave, taking on the likeness of men."

To defeat pride and build intimacy in my marriage, I need to compare my behavior to Paul's instructions. For instance, is my decision to spend a Saturday relaxing with a book rather than joining my wife for a walk really only considering my own interests—not those of others? When I am unwilling to forget a hurtful word after an apology is offered, am I guilty of vain conceit? And when I choose not to take over some chores so my wife can spend time with her friends, have I failed to take on the nature of a servant? When I realize I'm falling down in these areas, I ask Christ to let the power of His humility take over my thoughts, actions, and attitudes.

Not long ago I had a chance to test the power of humility. For the first time in 22 years of driving, my wife had a scrape with a cement pole while pulling out of a narrow bank drive-up lane. It slightly damaged our van.

When she called to tell me about it, I realized I had a choice to make. I could pace around the van with a furrowed brow and ask in an artificially calm voice, "Just what happened at the bank?" (Underlying message: this wouldn't have happened to me.) But that would have been pride talking, and fortunately that's not what I did.

Instead, as I put down the telephone receiver, the Holy Spirit reminded me of an experience I had years ago. When I was 18, I borrowed my sister's car for the spring prom. That evening, while driving up a parking ramp next to a restaurant, I scraped her new car against a wall. The incident ruined the night for me as I dreaded having to face my sister. What I needed most was someone to understand how bad I felt, not a lecture on safe driving.

It also occurred to me that I ought to be thankful that neither my wife nor our children were hurt. Christ helped me realize that intimacy was more important than insurance premiums. As a result, humility won the day and we dismissed the incident as one of those things that can happen to either of us.

Humility builds up, restores, heals, and deepens our bond.

The writer of Proverbs was onto something when he observed, "Pride goes before destruction" (Pr. 16:18, NIV). But the opposite is true as well: humility goes before exaltation. In marriage, that means humility builds up, restores, heals, and deepens our bond. As I learn to put aside pride and selfishness, we see joy and intimacy rush in to take their place. The benefits to our marriage are well worth keeping up my fight against pride.

Robert Moeller

5.14 WANTING TO SWITCH CHURCHES

When we got married, I left my church and began to attend my wife's church. I didn't think this would be problematic, but I've come across some serious doctrinal differences. It's been several years now, and my wife and kids are deeply involved in this church. I want to visit other churches, but my wife doesn't. Should I insist we "shop around" or just endure the situation?

Family unity and tranquility are usually more important than your personal satisfaction with a particular church. So if your difficulty is something like the pastor occasionally making a statement that you disagree with, you can probably live with it for the sake of your family. However, there could be reasons to look for another church.

When our children were young, my wife and I began attending a church where the preaching was very intellectually stimulating to me. But the Sunday school program was slipshod, and the teachers weren't really teaching from the Bible. In light of that problem, I had to give up my enjoyment of the pastor's sermons for the sake of my children. They needed Christian teachers who modeled their faith and teaching based on the Scriptures.

Small differences in the area of doctrinal preferences can be put aside for the larger issue of domestic tranquility, but you might want to talk with your wife about the more pivotal issues. Does your church offer good, biblical teaching on the central doctrinal issues, such as salvation through Christ? Are your children happy there? Are the doctrinal differences things you can offset in family devotions without undermining the family's relationship to church leaders? If you make a choice that pleases you but demoralizes your children and wife, you will lose far more than you will gain.

Jay Kesler

5.15 PRIVATE VERSUS PUBLIC EXPRESSIONS OF FAITH

I thrive on church involvement, but my wife is much more private in her faith. She enjoys Sunday morning worship, but during the week she prefers to stay home or take part in non-church family activities. She doesn't complain about my church responsibilities, but I suspect she wishes I were home more. And I wish she were more involved at church. What should we do?

Both of you need to compromise, to "give in" to the other. Maybe your wife could be more involved at church, and you could back off a bit. But that's much easier said than done.

You might begin by examining your motives. It sounds as though you are serving out of joy and love, but it's easy to fall into a trap of serving out of guilt or even habit.

It's easy to fall into a trap of serving out of guilt or even habit.

You'll also need to consider the nature of the church itself. You've probably read about the dangerous effects on a marriage of too much time spent on the golf course or excessive work hours over a long period of time. But too much church involvement can have a similar effect.

Some churches are places where programs dominate, and people are needed to lead and attend those programs. In those cases, the church can become an enemy of personal spiritual growth and of marriage and family.

So step back and look at your church with a little loving critique. Worshiping God is good; worshiping programs is not. People who are overly involved in church need to realize that there are times when God is better worshiped by spending time together as a couple or as a family rather than attending yet another meeting.

Jay Kesler

5.16 QUIETING THE TEMPTATION OF "WHAT IF"

Before I got married 20 years ago, I was engaged to another woman. She broke it off because she wasn't ready to make a commitment. A few months ago this woman called me and said she still loves me. I told my wife about the conversation, but not about the inner turmoil I've been feeling. I keep thinking about all the "what ifs"— how my life would be different now if I had married the other woman. My marriage is good, but it could be much better. Now that my old girlfriend has shown up, I'm tempted to rethink my commitment to my wife. What's the answer?

The temptation you describe is one of the most common, the most subtle and the most dangerous that married people face. It has the potential to destroy your marriage and your happiness.

Everyone has opportunities to rethink major life decisions. But once you've made a decision that involves another person—and your relationship with God—no good can come from looking back. When you married, you entered into an unbreakable covenant with your wife and with God, and second-guessing can lead to serious sin.

When you think of your old girlfriend or feel tempted to turn your back on your marriage, turn your heart toward God instead. Thank Him for the good opportunities and choices you had as a young person. And thank Him for the choice you made to marry your wife.

Beyond that, it is crucial that you cut off all contact with the other woman. You can be kind, explaining that long ago the two of you shared strong feelings and good experiences. But tell her unequivocally that your marriage is now your priority. Like a moth that flies too near a flame and then finds its wings destroyed, you risk your marriage and happiness if you agree to talk occasionally on the phone or maintain "casual" correspondence with her. Scripture's commands for confronting temptations of this kind involve words like "flee" and "avoid"—there's no gray area here.

Think of it this way: if your dog kept begging for food while you were eating dinner, you'd be a fool to think, "Oh, he'll go away if I just give him a little bite of something." The only way to keep the dog away from the table is to stop feeding him when he begs.

This "what if" game you mention is a game of dangerous fantasy. It seems this other woman is playing it too. During the 20 years you have been apart, she has no doubt been involved in other relationships. Perhaps she recently lost a man she loved deeply. Now she thinks of you and the past—a past uncomplicated by the daily realities and problems of living with another person. You're doing the same thing. You say your marriage could be better, and you contrast it with the fantasy of what life might have been with this other woman. None of that fantasy is real, and God is calling you to fulfill the real promise of your real marriage.

This "what if" game you mention is a game of dangerous fantasy.

Tell your old girlfriend that you're going to work on your marriage to make it even better. And explain that the first step is to cut off any further contact with her. It won't be easy, but if you want to escape major sin, you have to do it.

Jay Kesler

5.17 WEEDING OUT SELFISHNESS

Last weekend, I desperately needed to get to the store to pick up some materials for a project. When I mentioned that I'd be gone about an hour, my husband countered with, "I'm just about to leave myself. I can't watch the kids." He had never mentioned any plans before I announced mine. I was furious and astounded by my husband's selfishness. And yet, there have been times when my husband has graciously pitched in when I least expected it but most needed help. How can he be so self-centered one minute and then so selfless at other times?

That's a hard question to answer honestly. Selfishness is a natural part of every one of us—just look at any two-year-old! And it's scary to discover that same infantile selfishness reasserting itself in marriage, where it has the power to be the most destructive.

Underneath the problem of selfishness lies the issue of power. I was flabbergasted recently to hear of one husband who doesn't "allow" his wife to drive. Further, he does all the grocery-shopping, handles all the money, and even picks out his wife's clothes. I know another man who turns over his paycheck to his wife, feels guilty if he asks for anything for himself, and is so intimidated that he is reluctant even to make a sexual advance. Such heavy-handed control by either spouse is selfishness gone on a rampage!

When it comes to my own life, I find it's the more subtle forms of selfishness that slither their way in. I've found ways to get what I want—deviously—while keeping a "righteous cover." For example, I know my wife might prefer not to attend a certain social event, so I avoid asking her if she'll attend the event with me. That would require us to negotiate our differences. Instead, I go ahead and make the arrangements and then mention it to her later. If my wife expresses her displeasure, I can appear pretty unselfish when I offer to cancel the whole thing—even though I know she wouldn't let me go to all that trouble.

But after acknowledging the problem, how can we combat this kind of self-centeredness and turn it into other-centeredness?

Like a willful two-year-old, our natural bent is to seek our own gratification ahead of the needs of others. But as we "grow up" emotionally and socially, we should begin to learn other-centeredness. And, even more important, when we come to Christ and are spiritually reborn, we should dislodge "self" from the center of our universe.

The first step is to honestly admit that selfishness lurks within. It's helpful to examine your behavior and your motives, then make a list of the subtle ways you put your own desires ahead of your mate's. I have found that my wife is remarkably accepting of my needs—even some of the selfish ones—when I am honest with her. Being honest about what I want and need is a whole lot easier than reverting to scheming manipulations. It's my responsibility not to take advantage of my wife's love, but she will often agree to do something the way I prefer or put some of my needs ahead of her own.

Ironically, our own self-interest should help keep us from acting on our selfish impulses. I've learned that it's in my own best interest to act unselfishly toward my wife. It's one of those paradoxical spiritual truths the Bible talks about.

When I take an honest look at my own desires in marriage, what I want from my wife is, basically, a pleasant companion and fantastic sex. That is to say, I want to be affirmed and praised and have someone support me in my goals; and I want to have my physical needs met. In describing what she wants, my wife would probably use words like "cherishing," "emotional security" and "intimacy," but generally our lists of major wants and needs would be similar. The paradox is that the more I devote myself to meeting Melissa's needs, the more she seems to become the kind of companion I desire. Conversely, the more self-seeking I am, the more resistant she is.

The more self-seeking I am, the more resistant she is.

Louis McBurney, M.D.

5.18 WHAT MUTUAL SUBMISSION **REALLY** MEANS

My husband and I are studying the book of Ephesians and when we got to the verse, "Submit to one another out of reverence for Christ," we had quite a discussion about what this passage really means. Does being a submissive wife mean my desires and needs will go unmet? Will I become my spouse's doormat?

There are times it would help if the apostle Paul could walk right into my house to remind me, "Husbands, love your wives, just as also Christ loved the church and gave Himself for her" (Eph. 5:25). Those poetic-sounding words are verbal dynamite; they blow apart the way I want things to work. And when the dust settles, their wisdom remains: "Put your spouse first."

A wife is supposed to do that as well, the passage goes on to say, by showing respect, listening to her husband, honoring him, and not tearing him down. A husband is called, meanwhile, to sacrifice himself for his wife. Make her feel special. Help her become a more holy, gracious person because of what he gives up for her.

This is a frighteningly high standard. It means dropping whatever I'm doing if it stands in the way of my wife's well being. Not buying something I want, for her sake. Not working as long as I'd like, for her sake. The thing most essential to Christian marriage is to do the one thing I most want to avoid.

A lot of Christians stumble over this point. They can't accept that God would command them to do something so painful, so difficult, so outrageous as self-sacrifice. Most of us stumble over this command—"Submit to one another out of reverence for Christ"—because we're concentrating on what's fair. We expect our spouses to see how frazzled *we* are and give us a break. When there's a conflict, we demand what's rightfully ours: 50-50.

But if we play out marriage the logical, natural way, insisting on what's fair, we only bring pain to our spouses and ourselves. To paraphrase Tevye from *Fiddler on the Roof*, "If you insist on an eye for an eye and a tooth for a tooth, you'll both end up blind and toothless." God wants to spare us that pain, so he gives us a better way: "Submit to one another."

Mutual submission will look different in every marriage. My first clue that I need to start submitting to my wife in some area is when I feel irritable about doing it. Should I sit and talk with her when I've got a hundred other things to do? Do I really have to go out with her and a couple of her friends—who are not my favorite people? Why must I remain open to her when I'd prefer to close off?

For your marriage to go up, you must go down.

For your marriage to go up, you must go down. You have to descend into greatness. In the movie *The Poseidon Adventure*, the only people who are saved are those who do what doesn't make sense. The ship had flipped over, and because of the air trapped in the ocean liner, it floats upside down. Those who descend into the belly of the ship and pound on the hull are the ones the rescuers hear and cut free.

In marriage, it's as if God has turned the ship over and the only way for us to get free is to choose what doesn't make sense: We lay down our lives by serving, supporting and sacrificing for our spouses.

Kevin A. Miller

5.19 MAKING SURE SERVICE DOESN'T BECOME SERVITUDE

For the most part, we're happy with how we have divided up the duties necessary to share a life together, but sometimes I have my doubts. For instance, my co-workers were stunned that I take my husband's shirts to the cleaners. They say, "They're his clothes. You're being turned into a slave." How can I avoid being "used" in my marriage?

My husband and I, after 23 years of marriage, are still trying to work out what it really means to serve one another. One of the bigger issues in our marriage has been who stops at the cleaners. For some reason, my husband thinks I should drop off and pick up the dry cleaning even though 99 percent of it is his! For years I did so—grudgingly. Then one day I said, "I almost never have anything in the dry cleaning pile. Why am I the one taking responsibility for it?"

Basically his answer was, "You go past the shop more than I do" (which I do), "your schedule is more flexible" (which it is), "and I would really like not to have to worry about the dry cleaning. I guess I'm just asking you if you would do this for me."

Inside me, a voice was saying, "Like I don't have enough on *my* mind? Like *I'm* not busy?"

To this day I don't fully understand why my husband is so averse to handling the dry cleaning. And I still take care of it. Why? Because the few minutes it takes me isn't worth causing a strain in our relationship. Does my husband take it for granted that I make time to drop off and pick up the dry cleaning? Maybe. Is it worth an argument or simmering resentment? No way. And when I'm the one who is rushed and need him to do something for me, including picking up the dry cleaning, will he do it for me? Absolutely.

To some it might seem the situation was resolved by me "giving in." But giving in is a far cry from being trampled underfoot. Servanthood does not automatically involve a disregard for our own needs. Continually choosing to meet the needs of others *at the expense of our own* is neither a healthy nor a spiritually sound way to live.

Here are a few tactics that can help keep servanthood a central part of our relationships.

First, we need to decide who is going to shape the nature of our marriage: our friends, relatives, co-workers, society at large, the media—or us? Each of us is a unique individual, and marriage multiplies that uniqueness by at least two. While there are certain fundamental principles such as fidelity and trust that we know contribute to a successful marriage, no two couples are alike. If a woman finds it satisfying and pleasurable to have dinner on the table for her husband (or vice versa), it's not for an outsider to say she shouldn't do that. If a husband enjoys doing things that make his wife happy—perhaps attending cultural events that she enjoys but that leave him a little cold—then that's his choice to make, not his friends or co-workers.

Second—though this advice may seem overused—communication is essential. If you feel that the division of labor in your marriage is inequitable, discuss it with your spouse. But don't do it when you are tired and frazzled, or when an incident has caused hurt, angry feelings. Sometimes a person may not be aware that certain duties have fallen to his or her mate. As in other areas of life, making assumptions about what others know, think, or feel without asking is risky. But even when a couple has worked out a division-of-labor plan that's equitable, flexibility remains an important ingredient. Rules and "rights" should never be more important than people.

Third, servanthood is not a matter of "fairness." If I do something for my husband with the requirement that he "repay" the favor, it becomes an issue of keeping score. That's far from an act of love. A gesture of true servanthood has no strings attached and is not prompted by the expectation of reward or repayment.

Our society has talked so long and so extensively about gender equality and individual rights, it's no wonder the idea of servanthood has fallen out of favor. Yet we know that God calls us to demonstrate servanthood both in our relationship with Him and in our relationships with others. That's why I'll keep asking my husband one simple question: "What can I do to help?"

Alicia Howe

5.20 BUILDING A GOD-CENTERED MARRIAGE

Our falling in love kind of "just happened." We're very grateful we found one another and we're glad we're married, but it seems like we were called together for something greater. How can we make sure we don't miss out on what God wants us to do and be as a couple?

It helps to know where you're going, especially when it comes to marriage. "Let your eyes loook directly ahead, and let your gaze be fixed straight in front of you," counsels King Solomon in Proverbs 4:25-26 (NASB). "Watch the path of your feet, and all your ways will be established."

That's good advice whether you are trying to find your way through city streets or charting the course of your marriage. Of course, no matter how much planning you do, no marriage is exempt from a few missed turns. But you can do more than you think you can to successfully navigate the marriage journey and enjoy the comfort and confidence that comes in finding your way together.

No matter how much planning you do, no marriage is exempt from a few missed turns.

The answer begins with having a purpose, a shared marital *mission* that helps you chart a course. Too many couples get lost because they forgot why they got married to begin with. They had lofty ideals, plans, goals, and dreams when they were entering marriage. But amid the hassles of life, they gradually lost sight of their target. They ended up feeling frustrated and aimless, frittering away their married life.

We've experienced our share of matrimonial wandering. A couple of weekends ago, we were both frustrated and sulking because neither of us was getting our needs met. One person wanted some down time, a relaxing day with no demands. Another wanted a productive workday to tackle a long-overdue household project.

Finally, one of us said, "Why are we doing this?" The question took us back to the purpose statement we worked out for our marriage over the last few years. In quiet moments of contemplation, we had drafted this statement of shared purpose: "Understanding that only God meets all our needs, we will love each other with empathy and try to model a healthy relationship to the young couples we mentor." That's part of our marital mission, and it reminds us that we can't expect the other always to meet our needs—only God can do that. This simple truth enabled us to set aside our bickering and salvage a weekend that was about to be ruined. We each put ourselves in the other person's shoes, each of us made a minor compromise, and we stepped over our conflict.

Revisiting our mission statement reminds us of the reasons we got married, a reminder we all need from time to time. But if drafting a formal statement doesn't fit your style, there are countless other ways to keep your marriage's mission on your mind. We know one husband who carries a key chain attached to a small plaque that reads, "Love is a decision." It's a meaningful reminder that he *chose* his marriage. And that simple statement helps him cultivate his commitment to his wife.

We know of a woman who displays on her desk a copy of the prayer that was said at her wedding. Re-reading that prayer takes her back to the "mission" of her marriage. For some couples, the simple act of carrying a photo of each other keeps before them the reason they are married—to love sacrificially and to help each other grow in grace. Some couples repeat or revise their wedding vows every few years. Any time a significant change occurs—having children, changing jobs, any sudden turn in the road—you need to fix your eyes once again on your shared "mission."

> *Aristotle likened having a purpose statement to "archers aiming at a definite mark."*

Aristotle likened having a purpose statement to "archers aiming at a definite mark." When we do the same, according to the Greek philosopher, we are "more likely to attain what we want." And in keeping with Solomon's wisdom, we are also more likely to fix our gaze directly before us while making a level path for our feet, and our marriage.

Les and Leslie Parrott

5.21 REBUILDING SHATTERED TRUST

I thought my husband and I were as close as two people could be. But after we'd been married several years, he had an affair. Obviously, my sense of trust was shattered. We're trying to deal with it, but I'm angry and we keep arguing about the affair. He assures me it will never happen again, and he even bought me a one-carat diamond ring. I guess the love is still there, but what good is that without trust?

Your situation reminds me again of why God took so much care to underscore the importance of fidelity and commitment within a marriage. When those commands are violated, the resulting hurts are so deep they almost defy a cure. Rebuilding trust is going to call for more than just you willing it to happen. It will require forgiveness and a fresh start built on the basics of your life in Christ.

Don't try to push the facts aside and act as though it never happened. The best place to begin is with you and your husband each acknowledging your own sin. Your husband sinned grievously against you by committing adultery. And you have sins of your own (Rm. 3:23). All of us grapple with less-visible sins, like arrogance or pride, lovelessness, or a lack of concern for others. When we acknowledge our own sin, we agree that we—like our spouse—are the same in that we are all sinners. This concept of being on a "level playing field" is important because otherwise you both will have the sense that your husband "owes" you something to pay for his sin. (A diamond ring is fine, but not if the gift is intended to placate you.)

Think about the miracle of the New Testament church. Outsiders watched with great frustration and wonderment, trying to figure out what could bring together such a strange collection of failed people to live together in harmony. Through Christ, these religious leaders, tax collectors, prostitutes, and other kinds of fallen people found level ground and community through mutual forgiveness.

I can't promise that you'll never remember your husband's betrayal or that you'll both forget the other sins in your lives. But true repentance can bring you together before Christ. As your husband acknowledges his sin against you and as you offer genuine forgiveness, as Christ does, you'll begin to heal. Over time, faithfulness will cover the past layer by layer until the scar is old and the memory dim.

Over time, faithfulness will cover the past layer by layer until the scar is old and the memory dim.

As you move ahead, don't underestimate the power of the enemy. Satan will constantly bring this up in your interaction and your memory. When he does, tell him, "Rub your nose in this: Christ has forgiven me, and Christ forgives my husband. We're starting over!" Only Christ can make this superhuman forgiveness possible.

Jay Kesler

5.22 SPEAKING THE SAME SPIRITUAL LANGUAGE

I wish we had a more open and active spiritual life, and yet whenever we try to talk about this aspect of our marriage, our talks seem to stall out. We're both Christians so I'm perplexed as to why talking about our faith is so difficult. Shouldn't this aspect of our relationship flow naturally?

All couples run into "touchy subjects"—topics that stir up frustration and lead to awkward silences.

All couples run into "touchy subjects"—topics that stir up frustration and lead to awkward silences. Sex and money top the list in many marriages. But you and your spouse seem to struggle with a third area: how to talk about spiritual things.

Talking in-depth about spiritual issues can create significant anxiety. "Will I sound immature if I talk about my relationship with God? If I'm honest about what's going on in my life, will my spouse think I'm not spiritual enough?" Ever since sin came between the first married couple and God, fear, self-consciousness, and embarrassment have made spiritual intimacy a difficult proposition. The vulnerability it takes to talk about matters of faith leads many people to keep the conversation short or avoid it altogether.

A second obstacle is the way each spouse was brought up. Maybe when your mate was growing up, her family talked about Christianity as easily as they did the weather. But at your house, family members rarely spoke of spiritual things beyond saying "good sermon today" on the way home from church. And, of course, many people never even attended church until they became adults. Some people grew up with spiritual expressiveness being as natural as breathing; while to others, it's still a foreign concept.

Add to that a third difference: the natural tendencies of different personality types. In *Experiencing God Together*, David Stoop writes, "When we approach the subject of spiritual intimacy, our personality differences obviously predispose us to certain approaches to God...and to our basic understanding of how religion relates to life."

For instance, some people have a strong bent toward duty and responsibility. Their spirituality is shaped by their desire to serve and make the right choices. Others are more mystical, emphasizing the importance of experiences and leadings from God. A third personality type is more people-oriented. These folks think of their spirituality in terms of how it relates to the people they care about. Still others are problem-solvers. They are most interested in "how-to's" and identifying the best course of action from a spiritual perspective. A fifth group is more intellectual about faith issues. They emphasize learning facts and grasping spiritual concepts. Different personalities use different languages of spirituality. If a mystical type marries a problem-solver, it's understandable that they can easily end up talking past each other.

Tim Sutherland

5.23 THE LESS SPIRITUALLY INTERESTED SPOUSE

My husband and I are similar in almost every way except one. He's not as interested in spiritual issues as I am. I'm worried that our differing attitudes and interests in spiritual things will come between us. What should I do?

If your efforts to deepen your spiritual communication so far have failed, it's time to take a different tack. Try these approaches:

1. Learn your partner's language. By becoming more attuned to your spouse's spiritual personality you can learn to use the language that will communicate most effectively to him or her.

2. Appeal to your mate's spiritual strengths. If your spouse's spiritual focus is on people and relationships, ask for input and opinions from a relational perspective. If he or she has a more mystical bent, you might ask something like "How can I figure out what God wants me to do in this situation?" When we ask questions on our partners' spiritual wavelength, they'll be more interested in what we have to say.

3. Break the hide-and-seek pattern. Gently end conversations about spiritual matters when you notice your mate is withdrawing or becoming uncomfortable. It's better to try again later than to cause frustration by pressing to keep alive a conversation that's not going anywhere.

4. Catch your partner doing something right. When you do get spiritual input from your mate, jot him or her a note: "Thanks for your perspective." Expressing your appreciation can go a long way toward easing your spouse's discomfort. When less-interested partners know they'll get credit for the efforts they make to join in spiritual conversations, they are more likely to open up the next time.

Tim Sutherland

5.24 THE MORE SPIRITUALLY INTERESTED SPOUSE

My spouse is much more interested in spiritual matters than I am. How can I be understanding of her desire to cast everything in a spiritual light and not come off as insensitive?

Even if you don't feel urgent about deepening the spiritual communication with your spouse, chances are good that he or she *does*. To meet your spouse halfway, consider some of these steps.

1. Recognize the importance of your role. When it comes to spiritual intimacy, there is something your spouse values deeply that only you can give. Though talking about spiritual matters doesn't come easily to you, God has called you to be your mate's spiritual helpmate. That's an important role that belongs only to you.

2. Share your fears and uneasiness. Write a letter to your spouse to assure him or her that you know talking about spiritual things is important. Include the reasons you find it difficult to discuss your spiritual life. Don't assume your mate knows these things. Even the letter will count as a spiritual connection to your partner.

3. Recognize that questions are better than answers. Take some pressure off yourself by remembering that active listening and asking good questions both make for good conversations. The role of "spiritual sounding-board" is a valuable one, and it's easier than trying to come up with a lot of interesting things to say.

4. Cultivate spiritual expressiveness. You can even do this alone by putting your spiritual life into written words. As you write down your thoughts about God and His work in your life, consider which ones you could share later on with your spouse.

Tim Sutherland

5.25 WHEN LOVING FEELINGS TAKE EFFORT

There are times I find it nearly impossible to love my spouse. And yet I know I'm commanded, as a Christian, to do so. Should I put up a false front and act as if I have tender feelings toward my spouse, even when my feelings would dictate that I behave otherwise?

No one before or since has loved more—or sacrificed more for those He loved—than Jesus did. And following His example begins with the "good news"—the gospel.

I want to love my wife the way Jesus would, so I preach the gospel to myself every day. If I didn't, it would be easy to forget the impact of God's mercy on my own life. Knowing, *really* knowing, God's love and forgiveness toward me makes it possible for me to love my wife—especially during the times when it doesn't come naturally.

But I couldn't choose that loving alternative without God's power to fuel my actions. Paul said, "I am able to do all things through Him who strengthens me" (Php. 4:13). That's the secret weapon we obtain when we understand the gospel—the power of God to live His love through us.

Paul encouraged us to "be imitators of God, as dearly loved children. And walk in love, as the Messiah also loved us and gave Himself for us" (Eph. 5:1-2). A second clue to loving the way Jesus did is to see ourselves as God's "dearly loved children." The extent to which you believe you are dearly loved by God, that's the extent to which you can love others.

I recently received a letter from a woman who for years had felt trapped in a continuous cycle of guilt and confession. When she finally realized her guilt had already been taken care of by Christ's sacrifice, her life changed dramatically. She had discovered the freedom and power that comes with being God's dearly loved child, and it enabled her to start showing patience and kindness toward her husband.

I can't ignore the instruction in Ephesians 5 to love my wife with the love of Christ, who "loved the church and gave Himself for her." Sacrificial love sounds great—on paper. But every married person knows how tough it is to put into practice. Too bad the Bible doesn't say: "Love your wife as Christ loved the church, and here are ten easy steps for accomplishing that."

Christ set the example for sacrificial love when He left heaven's glory to live 33 years of grime, dust, humanness, and rejection, all without sinning, just so He could give Himself up for the people He loved. For Christ, love was a motive, not a duty.

For Christ, love was a motive, not a duty.

I admit that too many times I have served my wife out of a sense of duty or to keep peace, without the motive of love. Reality is messy, and I'm still learning what it means to love as Christ loved when my desires and my wife's conflict.

Jesus' sermon to husbands and wives delivers a tall order: "Remember my love and sacrifice for you, and do the same for your spouse. Love each other the way I did." It would be an impossible task if we didn't have our secret weapon: God's power to love, which He has freely given to His dearly loved children.

Jerry Bridges, with Annette La Placa

5.26 THE SPIRITUALLY INCOMPATIBLE COUPLE

My husband is a lukewarm Christian who often sleeps in on Sunday mornings or skips church to play golf. I find that I no longer feel close to him since we don't share what is a core part of my life. What should I do?

I empathize with what you're feeling. I watched my mother deal with a very similar situation until my dad finally made a serious commitment to the Lord.

Most of the time when Scripture deals with a spiritual mismatch, it refers to a Christian married to a nonbeliever, but the advice also applies to your situation. In 1 Corinthians 7, Paul talks about marital incompatibility, and he approaches the subject of intimacy by discussing sex. Paul is very clear that spouses should meet one another's sexual needs, despite any spiritual differences. He understood that a mutually fulfilling sex life had a lot to do with a couple's intimacy.

In another New Testament passage (1 Pt. 3), Peter describes how a Christian should respond to a spiritually incompatible mate. He advises such a believer to be the best possible spouse "as unto the Lord." That is, even though your mate's lack of spiritual commitment doesn't generate a sense of intimacy, you still are expected to choose loving behaviors that build intimacy because you're doing it for God.

My mother participated wholeheartedly in every aspect of my dad's life that she could share, while constantly praying for him, and maintaining her own commitment to God. She set an example for my father, but she didn't nag him or leave the Bible lying open on his pillow.

My dad loved a card game called Euchre, and my mom became an expert player. She moved among his unbelieving friends as an uncompromising witness for Christ, and none of them considered her hyper-spiritual. Over the course of 40 years, those fellow card players came to personal faith in Christ as a result of my mom's witness.

Those fellow card players came to personal faith in Christ as a result of my mom's witness.

Although nagging isn't the way to go, you should tell your husband you're concerned about the spiritual incompatibility in your marriage. You might use the visual image of your marriage as a triangle, with you and your husband at the two bottom corners and Christ at the top. The closer each of you comes to Christ, the closer you get to each other. As you talk, explore what he perceives to be the reason for the uneven growth. His perspective may give you both a starting place toward resolving the issue.

I encourage you not to give up your efforts to build intimacy while you do all you can to "bring your husband along" as you both grow spiritually. Pray for his growth, and pray for grace, perseverance and creativity for yourself as you try to build intimacy in your marriage "as unto the Lord."

Jay Kesler

5.27 FINDING STRENGTH TO PERSEVERE IN HARD TIMES

Within the last year, a friend's husband was laid off and later she was severely injured in an accident. Their marriage seems to be falling apart. How can we make sure our marriage remains intact when we eventually face the inevitable crises that come?

How you react during a crisis is important for the survival of your marriage. But the real battle is won or lost before the crisis occurs. A marriage that crumbles under intense pressure is similar to a china cup with a hairline crack. While sitting on a table, the crack goes unnoticed. However, when the cup is held up to the light, the tiny crack becomes visible. The light doesn't cause the crack; it only illuminates a fracture that already exists. External crises are like

The light doesn't cause the crack; it only illuminates a fracture that already exists.

the light, illuminating difficulties that lie under the surface of a marriage. So while the outside influence (the crisis) may seem like the problem, the real problem is what's going on inside the marriage before the crisis strikes.

Couples who survive share at least three characteristics. First, the couple is committed to marriage as an institution. They consider marriage a sacred institution, and their commitment brings stability and can provide staying power even during the most severe setbacks. Every marriage needs this resilience, but true survival requires more than simply bedrock commitment to an institution. If this is the only characteristic working in a marriage's favor, the relationship can easily become lifeless and devoid of emotion.

Second, survivors are committed to marriage as a relationship. I have friends whose daughter was depressed, even suicidal. "We felt so helpless," my friend told me. "When things were at their darkest, my wife and I found ourselves holding each other tight. Through tears, I told her things may get a lot worse for us, but we'll survive even if they do." He was trying to tell his wife he loved her, no matter what might happen. He was committed to more than the institution of marriage; he was committed to his wife.

For more than 20 years, this couple had practiced being sensitive to one another's needs. They had guarded their relationship against time pressures and striving for material success. And they had practiced mutuality—giving and receiving in roughly equal measure over the years. They shared a goal of looking for and doing whatever was in the best interest of their relationship, even if it meant sacrificing some personal comfort. They survived the pain of their daughter's depression, and their marriage was made even stronger because of it.

There's a third characteristic that enables a couple to weather the big storms of life: a vital faith and commitment to God. Vital faith appreciates "the big picture." Life doesn't operate on our agenda. Pain comes to everyone, and some of the greatest truths we learn come from experiences we wouldn't choose for ourselves. God uses personal circumstances, even negative ones, to develop our ability to deal with the crises of life. By learning to trust him in the little storms, we are prepared to trust him in the big ones.

Married Christians have to guard against the "Teflon mentality"—an expectation that pain, stress, and hardship can't really touch us, but will magically slide right off. It's true that Christians are not *of* the world, but we are definitely *in* it. We do feel pain and stress. But we don't have to be overwhelmed by them.

I don't totally understand the "all things" verses in Scripture: "all things work together for the good" (Rm. 8:28) and "giving thanks always" for all things (Eph. 5:20), but I believe them. God does not cause bad things, but He allows painful and unjust experiences. And there is a useful purpose found in them. The trials of life may cause us pain, but they refine our faith in a way nothing else can (1 Pt. 1:6-7).

It's time to face some facts: life is hard, and you and your spouse are not exempt. It's not an issue of if; it's a matter of when. And when the storms do arrive, they will stress your marriage.

But here's a second fact: you can survive the storms—and even be strengthened in the process. You can do it by winning the battle before it begins by strengthening your commitment to your marriage, demonstrating that commitment by building your relationship with your spouse, and growing a faith that embraces the big picture. God always has a future for His people.

Donald R. Harvey

CHAPTER 6

PARENTING
AS A
TEAM

PARENTING
AS A
TEAM

Have you ever wondered, "If raising kids is so important, why don't they come with directions?"

Actually the Bible is full of instructions on how to raise children. God said, "Be fruitful and multiply, and fill the earth and subdue it" (Gn. 1:28, NASB). And at the heart of this "multiplication" is God's desire to raise up men and women who love Him. "Has not the Lord made them (the married couple) one? In flesh and spirit they are his. And why one? Because he was seeking a godly offspring" (Mal. 2:15, NIV). God is calling people to Himself through Christ for His glory. His plan has parenting in view. We are called, therefore, to raise up a new generation that loves God with all their heart, soul, mind, and strength (Dt. 6:5).

Children are a gift from God (Ps. 127:3). They are like arrows in the hand of a warrior (Ps. 127:4). We must shape them and guide them, for one day we will pull back the bowstring and release them. By God's grace they will hit the target. The stakes are high—their souls are eternal (Ec. 12:5).

So how do we do this?

First, we need to aim at their hearts. Our task is to shepherd a child's heart so that by God's grace he or she will love God with all their heart, soul, and strength (Dt. 6:5). We must remember that children are sinners who need new hearts. As Genesis 8:21 (NIV) says: "Every inclination of his heart is evil from childhood." Thus, we must not allow other aspects of parenting to keep us from this central role. Through prayer and example, we must guide our children to see their need for a Savior.

Second, we need to cultivate our own heart. We can't impart what we don't possess. We are called to have God's Word (specifically His commands) on our hearts before we can impress them on our children's' hearts (Dt. 6:6). We need to model a vibrant walk with Christ before our kids. If we want our kids to love Jesus, we need to love Him.

Third, we need to use the Word. Teach God's Word to your children. When they look to the Word they learn who God is and how to live in relationship to Him. He is the Lord—sovereign ruler of all things. He is our Lord—a God who longs for us to know and love Him.

Fourth, we need to teach all the time. Our teaching should impress, or leave a mark in such a way that our children have an appetite for God. Teach your children throughout the day, formally and informally—at home, on the road, and again at bedtime. Use symbols and even the architecture of your home to help children grow to love God (Dt. 6:7-9). Paul says, "Fathers, don't stir up anger in your children, but bring them up in the training and instruction of the Lord" (Eph. 6:4). Dads need to take the lead.

Fifth, we need to pray for our children in detail. Specifically, we need to pray for godly friends, for those our children will date and for the one they will marry. Pray for their salvation, their protection, and for their security to rest in Christ. Pray for wisdom as you raise them.

And finally, we need to cultivate our marriage. One of the most important things we can do for our kids is love our spouse. A strong Christ-centered marriage is the bottom line when it comes to raising godly children.

> PRAYER: Thank You, Lord, for our children. Help us to love them in such a way that they will love You. Fill us with the wisdom of Your Word that we might parent well. Give us the joy of seeing our children follow You with all their hearts. Be gracious to them and to us that we might all live for Your glory. Amen.

6.1 MAKING THE MOST OF LIMITED TIME

I travel quite a bit for my job. Though I'm dedicated to my family, my time with them is limited. My kids are growing up so quickly and I want to be involved in their lives. How can we make the most of the family time we do have?

The idea of substituting quality time for quantity time is great in theory. But it doesn't work that well in practice. Based on my own experience and the experiences of people I've known and counseled, I have come to the conclusion that the less quantity time you find to devote to your spouse and your children, the tougher it is to create the quality time. If people could just sit down and say, "Now I'm going to have a quality experience," maybe it would work. But real life can't be manipulated that way.

Screen, stage, and literature all portray only a sample of life's experience.

Perhaps part of the problem is our distorted view of reality. Some people blame the media, and it's true that even the best of television compresses life into scenes portraying crucial action and dialogue. Screen, stage, and literature all portray only a sample of life's experience—more interesting than representative. They can show great moments of achievement, but not the years of preparation and work. We can very easily get a distorted view if we measure our lives by what we read and see.

Such distortion can even be a problem with our Bible study. It's easy to forget that the Bible is made up of *compressed* history. We have this patch followed by that patch, this important experience followed by that important event. The gospel writers don't recount everything that happened on those long walks Jesus and His followers took from one end of Palestine to the other.

If we're not careful we can, even as Christians, try to live our lives from one great experience to another. And it just can't be done. In real life, it's the mundane, day-after-day experiences that make the highlights stand out. It's the quantity time that makes possible the quality time.

I saw a survey that claimed the average father spent less than three-and-one-half minutes a day in conversation with his child. Let's assume that's accurate and you're about average. How hard would it be to double that figure? Or triple it? That's only ten minutes a day, a little over an hour a week. Even a father who's on the road most of the time could do that.

I learned I can't find enough time for my work, my marriage, my children—and still have a lot of personal time, at least not in large chunks. That means for me, certain leisure activities like golf (which takes hours at a time away from home) are out. My personal time is going to have to happen at home, where I'm close to my wife and family. Gardening and yard work can be done with my wife or my children. Woodworking projects in my shop can be done in small snatches of time or alongside my son. If I'm going to keep my priorities consistent, the use of my "personal" time has to be as purposeful as the use of my business and family time.

I've also learned that planning is crucial to making the most of the least time. When we're busy, there's a tendency not to take time to plan ahead. But there are two things wrong with that thinking. First, we let other things squeeze out the time we were going to devote to our spouse or our children. And second, we lose out on that wonderful thing called anticipation.

If you say to a little girl, "A week from Sunday we're going to do this," or you say to her mother, "Next Friday evening let's you and I plan that," then you and they have all the time between now and then to look forward to the event. Planning helps make the flavor last—kind of like taking a LifeSaver and working it down to that fine little ring on your tongue. Anticipation lets you savor it, and savoring something good is always better than gulping it down.

Planning helps make the flavor last.

Also, I consider it a part of necessary travel expenses to call every day. I call not just to touch base, but to find out what happened at home and to share what has happened to me.

It's true that our mobile culture presents some tough challenges to us in our search for quantity and quality time with our children. But if we seek God's help in establishing and maintaining our priorities, we'll not only beat those "typical" national averages, we'll strengthen our marriages and families as well.

Jay Kesler

6.2 TIME-CRUNCHED FAMILY LIFE

At this stage in our lives we feel like we're in a pressure cooker—there's never enough time for kids, house, even us. Seldom do we go to bed at night without thinking about all we didn't get done that day. What can we do to regain some sense of control over our daily schedules?

How *do* healthy families learn to control time so that it doesn't become a source of stress that affects their personal and family lives? I've found that these families tend to share the following characteristics: They view time as a controllable commodity; they balance work and family life; they balance couple and personal time; they recognize their stress level and take early steps to counter it; they play together; they prioritize activities.

People who have the most control and least stress over the issue of time are those who recognize it as a resource that needs the same attention as money. So they tend to use the same techniques in managing time as they do in managing money: talking about it; sharing feelings and needs that arise from insufficient personal, couple and family time; allocating time for certain activities; budgeting time; and prioritizing activities that eat up time. Some even have a savings plan for time—reserving time on their calendars for unscheduled needs.

While all families experience stress to some degree, some families live with stress at a peak level constantly. Here are the signs:

- A constant sense of urgency; no time to release and relax.
- Tension that underlies and causes sharp words, sibling fighting, misunderstandings.
- A mania to escape—to one's room, car, garage, away. A feeling that time is passing too quickly; children are growing up too fast.
- A nagging desire for a simpler life; constant talk about simpler times.
- Little "me" or couple time.
- A pervasive sense of guilt for not being and doing everything to and for all the people in our lives—our family, fellow workers, church and community.

I asked people to study these signs and respond to questions about them. I found that those least buffeted by time pressures recognized that the signs were a *result* of inattention. But those who acknowledge living with these at a high level tend to see them as a *cause* of daily stress and feel powerless to control them. Highly stressed people tend to seek a place to lay blame (the job, school, latest activity), while stress-effective people tend to seek solutions (budgeting time or prioritizing activities).

Blaming is an easy trap to fall into because it alleviates personal guilt.

Blaming is an easy trap to fall into because it alleviates personal guilt, at least temporarily. I recently directed two workshops at a conference center a couple of hours from home. One was held on Wednesday and the other on Friday, and both required a lot of energy and attention. But instead of giving myself Thursday to relax, I filled it with meetings, figuring it would save me a couple of trips later on.

My schedule was brutal, and I found myself complaining to whoever would listen. Finally, a friend at the center said gently, "But you scheduled yourself." She was right. I knew that, of course, and recognized my foolishness, but it was more comfortable blaming those nonexistent "theys" than admitting I was at fault.

Dolores Curran

6.3 BECOMING SUPPORTIVE PARENTS

Our 16 year old just learned he didn't make the football team—a dream of his since junior high school. We share in his disappointment and wish we could change the situation, but obviously that's beyond our power. How can we be supportive parents to a crushed teenager?

You can't shield your teenager from the sting of failure, but you and your spouse can help him cope and, ultimately, triumph over it. Some suggestions for how:

Be role models. One of the most powerful ways to teach your children how to cope with failure is to show them how you handle it yourself. "Kids absorb more by watching you than you may realize," says therapist Brenda Wanner. "So when you don't get the job you want, say, 'I'm really disappointed, but here's what I'm going to do instead.' Point out the benefits of the alternative."

Accept your child's limitations. Most young people have a hard enough time dealing with their own expectations of themselves, let alone what may be the unrealistic expectations of their parents. Parents who accept their children's limitations help them avoid a sense of failure in the face of what for them would be impossible standards. Wanner points to the example of a highly educated couple whose son had a learning disability. "Instead of going to college," she recalls, "he learned auto mechanics. In some families, the parents would have been hysterical, but this family accepted the fact that their son couldn't be what they are."

Encourage your child to identify whose expectations he or she is trying to live up to. "Parents can help their kids by talking about expectations and who they

Encourage your child to identify whose expectations he or she is trying to live up to.

belong to," Wanner says. "It's important to help your children realize that if an expectation belongs to someone else—a parent, teacher, peer, whoever—it has less meaning and they're less likely to achieve it." By the same token, she says, it's important for parents to allow their children to set their own goals.

Help your child examine whether his or her goals are realistic. Parents can help their children set realistic goals by pointing out their natural abilities and helping them examine their interests and motivations. If they have to give up an unrealistic goal, ask them, "Where are your skills and how can you redirect your interests?" In a suicide-prevention seminar she offers to church youth groups, Wanner asks teenagers to catalog their strengths, weaknesses, successes and failures. "Usually they find they have more strengths and successes than they thought," she says. Consider informally going through the same exercise with your teenager.

Be a nonjudgmental resource in times of crises. When your children experience what may be to them an excruciating failure, curb whatever instincts you may have to sermonize. "Let them talk through it and express their emotions," advises Wanner. "Don't tell them they shouldn't feel the way they do. Especially in the initial period after the failure, do some active listening. Don't give a lot of advice. Let them mourn their loss for a while. Recognize that for him or her, it's a big deal, even if you don't think it should be. Later, when you think they're ready to move on, be available as a resource."

Finally, she says, help your child understand what she calls the "God/scum continuum." Some kids have a hard time accepting that only God is perfect and because they're not perfect, they assume they must be scum. They don't realize that there's anything in between, so they label themselves as failures. But even Jesus, who was perfect, was considered a failure in the eyes of the world. We need to teach our kids that what looks like failure today may ultimately lead to success.

Janis Long Harris

We need to teach our kids that what looks like failure today may ultimately lead to success.

6.4 APPREHENSIVE ABOUT STARTING A FAMILY

My husband and I have been happily married for seven years. My problem is that I don't know whether God wants us to have children. Sometimes I want children very much, but other times I look at all the difficulties involved and think I should accept the fact that my husband and I aren't cut out to be parents. Do you think the Bible teaches that it's God's will for couples to have children in order to experience all the blessings and challenges of life?

No, I don't believe the Bible teaches that. There does seem to be ample evidence that God intended children to be a natural result of marriage. And yet there are numerous examples in the Bible and throughout history of godly couples who never experienced parenthood—just as there are examples of godly people who never experienced marriage. There is much to be learned from marriage and parenthood, but experience doesn't guarantee greater wisdom or sensitivity.

Parenthood is a personal choice God allows us. Unfortunately, it's often people like you—wanting to be thoughtful and sensitive to the significance of parenthood—who decide not to be parents, when in fact your thoughtfulness and sensitivity might make you the best parents of all.

Don't be too hasty in your decision or too harsh in judging yourself as a potential parent. I also would caution you about making irreversible decisions regarding birth control. I've known too many couples who thought they didn't want children, took permanent measures, and later deeply regretted that decision.

> *God doesn't want us to have the spirit of fear; that's not a good basis for a decision.*

It sounds from your letter that you may be a tentative person—someone who can be immobilized by too much thought and sensitivity. I'm not saying you shouldn't be thoughtful and prayerful about such a big decision. But you can spend so much thought and prayer trying to decide that you're unable to make a decision—until eventually you've made the decision by default. I don't think God wants decisions to be made that way.

Some couples decide not to have children out of fear—fear of the future, fear that they won't be able to handle the demands of parenthood. God doesn't want us to have the spirit of fear; that's not a good basis for a decision.

Other couples decide against having children because they don't want to change their lifestyles or make the necessary sacrifices. If the root of such a decision is selfishness, that's not a good basis for making it either.

So I'd challenge you to make sure you discover the true reason for your uncertainty. I'd even suggest seeing a marriage counselor who can administer a parenting test to help you and your husband carefully consider this decision together. Whatever you ultimately decide, you need to make it for good reasons, reasons you understand.

Jay Kesler

6.5 BABY GETS ALL THE ATTENTION

We've been married four years, and we have a one-year-old son. My wife is so wrapped up in taking care of the baby that I sometimes feel left out. Even when I just want her to sit with me for a while, she keeps jumping up to check on the baby. How do I tell her I need more attention?

You could begin by telling her just that. It would be a good start, but not an easy one. Who wants to admit he feels as if he's in competition with a baby, especially if that baby is his own? It seems unworthy of a grown man, even immature.

I doubt there's any man who hasn't felt a little left out after a child is born.

And yet I doubt there's any man who hasn't felt a little left out after a child is born. Young children are usually so mother-oriented that whatever efforts we make, there's a bond between mother and child that we naturally envy. So step one is to admit your feelings and recognize this natural tendency.

Step two is to realize your son may feel some competition with you, too. He has Mom's undivided attention when you're not around. But when you come home he may get fussy or demanding just to recapture her full attention.

You and your wife not only need to talk about your feelings, you need to develop a strategy for easing your son's sense of competitiveness. One possibility: You may need to become the one who jumps up to check on the baby when he fusses. When fathers get up when the little guy cries in the night, the child begins to develop a new kind of bond with the father, seeing him not as another person competing for Mom's attention, but as someone concerned about meeting his needs.

A side benefit is that Mom's load is eased and she has more energy to devote to her husband. Sometimes the issue in a situation like this is that a mother feels as if she's carrying a lopsided share of the parenting load and doesn't have the emotional reserves needed to meet her husband's needs, too.

You both need to realize the best thing you can do for your son is to have the strongest possible marriage relationship. You can best do that if you face your feelings and develop a strategy that will meet everyone's needs. It will take work, but it's possible.

Jay Kesler

6.6 INFERTILITY IS DRIVING US APART

My wife and I have been trying unsuccessfully to have a child for about three years. We've prayed a lot and have asked God to remove the desire to have children if it's not His will for us. I'm becoming reconciled to the idea, but it's much harder on my wife. Tears always seem close to the surface when we try to talk about the situation. This problem hangs like a storm cloud over our heads, darkening our relationship. I don't know what to do.

It seems every year I'm meeting more and more couples struggling with infertility. I've done a little research on the subject, and my sources say 90 percent of infertility has a physical cause. Of this 90 percent, 35 percent are female problems, 35 percent are male problems, and the remainder are a combination of male and female problems. About half of these can be corrected.

If you haven't sought medical solutions to your problem, I urge you and your wife to see a fertility specialist to learn if the problem can be corrected. This can be a difficult step—often harder for husbands than wives—perhaps because men often see their fertility tied to the ego issue of male identity. There's an unspoken attitude that "real men" can have kids. There's also an underlying fear that going to a doctor will uncover a problem that can't be solved and will destroy all hope of having children. But seeking medical treatment is essential, nonetheless.

> *You and your wife are not alone.*

In addition, let me encourage you to remember that you and your wife are not alone. Millions of people are struggling with the issue of infertility. The two of you should try to get in touch with other couples in your situation. A doctor or a marriage counselor might be able to recommend a nearby support group. Your pastor may be able to suggest some couples in your church whom you and your wife could talk to.

Another fine resource is the *Stepping Stones* newsletter, put together by a committed Christian group that is trying to deal with the ethical issues raised by such infertility treatments as in vitro fertilization and artificial insemination. The newsletter also addresses the important issues of adoption. You can get information by writing to Stepping Stones, 2900 North Rock Road, Wichita, Kansas 67226.

I'd also suggest two books on this subject: *The Infertile Couple* by Beth Spring (David C. Cook) and *Give Us a Child* by Lynda Rutledge Stephenson (Harper & Row). Both are written by thoughtful Christian women who speak to this subject from personal experience, as well as offering information and practical advice on steps that might be taken.

Finally I'd like to offer a word of caution about your prayer that God would take away your desire for children if you aren't meant to have them. I don't think God usually works that way. He created humankind with a strong desire to multiply and create children. While I have no doubt that God is capable of removing your longing, it's been my observation that He rarely overrules or negates those basic human desires He created in us just because those desires don't seem to be fulfilled.

What I have seen, time and again, is how gracious and loving God is to answer prayers for His presence and help and to enable His people to overcome their circumstances in this imperfect world. Whatever happens, God wants to help you face it as a couple in a way that will make you, your wife, and your marriage stronger for the experience.

Jay Kesler

6.7 GRIEVING OVER INFERTILITY

I'm still hopeful that we'll someday be able to conceive a child, but just learning about and dealing with our infertility is causing us such feelings of grief. Is this normal? How can we keep it from damaging our marriage?

Infertile couples are grieving the death of a dream, and it's important to understand that people grieve in cycles. That is, they may feel they have resolved the anger or sadness over their loss, but then sometime later they will re-experience the same feelings, perhaps less intensely, perhaps more so. This is a healthy sign that they are continuing to cope with their loss.

However, the grief process is stifled when one or both partners tries to act as if everything is resolved too quickly. It's only a matter of time before the pain manifests itself, and typically it will come out in the form of overworking, overeating or depression. Partners can also get stuck in the grieving process when they fail to resolve some aspect of their experience, like anger, bitterness or sadness.

If infertility is causing a significant amount of stress in your marriage, such as an increase in conflict or a noticeable withdrawal from the marriage relationship, counseling may be in order. While infertility is never a situation anyone would hope for, I have seen many couples derive long-term benefits from working out the issues that surface as a result of the crisis.

It's important for spouses to relate to each other as whole persons and not just potential baby makers. To maintain a well-rounded view of your spouse, make time to be alone as a couple during non-crisis times. Go out to dinner or take a walk in a park and use the time to share what you're feeling about your relationship and your infertility experience.

Couples who choose to see infertility as both a challenge and a loss are more likely to come through the experience with a stronger relationship. Infertility for them becomes a road to deeper intimacy, understanding, and acceptance. And, in the end, they will have a greater sense of purpose for their lives together— whether or not it includes children.

Daniel Green

6.8 BUILDING A RELATIONSHIP WITH STEPCHILDREN

I've worked hard to build a relationship with my husband's two children from his previous marriage. We now have a baby of our own and I'm surprised that I feel such intense love for her and yet not for my stepchildren. What should my role be as a stepmother? And is it really possible to blend two families into one?

It's also quite natural that you don't feel intense love for your husband's children.

Your feelings are all quite natural. It is right that you feel a love for your own child. Don't feel guilty about that! And it's also quite natural that you don't feel intense love for your husband's children. It's common to have the sentimental notion, when marrying a divorced person, that it's possible to love the new spouse's children like one's own. But that's unrealistic.

There are several unpleasant realities of divorce. One is that a stepparent doesn't usually feel automatic love for another person's children. Another is that the non-custodial parent cannot have the same kind of relationship with his children that he had when he lived with them every day. Sometimes, out of guilt, he'll try to prove that nothing's really changed. But inevitably the fact that they're not living together much does alter things. New interests and responsibilities, such as a new child in your case, make it even harder to maintain strong bonds.

Your husband needs to face some of these realities. I suggest you talk with him about how you feel. Remind him that his children are his responsibility, not yours. Your duty is to extend ordinary kindness and fairness to his children; it's not necessarily to forge a close emotional bond with them (although that certainly may happen). If your husband expects that of you, you need to help him rethink the realities of the situation. When his children come to visit in your home, he is the one who should be investing time and energy in them.

You're also right about the need to concentrate on your own new family. That child will be just as much your husband's child as the other children, and as the at-home father of that baby your husband needs to let a strong bond develop. He may feel guilty that his new family takes time away from his other children. He'll have to deal with his guilt and find a way to redefine his responsibilities to his older children, realizing that you and the new baby must now be a more primary focus. Blended-family situations are not easy to deal with. But you're on the right track; trust your own feelings and don't let misplaced guilt interfere with the joys that lie ahead.

Jay Kesler

Blended-family situations are not easy to deal with.

6.9 EASING MOTHERHOOD GUILT

I work fulltime and I'm finding it increasingly difficult to spend the kind of time I'd like to with my preschooler and my husband. It seems like one or the other is always getting shortchanged and I end up feeling guilty. How can I stop feeling so torn?

By not worrying about it. We get unduly stressed out when we feel we must allocate time evenly between our spouse and our children. One harassed mother told me she kept a list of minutes spent daily with each member of her family. Small wonder she didn't enjoy them!

Children and spouse alike resent it when we're spending time with them only because we feel guilty. I suggest you try being more spontaneous, and meet your need for quality time, as well. "This is Mommy time," "this is Daddy time," and "this is your time. What would you like to do?"

Women in earlier days didn't worry about fairly dividing their time between children and husband. As a result, they were probably more effective wives and mothers. We get hung up on the shoulds—a good mother should, a good wife should. There's really only one should: we should be available when needed. That's when we put aside our schedules, calendars, and lists, and make ourselves available to our children and spouse. But those times aren't daily and they can't be scheduled.

One husband told me, "I go crazy on this 'couple time' thing. It's like a performance objective. I just like being at home, around my wife and children. Why can't my wife understand that *that's* good couple time?"

Many healthy couples establish a weekly night out, a time to share thoughts after the children are in bed or before they get up, or even good conversation during their child's interminable T-ball games. They know they care about each other, that they would like to have more time together, and that someday they will have it. But meanwhile, they aren't going to put it on their list as one more duty to cross off.

> *A healthy wife and mother does not operate from guilt, but confidence.*

Like Parkinson's Law ("work expands to fill the time available"), children will consume the amount of time you make available to them and more. A healthy wife and mother does not operate from guilt, but confidence. "I need to be alone for an hour," is not an unreasonable request. Nor is, "I need to spend some time with Daddy now." This teaches children that individual and couple needs are to be respected.

When your children sense that life between you and your spouse is good, and that you will be there when they really need you, they will feel far more secure than they will with all the quality time in the world.

Dolores Curran

6.10 LIVING WITH A NIGHT OWL

I suspect our first grader is a night person. She dislikes going to bed and doesn't want to "miss anything," as she says. Even if I put her to bed at 8 P.M. it still takes her until well after 9 P.M. to fall asleep. Her bedtime tactics are certainly creating a wedge between my husband and me—she encroaches on our couple time and the resentment is building. Is there any hope for getting her to bed at a decent hour?

Begin by observing how your daughter functions in the morning and during the day. If you don't have undue difficulty getting her up and off to school and if her energy level meets her needs, she may merely be responding to her own unique body rhythms.

Some children require more sleep than others. Some are born night owls and others morning larks. Parents can't control when a child falls asleep, but you can control the environment conducive to sleep by setting rules on when she will be in her room and when the lights go out.

The disturbing part of your question is her statement that she thinks she might be missing out on something by going to bed. Might she be subconsciously sabotaging your time with your husband? Does she resent the need for you two to want to be together without her? Does she feel an undue need to be the center of your attention?

I suggest you try a simple set of rules. "Eight o'clock is room time; nine o'clock is lights out." This gives her some power in choosing reading or playing in her room (no TV) while you're stating clearly that running about the house looking for stimulation is unacceptable. At 8:45, you might go in and read her a story, pray with her and tuck her in.

Make it clear that you are not setting these rules as punishment but as a response to her inability to go to sleep. You are simply furnishing a quiet environment to avoid that overstimulation that often prevents her from sleeping.

Dolores Curran

6.11 ASSESSING A CHILD'S KNOWLEDGE ABOUT SEX

Is there some delicate way to determine how much your child knows about sex, without launching into a heavy-handed discussion or being inappropriately graphic? My daughter is a fourth-grader and I'm beginning to wonder just what she's picking up at school and from TV—because, let's be honest, they do pick up ideas, images, and misinformation. How should I proceed?

Congratulations for tackling an issue most parents prefer to avoid. You're right; ten-year-olds know a lot about sex. Sadly, they are affected by news stories and TV programs, particularly the soap operas, promoting unhealthy sex and un-Christian values. AIDS, rape, infidelity, surrogate parenting, the gratuitous use of sex in advertising, pornography, molestation—all are open subjects to today's children.

You're right; ten-year-olds know a lot about sex.

The best way to find out what your daughter knows or wants to know is to include her in your conversation with your spouse over some current news story that involves sex. Perhaps you could bring up an abortion protest, a child molestation case, or a date-rape case. At first, she is likely to listen quietly to you and your spouse, but soon she will begin making comments and asking questions. If she doesn't, you might ask, "How do you feel about that? Do you think kids really know the difference between being hugged and being molested?"

Ten is not too young for the direct approach, either. When you're in an intimate conversation over something else—friends, school, sports—you can say, "Sometimes I wonder if we're doing a good-enough job of teaching you about sexual issues. We just want you to know that we are open to talk about sex, AIDS, pregnancy and so on, and to answer your questions when and if you want to talk about those subjects. But we won't push you."

Dolores Curran

6.12 SPOUSE AMBIVALENT TOWARD STARTING A FAMILY

My husband and I have been married for six years and we're trying to decide whether to have a child. My husband says he doesn't care, so it's my decision. It upsets me that he's so passive. I want him to participate in the decision-making process, since a decision as important as this one should be mutual. But the more I try to get him to discuss it, the more he withdraws. Should I keep trying to get him to talk about it, or should I give up and make the decision myself?

Sometimes the idea of fatherhood can be very threatening to a man.

In former generations, most pregnancies were announced by the husband shouting over the breakfast cereal, "You're what?" He then had seven or eight months to get used to the idea. The process is much easier for the mother, who, after all, is carrying—and beginning to bond with—a living human being inside her body. But men have to learn to love, to share, and to adjust to economic realities. And sometimes the idea of fatherhood can be very threatening to a man, because it doesn't yet seem real.

A man can share the delights of pregnancy—the shopping, the nursery renovation, the trips to Lamaze class. But it's still not the same, not until he holds that newborn in his arms, marvels at perfect little fingers and toes, finds familial resemblances. These things stir a sense of mystery in men.

In a computerized, calculating generation, when we try to get the answer to whether we should become parents by reading *Money* magazine, men tend to be afraid of family commitments. But there are some questions that can't be answered on a financial projection sheet. I suspect there may be an element of "paralysis by analysis" in your situation. There are those who would point out to me the terrible potential consequences of parenthood by surprise but, having observed a couple of generations, I'm not convinced that parenthood by analysis is superior.

So let me offer a radical suggestion: consider leaving this decision up to God. If it's His will that you have a child, you will. But give Him a chance. Don't head His decision off at the pass.

Jay Kesler

6.13 MINIMIZING MOTHERHOOD STRESS

My wife has assumed the majority of the parenting tasks since she's at home full-time. I know her job is demanding and at times very stressful. How can I really help my wife when it comes to caring for our kids?

To begin with, we have to recognize the validity of the "job stresses" that bother most mothers. Then we ought to talk to our wives about it. Recognizing and understanding stress is the first, perhaps most important step in dealing with it.

We had a birthday party at our house for our four-year-old. I helped organize some of the games and even dipped a little ice cream when it was time for refreshments. When it was all over my wife and I talked about how much we enjoy kids' birthday parties, and she told me she appreciated my help and complimented me on being "such a good daddy." When I replied that she was "a good mother, too," she responded, "Thanks, I need to hear that more often."

"Thanks, I need to hear that more often."

I realized again what I've realized before: I don't compliment my wife on her mothering nearly as often as she comments on what I do as a father. When we give our wives positive feedback on their mothering, we relieve one stress and at the same time provide encouragement that helps them better cope with other pressures.

A number of husbands have found specific ways to help their wives. For example, getting up at night with kids was becoming a major headache for the wife of a friend of mine. She'd take a child to the bathroom or get someone a drink, then be wide-awake for two hours before she could fall back to sleep. The result was constant exhaustion.

Once my friend understood the problem, he volunteered to take night duty. He can get up, care for a child's needs, and fall back to sleep the minute his head hits the pillow. His wife now feels more rested, and he thinks a few minutes a night of lost sleep is a small price to pay for a happier, healthier wife.

Some men give their wives regular breaks. One dad I talked to takes charge every Saturday morning and sends his wife out by herself for breakfast. It's her time—time she can count on and look forward to every week, time when she can have peace and quiet to read and think. Another husband made it a priority to spend money on a babysitter/housekeeper one afternoon a week so his wife could enjoy a respite from mothering.

Some people we know do the "motherhood break" idea in even grander style. Once every three or four months, one friend gives his wife a coupon for a one-night stay at some large, nearby hotel. He comes home on Friday afternoon to take over the house and the four kids, and his wife is on her own for the next 30 hours to read, sleep, browse through local malls, or do anything else she wants to do. She comes home so energized and rested and appreciative of his support that my friend considers the expense a very worthwhile investment in his wife and their marriage.

Even if you don't feel your budget can afford a day's worth of meals and an overnight hotel stay for your wife, you could still try the mini-vacation at home idea. Just notify your wife that you'll take over all her responsibilities for a day, an afternoon, or even for a couple of hours. Then she is free to do whatever she wants.

Gregg Lewis

6.14 KUDOS KIDS NOTICE

We praise our children often, but we're beginning to wonder if our praise is a little hollow at times. When we point out something our kids did well, they usually shrug their shoulders and don't seem to care about our words of praise. What more can we do?

I prefer the idea of affirming and supporting children by encouragement rather than praise. Praise affirms the result, encouragement the effort. If we praise a child for his good game one weekend and don't say anything when he plays poorly the next, we are stating our expectations: if you want our praise, play well.

Far better to say, "You're a real team member. You care about those who feel bad when they strike out. I really admire that in you," than "Two base hits. You're great!"

Nonverbal affirmation is easy, too. When children show fairness or receive a hurt without reacting, we can give them a squeeze on the shoulder, a smile and a wink, or an "okay" hand signal.

Praise affirms the result, encouragement the effort.

I remember the time my then-teenaged, always laid-back son watched my stress level go sky-high in minutes. I was trying to get dinner and was running late for a meeting when the phone rang. He reached up, closed his hand around the phone so I couldn't answer it and said, "Don't sweat it, Mom."

My anger at having to deal with this final stress-inducing straw began to erupt, but he winked and gave me such an impish smile that I burst into laughter instead. He was giving me permission to relax—a gift he has given our fast-track family many times. What a God-given gift that is, and how rarely we affirm it.

Dolores Curran

6.15 COPING WITH TEENAGE MATERIALISM

Our teenagers are asking for some things that are clearly beyond our family budget. Last week I got angry looks and the silent treatment because I wouldn't give in and buy our 15-year-old a pair of outrageously expensive tennis shoes. I stuck to my guns but the battle is getting tougher. How can my husband and I firmly and effectively deal with their requests?

There are four avenues to dealing with a teenager's demands without alienating your child or making you out to be a mean miser.

Basic capitulation. "Look," I've been told by a parent, "my daughter is at the most crucial time of her life. Who knows how her personality will form? I'm not about to jeopardize her fragile self-esteem by forcing on her my view of fashion. "She's the one who has to walk down those school corridors each day, vying for recognition. She's the one who feels the sting of being out of it, not me."

This may seem more like shortsighted capitulation than a creative solution, but it may lower the decibel level in a house where parents have to live with teenagers. And yes, clothes are expensive, especially the "must" labels. Yes, kids grow out of them or discard them before they wear them out. No, it doesn't really seem like such great stewardship. But the thought remains, "Do I want to mess with my child's self-esteem at his or her point of greatest vulnerability?" I can't criticize parents who are unwilling to sacrifice their adolescents to the standards of a past era.

Cagey compromise. I'll admit, this has been our basic strategy for our near-teens. I want my kids to have clothes they're proud to wear among their friends. I want to give them everything they truly need (and not judge their needs by what mine were), even if I refuse to give them *everything* they want. To do that, we've used a threefold plan.

First, we try to discern reality. "Everybody" doesn't have Air Jordans, as much as it may seem that way at times, and my kids don't necessarily have to *set* the fashions.

Second, we try to determine genuine needs versus vigorous wants. By *needed* I mean needed emotionally and socially along with physically. For instance, my son needs shoes. I'll also concede he *needs* unembarrassing shoes. But he doesn't really *need* Air Jordans.

Third, we wait to search out the best buys. My kids can be uncool for a few weeks. We'll eventually buy them a few top-line togs, but we'll rarely pay a premium price. Almost-perfect fashion items have to move to make room for the next wave of the latest, so we find the sales. Upscale resale shops also are big now, and they offer surprising bargains on fashionable, "gently worn" garments.

We wait to search out the best buys.

Negotiated sharing. "All right," one father tells his daughter, "if you have to have an Esprit top, you can have it. Here's $25, enough to buy a perfectly acceptable top. You can pay the remainder if you must have Esprit." Such sharing of expenses isn't uncommon. Today's teenagers spend more than $50 a week on the average, and it might as well go for clothes as for CDs and posters.

"It's amazing how kids' needs' change when they share the cost," adds the father. "They learn they can live with less. And this method teaches my daughter the value of money. She knows how much work is needed to be able to plunk down 50 bucks for a blouse."

Total budgeting. One family with older teens takes an educational approach. About two years ago they sat down and figured what they spent for each of their two teens for clothes, movies and other entertainment, lunches bought at school, and various other expenses. With a little negotiation the kids and the parents arrived at a reasonable monthly figure. The bank now automatically transfers that amount monthly from the parents' account into an account for each child. The kids use withdrawal slips (signed in bulk by their mother) to withdraw the cash they use to get themselves through the month.

The decisions belong to the kids now. "Some months they pay so much for clothes that nothing is left for movies," says the mother. "And when something special comes up, we just say, 'Sorry, but you knew how much money you had, and you spent it.' We do sometimes give them extra jobs to earn money to get them through the month, though."

This option obviously works best for older, more responsible teens (if that isn't an oxymoron), since money management makes monkeys even of many adults. But although the risks are palpable, so are the benefits.

James D. Berkley

6.16 SECOND THOUGHTS ABOUT CHOOSING CHILDLESSNESS

Before my husband and I got married we decided we wouldn't have children. We've been married a few years now, and just recently two women at work had babies. I didn't think this would affect me, but it has. I've started thinking I might like to have children after all. But when I mentioned that to my husband, he said I was trying to change the agreement we had when we got married. My change of heart is driving us apart. What should I do?

Your question illustrates a basic fact in marriage: people change. The two people who made those vows on their wedding day are not the same two people today. Once your husband realizes that you have not purposefully backed out of your original agreement, but your feelings have simply changed because you have changed, it might help you regain the closeness you used to share.

You might say something like, "Yes, I did make this agreement when we got married. However, I have changed. This is how I've been feeling." Tell him the purpose of your sharing this is not to change his mind, but to keep the lines of communication open. Your husband should be able to acknowledge that people do change and that you have not become a traitor.

However, I suggest you keep your word. Nagging or pushing your husband into a decision he doesn't really want to make will only drive a deeper wedge between you. You can pray that if God is leading you in a new direction about having children, that He would also work in your husband's life and heart. Often, resistance to having children is based on fears created by one's background or by society, and these prove weaker than whatever biological or spiritual urges kick in once a couple starts spending time with friends who have babies. Pray that if God is behind the changes in your heart, He would help your husband overcome whatever reluctance he has about becoming a father.

If he doesn't change, however, this doesn't mean that your desires can't be fulfilled, at least in part. I know many students who are in college today because a childless couple has taken them under their wing and acted almost as a second set of parents to them. I have known single or childless teachers who have become involved in children's lives almost more closely than the biological parents. Perhaps there are some children in your life with whom you could develop a special relationship and fulfill some of your emerging desires to nurture a new generation.

If he doesn't change, however, this doesn't mean that your desires can't be fulfilled.

Jay Kesler

6.17 KIDS BARGING INTO PARENTS' BEDROOM

Boy are we ever embarrassed! Our two children, ages seven and four, came barging into our bedroom the other night and caught us making love. We didn't know what to say or do, and now I'm afraid we've perverted them or something. How should we have handled this?

To prevent something like this from happening again, we recommend putting a lock on your bedroom door and using it every time you are going to engage in any type of love play. But since your children did walk in on your lovemaking activity, it would have been most appropriate to have asked them to leave. Then, when you got yourselves presentable, you could have gone out and had a talk with them.

You could have explained that what the two of you were doing was loving each other sexually—a time of pleasure for both of you designed by God for marriage. But it is private, so it probably made them and you uncomfortable. Allow them to talk about their feelings and ask any questions they might have. If this type of exposure is handled with care and openness, damage is not likely to result.

To avoid further embarrassment, however, you need to remember to lock your door whenever you're enjoying sexual activity. It's also a good rule for your kids to learn to always knock before they enter.

Clifford L. and Joyce J. Penner

6.18 DOING BATTLE WITH THE "GIMMES"

It seems that every time I take my six-year-old to the store, she wants something. When I refuse, she says her father and I never get her anything. To compound the problem, she sometimes seems ungrateful for what she does receive. What should we do to control our daughter's escalating demands?

Many couples are dealing with the frustration of rearing kids who see parents as dispensers and know how to load on the guilt by implying, "If you love me, you'll buy me something." Unless you put a stop to it, your daughter will up the ante and you'll find yourself caught in an unhealthy dance with her later on, when she will equate your love with your largess.

In your case, this is a habit you have reinforced by dancing to your daughter's tune. If she was diabetic and you brought her chocolates, you would be considered a negligent parent. The same principle applies to her incessant demands for proof of your love in the form of surprises and rewards. Mark Twain wrote, "Habit is habit, and not to be flung out of the window, but coaxed downstairs a step at a time." So let's look at the stair steps you can take with your six-year-old.

First, I suggest you gradually stop bringing her things from the store and—most important—refuse to apologize when she accuses you of neglect. Simply say, "What did I bring you? Let's see...a big hug. Come and get it." If she begins to complain, simply give her a smile and walk away. Don't get hooked into an argument.

When you do this, you are changing the dance. And as you continue to show her that you are not going to habitually bring her things, she will be forced to relinquish the power she has over you. You must take charge now, as unpleasant as it may be for you.

After a few weeks of "forgetting" to bring her things, you can move on to the second stair step. If she gets angry, react by saying calmly, "You may be right. I do seem to be forgetting a lot lately. So let's set one time a week when I won't forget to bring you something. You're getting so old and grown up now, you don't need a surprise every time. What day do you want to choose for your surprise?" If she makes a scene, simply smile and say, "Let me know which day you choose," and walk away.

> *You and your husband need to be together in this strategy.*

You and your husband need to be together in this strategy. It won't work if one of you is more lenient than the other. So encourage him to join you on your journey down the staircase of change.

Dolores Curran

6.19 SETTING LIMITS FOR A TEENAGER

Last night our 17-year-old daughter went out on a date. We had told her to be home no later than midnight, but she finally strolled in around 1:15. My wife and I had visions of her being injured in an auto accident. We've told her, "Call if you're going to be late." She knows the rules, and until recently she was pretty good about obeying them. We tried not to overreact, but she didn't seem remorseful—and this is the third time she's been late. My wife and I feel like she's taking advantage of our trust. How can we make her understand that as long as she lives in our house she must follow our rules?

You have set reasonable rules and limits, but your teenager may be testing them. Her lack of remorse is deliberate behavior on her part to challenge your rules, your fears, and your reaction to her disobeying. Older adolescents often use conflict and emotional separation to offset the pain of the physical separation from their parents that they know is coming. They are also putting parents on notice that when they return home from college during summer and Christmas holidays, they plan to set their own hours and limits.

I sometimes wonder if God doesn't send us this familiar but frustrating "last-year-at-home" behavior to get us used to living without our kids. As young adults take on more autonomy, parents must gradually relinquish authority if there's to be an eventual mature relationship between the two generations.

At this point, I wouldn't overreact unless your daughter's behavior drastically changes for the worse. At an unhurried time, I would tell her you were disappointed that she didn't call because you were concerned about her safety. You should ask if she feels such a request is unreasonable. She is likely to say no and apologize.

As young adults take on more autonomy, parents must gradually relinquish authority.

But even if she doesn't, you will need to restate your expectations, the limits, and the consequences that you will enforce as long as she is living at home. You might say, "We know you are maturing and we're pleased that up until now you've been pretty good about sticking to the rules. But it's our responsibility to know where you are and whom you are with as long as you're living under our roof. This means now and in the future when you're home. Do you think you can respect these rules without our setting consequences in advance, or would you rather have us set up the consequences now in case this happens again?"

This gives her some face-saving power while letting her know that you're still in charge. That's what she's testing and, while parents may find it hard to believe, she may feel a sense of relief. Adolescents, particularly those facing separation, don't want their parents to stop caring about their welfare.

If she doesn't cooperate, state some consequences and stick to them. One might be that if she doesn't respect your curfew and subsequent anxiety one weekend, she is not to make plans to go out the following weekend. It usually takes only one weekend at home for a teenager to get the idea that you're still in charge and that you are serious about her welfare.

Dolores Curran

6.20 OVERLY STRICT PARENT

My husband is too strict with our children. He's quick to raise his voice and often orders our children to their rooms over a small infraction. When I talk to him about his strictness he accuses me of being too lenient. While our kids are doing fine so far, I'm worried that as they get older they'll start to rebel. I try not to argue in front of the kids about our differing parenting styles, but it's getting more and more difficult to hold my tongue. Will we ever be united in how we parent? I'm tried of fighting about it.

You are describing a classic situation in many marriages, one that hearkens back to an outdated belief that mom is the nurturer and dad the disciplinarian. Research has shown that children fare best where both parents are nurturers and disciplinarians. So I must ask, are you doing your share of the disciplining, or are you leaving it all to your husband? If the latter is the case, you are forcing him to be the tough guy while you remain the nice guy.

If, however, you are doing your share of behavior monitoring and you are fearful that his harshness will drive the children away, I suggest that the two of you seek out some parenting skills workshops or courses where your husband can hear someone else say what he isn't hearing you say. If none are available, I recommend the book *Parenting by Heart* (Addison-Wesley) by Ron Taffel. This is a fine book on the over-controlling, under-nurturing parent.

Another good resource is pastoral counseling. A good pastoral counselor will be able to hear the fears both of you have, and will help you move closer together in discipline practices *and* in your marriage. A counselor can also help your husband deal with what he believes are the duties of a father as a disciplinarian.

When couples are courting, they usually don't discuss how they will discipline their children. Yet, it can easily become a wedge in the marriage. The paradox is that the more controlling one partner is, the more likely the other is to become protective of the children, thus increasing the emotional distance between the spouses. The goal of learning, reading, or seeking counseling is to begin to take small steps toward each other's parenting style—and minimize that distance.

Let your husband know, lovingly, that you two are going to spend a lot more time together as a couple, *without* the children. Let him know, too, that you are feeling a distance growing between you and him over how he treats the children, and that this is a problem that can affect your marriage.

I suggest you move quickly. Once your children reach adolescence they are going to rebel against their father's treatment of them and express resentment toward you for not moderating it sufficiently. This will increase your anger toward him and create more tension in your marriage. I have seen formerly healthy marriages disintegrate during the adolescent years over this issue. If you begin praying together daily for more balance in your parenting styles, it will give the issue the grace and attention it deserves.

Dolores Curran

I have seen formerly healthy marriages disintegrate during the adolescent years over this issue.

6.21 GRANDPARENTS WHO PLAY FAVORITES

My parents, who live in the same city as we do, are very generous with their time and money toward our children. But there's no question they favor our elder daughter over our other child—and over all the other grandchildren in the family. (She was their first grandchild.) We've tried to encourage a better balance between the time they spend with both of our girls, but it's still skewed. Though our children are too young to realize what is happening, this has put us in an awkward position with my brothers, who also have kids. They sense our parents' favoritism and I know it makes them feel bad. How can we handle this so it doesn't become a divisive family issue and so it doesn't hurt my younger daughter?

You need to address this immediately, even it if means hurting your parents' feelings. I know a family where this identical pattern occurred years ago and to this day, the grown children refer to "Tommy's grandma" and "Tommy's grandpa" rather than "our grandma and grandpa."

Children sense favoritism at a very young age and it can become a lifelong barrier between them. Look at the mileage the Smothers Brothers continue to get out of the line "Mom always liked you best."

Let your parents know you are concerned about the favoritism. But assure them that you are also concerned about their feelings. Explain that you are very grateful for the love and attention they give your oldest daughter, but that you want their help in offsetting real or fancied favoritism.

Together you can work out some rules: equal time, gifts, hugging, and so forth for *all* the grandchildren. While many grandparents secretly admit to favoritism, they don't realize it is obvious to their children and grandchildren. Often they will put a stop to overt favoritism if it's called to their attention.

If your parents are unwilling or unable to reduce these tendencies, then you may want to restrict times your daughters spend with them to those occasions when both children are present.

Finally, let your brothers know that you are aware of what's going on, that you don't like it and that you are taking steps to alleviate the situation. Your sensitivity and frankness can strengthen a potentially strained sibling bond.

Dolores Curran

6.22 LACKING ROLE MODEL OF GOOD FATHERING

We just had our first child and I really want to be a good father. The problem is I was raised in a single-parent home by my mother and I'm not sure what characteristics are essential for becoming a good father. What should I strive for?

I consider the following guidelines to be a good starting place for any dad.

Men are never manlier than when they are tender with their children.

Show tenderness. The overall idea of tenderness is to speak to your children with gentleness and friendliness. When I was a teenager, my best friend's father was a man's man. He had spent 32 years in the U.S. Coast Guard and in his prime he had put on the gloves with Joe Louis. He could be rough and tumble, but do you know what he called his 265-pound son? "David dear." I was "Kent dear," and I didn't mind at all. In fact, it made me feel great. He was not hung up on "real men don't show affection." We are to be tender. Men are never manlier than when they are tender with their children—whether holding a baby in their arms, loving their grade-schooler or hugging their teenager or adult children.

Discipline your children when necessary. "Training" is a strong word that means "discipline, even by punishment." Discipline certainly includes corporal discipline as needed. But it encompasses *everything* necessary to help "train a child in the way he should go." The tragedy is that so many men have left this to their wives. Not only is this unfair to the mother, but it robs the child of the security and self-esteem that come from being disciplined by the father.

Instruct your children. "Instruction" literally means, "to place before the mind." Often this involves confronting your child, and thus is related to discipline. If we are to own up to our responsibilities we must be:

- Involved in verbally instructing our children.
- Regularly leading them in family devotions and prayer.
- Monitoring and being responsible, along with our wives, for the input that enters their impressionable minds.
- Taking responsibility to help ensure that church is a meaningful experience for them.
- And above all, we must make sure that the open book of our lives—our example—demonstrates the reality of our instruction. They will learn the most from watching us.

Be there for your children. The "do's" of fatherhood cannot be lived out by proxy. You need to participate in putting your little ones to bed and praying for and with them. You need to be at their plays, speeches, recitals and sporting events. You need to schedule regular time alone with each of your children. You need to take the lead in planning terrific family vacations and in celebrating and cementing family solidarity.

We all go through periods when we have little time for our families—it's part of the natural rhythm of life. But excessive "busyness" must not be by choice. We must beware of packing our schedules by saying "yes" to things that mean "no" to our families. Now is the time to take time to be with our children. And now is the time to become the father God wants us to be.

R. Kent Hughes

6.23 UNINVOLVED GRANDPARENTS

We have two daughters, three and six. My husband's parents and my parents all live within a few hours' drive, but his mother (a widow) is a more involved grandparent than my parents are. She is good about babysitting, remembering birthdays or holidays, and visiting. I know my parents love their grandkids, but they visit less often and in general are less involved. I've tried to talk to my mother about my concern but since she isn't as child-centered as my mother-in-law this isn't an issue for her. Meanwhile, I'm worried that my kids are going to grow up favoring one grandparent over another. Isn't there something I can do to help even out the grandparents' involvement?

In short, the answer to your question is no. I would advise you to relax and accept the reality that you aren't going to change your parents. Your expectations differ from theirs. And at any rate, your daughters, just like other children, will develop their own relationships with each grandparent. You can't invade those boundaries by trying to explain your parents' behavior, or by apologizing to your children for their seeming lack of interest.

In addition, overemphasizing your disappointment with your parents could rupture your relationship with them. The more you express your hopes and expectations, the less often they might visit and that will intensify the issue. It may be that as your children age and your parents wind down their busy lives, the relationship will become closer. Realize, too, that they have each other while your mother-in-law is alone and is likely to place a higher priority on close relationships with the grandchildren.

Finally, most children *do* favor one grandparent over another. But this doesn't mean they don't love them all. They just love them differently and that's their right.

Dolores Curran

6.24 WORRIED THERE WON'T BE MARRIAGE AFTER CHILDREN

I'm a little concerned about our marriage now that we have our first child. All of our energy goes into our son and I'm worried there isn't really marriage after children. Is there any hope we'll ever feel like a couple again?

Studies indicate marital satisfaction declines with the birth of the first child and remains lower until the last child leaves home. In doing research for my book *Stress and the Healthy Family* (HarperSanFrancisco), I found that couples ranked children as the third-highest source of family stress. Parenting trailed only money pressures and insufficient couple time, both of which are intensified by having children. No wonder couples find themselves longing for their earlier, pre-children relationship.

When you have a child, you swap one kind of married life for another, and the transition embodies both temporary losses and gains. The losses are multiple: money, control, couple time, playfulness, energy, lovemaking, and freedom. Most parents endure a period of chaos during which they are forced to relinquish the rewards of life without kids before they can experience the multiple rewards of parenting.

No wonder couples find themselves longing for their earlier, pre-children relationship.

Our society is big on personal freedoms, so it tends to focus on the losses couples encounter when adding a child to their family. Contrary to popular opinion, the rewards of parenting are many. The first, and one of the most important is, *greater intimacy and shared pleasures.* My husband and I were partners in delighting in our first child's development. Before the baby arrived, we had anticipated some of the losses, but we didn't expect the deeper intimacy God gave us. This added a dimension that lifted us up and sustained us over the years. Even today when our grown children call to tell us of new developments, achievements or happiness, we listen on separate phones, then replay the conversation together afterwards.

A second reward is *the chance to observe each other in new roles.* It's the emotional catch in the throat as a man watches his wife nurse their baby; or a woman's rush of pleasure at seeing her husband's tender interaction with their child.

Before becoming parents, we play multiple roles: spouse, employee, son/daughter, neighbor and so on. But the role of parent affects all our other roles. Good evidence of this is the way a baby can change a couple's work ethic. A new father finds himself drawing more strength and fulfillment from his family and less from his work. He might shift his priorities or cut back his work hours because he recognizes different values and joys. New moms often reconsider going back to work or choose part-time work once they experience the pleasure and challenge of being a mother.

A third benefit that is too easily missed is *the opportunity to recapture a childlike sense of play and optimism.* In the pleasure of day-to-day contact with their children, couples can renew a lost sense of awe and fantasy. One parent told me:

"Playing with my young children gave me a second chance to be an optimist in a pessimistic world."

A fourth reward is that *as parents watch their child develop, many enter a new phase of self-discovery.* Adults often see themselves in the mirror of a "child just like me." This process can be painful, but it's always insightful and can contribute to more empathetic parenting.

There is a fifth benefit inherent in nurturing a child: *It brings the awesome realization that parents are part of God's larger plan.* People experience this feeling whenever they create something that will outlive them—a book, a work of art, a new idea or product. Carl Sandburg observed, "A baby is God's idea that the world should go on." Parents become aware they are co-producers in God's great idea, and the partnership is exhilarating and intimidating.

Finally, *the challenges of raising children provide a great opportunity for renewed spirituality.* The wonder of a child's uniqueness, the powerless feeling that comes with a child's sudden illness, and the irrational love the child engenders offer a deep understanding of God's power and unconditional love. I've heard parents say the overwhelming impact of their love for their child was the first time they really believed in God's unconditional, passionate, and constant love for us in spite of our failings.

If couples joyfully make the tradeoffs between life without children and the world of parenting, they receive unexpected rewards. Those who focus on these gifts, rather than the sacrifices, weather the transition well and find greater joy in their relationship.

Dolores Curran

6.25 BUILDING A DAUGHTER'S SELF-ESTEEM

My wife says it's important that I affirm our daughter, since much of a girl's self-esteem is based on how her father relates to her. But I honestly don't know how to go about it, other than to show an interest in her activities. What else should I be doing?

I'm glad you want to be an important presence in your daughter's life. Your involvement, interest, and love will be the best gift you'll ever give her.

In the past, fathers were taught that their parenting role involved turning adolescent boys into men. Girls and younger boys were considered Mom's domain. But we know now that while mothers are important as role models, fathers are fundamental in nurturing a daughter's healthy self-image. It's Dad's interest, support, and affirmation that give girls a sense of self-worth, confidence and trust in themselves and ultimately in others.

When girls grow up with high self-esteem, they make wiser choices in moral issues, marriage, and career. Studies of high-achieving women have found that most had fathers who treated their children as whole people, investing the same amount of time and interest and applying the same standards to both their daughters and their sons. They didn't coddle their daughters or lower their expectations of them, but let them know they could meet almost any challenge.

Your task as a father is simply to love and challenge your daughter to her fullest potential. View her as a child of God with unique gifts to be nurtured rather than a young girl to be shielded and protected. Take an active interest in her activities. Give her one-on-one time that shows her she's valued and loved for who she is, not for what she is.

Your task as a father is simply to love and challenge your daughter to her fullest potential.

Your rewards will be both immediate and long lasting in your daughter's positive self-image and in her future wise decisions. And she will count herself blessed in having a loving and involved father like you.

Dolores Curran

6.26 BAILING OUT A PROCRASTINATOR

Our sixth-grader tends to wait until the last minute before she asks for help on major school projects. Then my husband bails her out by staying up all night doing her work. I've told him to let her "pay the price" of her procrastination. But he says he doesn't want to be mean or let our daughter's grades suffer. Sometimes I don't know whom I'm angrier with—our child who procrastinates or my husband who always saves the day. How can I help my husband see he isn't really helping our daughter but instead hurting her?

Your husband is rescuing your daughter at a stage in her life when she needs to accept responsibility in order to develop confidence, maturity and self-esteem. Perhaps if he understands that he is blocking growth in these areas, he will worry less about being "mean" or seeing her get a low grade.

Projects and papers are assigned, in part, to teach children to develop time management, responsibility, and pride in their accomplishments. I encourage you and your husband to visit your daughter's teachers together. I suspect that if you ask for their counsel on your daughter's study pattern, they will encourage you to let her suffer the consequences of her procrastination as a learning opportunity.

On the positive side, be grateful that your husband cares enough about your daughter to rescue her. I receive letters from women who are far more anguished because their husbands are disinterested in their children's lives. The practice of rescuing springs from a parent's love; and while it may be deleterious, its motivation is pure.

God loves us constantly, passionately and unconditionally but he lets us suffer the consequences of our behavior. He lets us learn from our actions and inactions so we can grow in his Spirit. As parents, we need to follow his example.

Dolores Curran

6.27 DISAGREEING ON WHEN TO START A FAMILY

I'm ready to have children, but my wife says that once we have kids we won't have much time or energy left for just us. She feels that a child will fill every available minute. We've been married more than three years, and I don't think we should wait any longer. I don't want to pressure my wife, but I would like to encourage her a little. What should I do?

In marriage, two become one. This is the opposite of mathematics, where one plus one equals two. However, the oneness that occurs in marriage requires a spiritual commitment. A husband and wife have to choose to merge some of their aspirations and not simply remain two separate individuals.

With a subject as important as having children, that type of mutuality is essential. Both of you must feel comfortable with your choices. So I encourage you to give your wife time to become comfortable with the prospect of parenthood.

She may be wrestling with some issues that are deeper than the ones she has mentioned to you. From observing other parents, she may have developed some deep fears that need to surface and be discussed. Be patient as you ascertain what these fears might be, and then do your best to work through them together.

Perhaps your wife is weighing the trade-offs. Many of today's young couples want to have it all, and some are too quick to add a child to an already over-crowded life. It's a myth that you can add a third person to a household without making some trade-offs in time and energy. Those trade-offs indeed are sobering, and both of you must seriously consider them. Many parents find they have to give up golf or tennis for a while, or Sunday-afternoon football games, or late dinners with clients. Something has to go when a person takes on the responsibilities of parenthood.

But there is a limit to the trade-offs. Your wife might know young mothers who believe their children should totally occupy their time and attention. She may be thinking, "That looks too demanding, and anyway, I don't want to lose myself in a child!" But that image is a false one. Of course, there will often be needs that require immediate attention. But a good mother must preserve some time for herself—and her husband. It's good for children to learn to play creatively on their own, and it's healthy for them to develop some independence. A mother who is constantly focused on her child's every whim gives the child a skewed understanding of his relative importance. Be patient as you talk together about the challenges of parenting. As you both become more comfortable with the idea of having children, you may be able to make a mutual decision to go ahead.

Jay Kesler

> *A good mother must preserve some time for herself—and her husband.*

6.28 MOUTHY TEENAGERS

My 15-year-old son has been getting increasingly "mouthy" over the last couple of years. My husband doesn't realize the extent of the problem, since our son doesn't talk to him the same way he talks to me. Our son is nearly grown and I feel rather help-less when it comes to influencing his behavior. What should I do?

Something happens between teenage boys and their mothers—it's called sep-aration and individuation. Psychologist Joan Shapiro refers to it as the "not Mom" stage. Around this age, the developmental force that drives a boy is the urge to separate from his mother. That's why anything Mom does is likely to be argued, scorned, or belittled by the teenager.

Because your son is following the normal male adolescent development of separating from you and identifying with his father, he's in a bind. He wants to be like his father; yet his father doesn't treat you with disrespect, the way your son does. It will take time for your son to sort this out. (In the case of my two sons, it took about two years.) As your son becomes more comfortable with the idea that you are allowing him to be "not Mom," and as he identifies more with his father, he will gradually adopt his father's more respectful behavior toward you.

Some boys turn mouthy toward their mothers at this stage and others withdraw into stony silence. I had one of each, and both were frustrating. I do know that when I refused to allow my eldest son to say anything even slightly disrespectful to me, he withdrew into himself and behaved as if I was invisible.

God uses our mistakes to help us grow, so when my second son reached this stage, I tolerated more mouthing, but I set clear boundaries. I told him, "You can disagree with me, but you must show respect." This meant he had to abide by clearly stated prohibitions of certain language, comments and behaviors, like leaving the room in the middle of a conversation.

He retained the right to argue with me, and to express his feelings, but with respect. In spite of their sometimes-unpleasant behavior, kids want boundaries. Your son needs you to set clear ones so he will not stray too far and increase his inner confusion.

It may help you get through this by knowing that your son doesn't much like himself during these difficult years, and he needs more than ever to know that you still love him. Some reassuring response to his mouthing might be, "If I didn't love you so much, I'd be tempted to put you out the door" or "It's hard to like you when you act like this, so I'm glad I love you." This gives him the security of your love but lets him know how you feel about his behavior.

Your husband is your best ally in this situation, but dads often minimize their sons' disrespect because boys are careful not to exhibit it in their fathers' presence. The father's task at this stage is to help his son identify fully with him as a man and to initiate him into adult male behavior. Your husband may need to talk man-to-man with your son about how real men respect and treat women. In families where this takes place, conflict is lessened as the boy grows through his separation struggles with his mother and begins his journey to manhood. Hang in there, thank God that your son is normal, and take comfort in the fact that the two of you will laugh about his behavior in ten years.

Dolores Curran

6.29 CHOOSING TO HAVE AN ONLY CHILD

My wife and I decided to limit the size of our family to one child. Because of our personalities and our limited financial means, we felt we could do the best job as parents if we stopped after our first child. But some people at church—especially couples with two or three children—treat us like we're selfish. Their implied criticism of our choice stings. Are we really being selfish or just sensible?

A couple's decision about whether to have children at all—or how many children they feel they should have—is between them and God. There is no mention in Scripture of an "ideal" number of children to have. The biblical pattern for families is that we're supposed to be responsible toward each other as spouses and toward our children, if we have any.

I believe different family sizes work for different people. Your problem really lies with the criticism you are sensing. I would caution you about "perceived criticism." Are you sure these church friends are being critical, or are you jumping to that conclusion because you and your wife aren't completely settled in your decision about family size? Take some time to discuss your level of confidence in your decision.

On the other hand, I wouldn't be surprised if you have received actual criticism. It's common for insecure people to have trouble accepting a conflicting point of view. They tend to demand that others conform to their preferences in order to bolster their own position. They'll peck away at the person who chooses to do things differently, and they might even reject you because of their insecurity.

In church life, issues that fall into the realm of personal judgment can be troublesome. You may have heard the motto: "In essentials, unity; in nonessentials, liberty; in all things, charity." It's an excellent standard for getting along in the church. There may be some disagreement over establishing the "essentials" on which we must be unified. But there is no question in the area of charity; loving each other is a clear command of the Lord.

Make it a habit to pray through your decisions with your wife, then follow God's leading.

For your part, resist giving in to the pressure to conform to the wishes of your insecure critics. Make it a habit to pray through your decisions with your wife, then follow God's leading. Sometimes, by the gracious way we live out our choices in obedience to God, we can convince others that Scripture allows us the freedom to be different.

Jay Kesler

6.30 TEACHING KIDS ABOUT SEX

At what age should our kids have a full understanding of sexual intercourse and how the reproductive system works? And how should we go about educating our kids apart from what they'll learn (both formally and informally) at school?

For a long time, I have endorsed church-sponsored parent-child sex education. More churches could offer Christian-based sex education classes where parents and children would learn together. This would relieve parents of the fear of giving their children erroneous information, and it would offset some of the usual embarrassment inherent in this teaching.

However, most churches are reluctant to get involved in sex education, so parents struggle alone with questions like yours. I am presuming you are talking more about the physical aspects of sex than the issue of "sexuality"—-what it means to be a male or a female—which begins at birth.

With puberty beginning at age eleven for many children today, our sex-laden media, the drug culture, AIDS and pressures and temptations unheard of in earlier times, I believe children should know the biological facts of reproduction, including sexual intercourse, by age ten.

If you're lucky, your children's school might offer a good unit on the biological aspects of anatomy and reproduction geared to a student's learning level. These teachers are trained in content and terminology, but they are also trained to avoid moral and religious teaching, so that part of the process falls to you.

Check out exactly what your children are getting in school.

Check out exactly what your children are getting in school. Ask the teacher or principal for a copy of the health curriculum that includes sex education. You might also talk with your children's teachers, asking them how to "teach" what your children need to know at a given age and to suggest resources.

Also, go to a Christian bookstore and ask for help in finding value-laden books and other resources for both parents and kids in this sensitive area. (Videos are particularly effective because you can view them with your children.) If you have a pastoral counselor or a family life minister in your church, ask them to recommend additional resources.

Dolores Curran

6.31 EXPOSURE TO HOMOSEXUALITY

My husband's brother is a homosexual, and my husband wants to have him over for regular visits. The problem is that he doesn't keep his homosexuality a secret. Because we have a young son, I am uncomfortable having my brother-in-law in our home. My husband thinks I'm being paranoid. Are my reservations out of line?

Because a respected adult, such as an uncle, can have a far-reaching influence on a young boy, you should be forthright in discussing this matter. Together with your husband and his brother, you need to agree on some rules for the brother's visits.

For instance, any sexual double entendre, suggestive language, or arguments in favor of homosexuality should be off limits. Also, he should not be allowed to baby-sit your son. Even when predatory sexual behavior is not a problem, some gay adults feel a responsibility to convince young people that homosexuality is an acceptable lifestyle.

> *Together with your husband and his brother, you need to agree on some rules for the brother's visits.*

Friends and relatives come for visits all the time without discussing their sexual orientation, so these should not be seen as unreasonable requests. If your brother-in-law's motivation is really to be a participating family member, then he should be able to comply with your decisions. However, if he seems bent on converting others to his way of thinking, you have a right to refuse at-home visits.

Jay Kesler

6.32 VERBALLY LASHING OUT IN ANGER

Our kids are generally cooperative and well behaved. But sometimes they push and push and we get angry and boil over. I'm always ashamed after we raise our voices in anger and say things we shouldn't. How can we get control over the volume and tone of voice we use when the kids push us over the brink?

The first step is to relax and accept your humanness. All of us explode at times, especially when we've been pushed to the limit by our children. Guilt has been labeled "the parent hormone" because parents have been taught we should never lose patience or control. Don't believe you are an inferior parent because sometimes you do. It's all part of the parenting package.

The most effective technique is to state a consequence and stick to it.

It sounds as if your kids know how to "push your buttons." If you want to control this ability of theirs, you need to learn how to become more detached. The most effective technique is to state a consequence and stick to it. "If you ask again, it means you're too tired to understand my 'no,' so there will be a 7:30 bedtime tonight instead of eight." When they ask again, simply sympathize, "I knew you needed more sleep," and walk away.

Another response is, "I'll think about this and give you my answer later. But if you ask again, the answer is no," and walk away. Or, "I am starting to feel angry so I'm going to stop and pray about it now." Then walk away.

Walking away is a very effective response when kids push their parents. It tells your children that you have already responded and the matter is closed. If they follow after you, whining and arguing, don't indulge them by listening to them. Simply smile at them, wink, or even yawn. Play the statue on the outside even if you're boiling on the inside.

A mother in one of my parenting workshops keeps a yo-yo in the pocket of her jeans, and when her three young children begin pushing she takes it out, concentrates on it, and spins it up and down. When she gets out her yo-yo, they stop pushing because they know she will no longer argue.

Another technique is to make a little sign reading, "Argument's over," or simply "No" and put it on the refrigerator. When they push, hand it to them, and engage in some other activity. When they continue to argue—and they will—

simply walk away.

Sometimes—at a time when you are close and enjoying one another—it helps to talk about how you feel when they keep pushing. Too often, we wait until we're in the middle of a battle to deal with ongoing and annoying behaviors. Then we tend to blurt out impossible consequences and threats.

In contrast, when you're outdoors sharing a Popsicle with them, you might say, "This is fun. Wouldn't it be nice if we could always be like this? I don't like being angry with you because I love you. What do you think it is that makes me angry?" Give them a chance to list their offensive behaviors and then ask, "What do you think I should do when you keep begging after I say no?"

Kids can come up with ingenious responses for their own discipline, given the opportunity. But even if they don't, you can suggest consequences, timeouts and withdrawal of privileges and ask which they think would work best. Then, later, when the pressure is on, you can refer back to their suggestions. Just be sure to carry them out or they will become merely ideas, not action.

Dolores Curran

6.33 RESTORING A CHILD'S DAMAGED SELF-ESTEEM

On several occasions, my 12-year-old has come home in tears because kids at the junior high ridiculed him about his hair, his struggles in class, his small size, whatever they can think of to use against him. He's absolutely devastated by these thoughtless and cruel comments. My wife and I tell him he's not a klutz or a dummy, but at his age a kid pays more attention to his peers than to his parents. His self-confidence is shaken. I know we can't protect our son forever, but what can we do to restore his damaged self-esteem?

You have described a common, though very painful, situation. It's quite normal for you and your wife to want to lift your son's unhappiness—all the while knowing this is merely the onset of healthy adulthood that requires skills to deal with such issues. If we remove that experience and the attendant pain from our children, we also remove the opportunity for them to build confidence in their ability to handle negative situations. Overcoming painful rejection is actually a first step in building a strong self-esteem.

When a child reaches the age of 12, 13, and 14, he or she has entered the prime-time misery years for many children. At that age, kids judge themselves against their peers and when they come up wanting in any area—and they always will—they feel incompetent, ugly and inferior. Their self-esteem plummets.

Preteens react with a variety of behaviors—withdrawal from family and friends, rebellion, cruelty to those even less-favored than they are, depression, false bravado or even being attracted to a gang mentality. It's as if they're saying, "If you don't like me, I'll just find someone who does."

> *Fortunately, these years are as temporary as they are painful.*

Fortunately, these years are as temporary as they are painful. But they can be tough on families. I could have retired in luxury years ago if I had a dollar for every parent who had confided to me, in anguish, "He used to be such a nice boy. I don't know what happened."

The simple answer is: puberty happened. Puberty is God's way of saying, "It's time to start separating as a limb of your family and to start being your own person so that eventually you can leave the nest whole and competent." This journey from carefree childhood—where children didn't worry about their looks, size, muscles and popularity—into adolescence (where peer approval becomes all consuming) is traumatic for almost everybody.

The good news is that parents can help smooth the path. Your own attitude is crucial. If you accept and project the attitude that this is normal and temporary pain—that you, too, experienced it; that ridicule is typical behavior for many insecure preteens; that you know he has the strength to withstand it—your son will be able to stand up to it, too. If, on the other hand, you show undue concern over his rejection by some of his peers, his anxiety will increase.

Together, you can develop some creative and nonabrasive responses to the ridicule, something along the lines of: "If I weren't short, you wouldn't be tall," or even a simple shrug, a smile, rolled eyes, or cupping a hand to the ear as if he has a hearing problem. If he's nonchalant in his reaction, the scoffers lose their power over him and will soon move on.

If your son is struggling with schoolwork, get him some help. If you are unable to furnish the help he needs, check the area for a gifted high school student who can be on call when he needs it. Peer tutoring can be tremendously effective during these years.

Finally, church youth ministers and leaders of Christian youth organizations can be immensely helpful. They are familiar with problems of preteen self-esteem. If your church doesn't have an active youth ministry, ask your pastor for help in finding one. Groups like Young Life, Youth for Christ, and Teens Encounter Christ offer fellowship, fun and support as well as spirituality with peers whose values do not typically include ridicule and rejection. Many a young teen has found his friends and self-worth in such groups.

Dolores Curran

6.34 SEEING THE POSITIVE SIDE OF PARENTING

There was a time I felt I could go anywhere and do anything whenever I pleased. Marriage and kids, however, have changed all that and every so often I feel a sense of being resentful about my reduced personal freedoms. What are some ways I can begin to see my choices in a positive light?

You're describing a common feeling among parents. To relieve your resentment, try some of these approaches.

First, reshape your dreams to fit reality. Exploring an opportunity, perhaps on a smaller scale, can ease the sensation of being restricted by marriage and family responsibilities.

I have friends who have a toddler. They find themselves resculpting the features of their personal and professional lives. One sensitive area is their love of travel, which they have had to rethink.

"Last summer we visited the Grand Canyon," my friend said. "My personality would have taken us down into the canyon for a week of wilderness camping. I would have experienced the Grand Canyon from top to bottom. Instead, with an 18-month-old and a car full of baby paraphernalia, we did the Grand Canyon in six hours. We trimmed our expectations to fit reality, and we were content. We did it, but we did it differently."

Second, recognize that some of the limits won't last forever. Nearly all of us have put some area of life on hold. "We put off having kids to pursue careers, or we put our jobs on hold to raise children," says one wife and mother. We can't have it all at once, but the time will come when we can stretch ourselves in areas that, right now, are in suspended animation. We can use that time to test the validity of our ambitions and process our dreams into concrete plans. We can take the small steps that turn hopes into reachable goals.

Third, "bloom where you're planted." As sappy as that phrase is, it still contains some useful philosophy. While this doesn't seem to be the year to incorporate my own communications agency, I *can* approach my mothering with flair. And I can find creative challenge in writing freelance advertising copy, as well as doing volunteer work on a publicity campaign. I can put down deep roots in this community and invest myself in the lives of friends and family.

> *"Bloom where you're planted."*

Fourth, count the cost and make needed changes. It's too easy to allow the apparent limits of one's circumstances to be an excuse to cover laziness or fear of the unknown. I respect one couple for their conviction that is leading them and their four children to Venezuela to teach in a school there. And I look up to the tenured professor and his wife who left their home in Florida to help establish a university in a remote area of Africa.

To be honest, I'd like to see more of their daring spirit in my own life. Some of us are hiding behind closed doors when we should simply count the cost and then pay it—considering it a worthwhile investment in the future. Marriage and parenting can limit our options, but lives are shaped by committed relationships that encourage us toward lasting values and toward exercising our options in light of an eternal perspective.

Nancy Sommerville Langham

6.35 PREPARING FOR PARENTHOOD

We're thinking about starting a family in the next two years, but frankly the thought of adding children to our lives overwhelms us. How can we prepare ourselves to be parents? And most importantly, how can we make sure our marriage will withstand the pressures of parenting?

To begin preparing for parenthood, a couple should discuss such questions as "Will children come between us and hurt our relationship? Can we afford kids? Will we both continue to work outside the home? What about paternity leave? How many children do we want and how close together? If we can't have children, would we want to adopt?" All are good questions to ask, and answer, before becoming parents.

With regard to minimizing the stresses that children can bring to a marriage, here are two areas to work on before the kids arrive.

Solidify your bond. When you have children, your marriage will become less partner-focused and more child-focused, so your relationship needs to be strong before the kids come along. Get comfortable with each other, explore your roles and work at understanding the ways you are alike or different.

Learn how to really talk. Many couples who had few problems communicating before the wedding find it difficult to talk about their feelings now that they're married. If that describes you, try some of these tips to help you discuss your hopes and fears.

Learn to listen and not simply react. Apply the advice in James 1:19: "Everyone should be quick to listen, slow to speak and slow to become angry." In our family, we condensed this verse to three words—"listen, don't react."

Be aware of your total message. Nothing is worse than speaking the right words but contradicting the message with signs of underlying hostility, bitterness or anger. Make sure your words, your nonverbal cues and your tone of voice all communicate the same message.

Stress the positive. It takes five positive statements to offset just one negative statement, so go slow in expressing your negative feelings, and emphasize the positive ones.

Avoid finger pointing. Don't begin sentences with the words "you" or "why," since they usually lead to statements or questions that accuse or attack. Instead, take responsibility for your own feelings. There is a big difference between "I feel so alone. Can we talk?" and "You always ignore me. Why don't you ever talk to me?"

Ask questions. It keeps the communication cycle going until you both agree that what you said is what the other person heard.

Becoming parents creates such a drastic change that most couples experience moderate, or even severe, crisis. The added stress can exacerbate any existing tension between partners and drive them farther apart. Too easily, the marriage can drop on the priority list down below washing windows and cleaning toilets.

David and Claudia Arp

6.36 FACING THE EMPTY NEST

I'm looking forward to the empty-nest years and so is my husband. And yet I'm a little concerned about this season of life, especially after watching several couples at church experience a very rocky transition from a home filled with kids to an empty nest. How can we make the transition to this stage of our life smooth and the later years rewarding?

When the last child moves out many couples go through a period of major crisis.

Over a lifetime, most couples will spend as many years together without children living at home as they do with kids underfoot. Unfortunately, when the last child moves out many couples go through a period of major crisis.

We entered this stage with a low supply of emotional energy. While our kids were growing up, we did our best to support one another. But we were often overwhelmed by the demands of our three adolescent sons. There was little time left to devote to our friendship, let alone intimacy. So when our sons left home we had to redefine our relationship, renew the love, and try to regain the close companionship that characterized the beginning of our marriage. Here are the three most important steps to take.

Redefine your marital focus. When the kids leave, you are faced with a difficult shift: the transition from a child-focused marriage to a more partner-focused relationship. As couples redefine their relationship, it either becomes more intimate or it slowly disintegrates.

In her book *The Good Marriage: How and Why Love Lasts* (Houghton Mifflin), Judith S. Wallerstein writes, "The sense of being part of a couple is what consolidates modern marriage. It is the strongest rampart against the relentless threat of our divorce culture. To become partner-focused means continually adjusting to each other."

It also requires readjusting your relationship with your now-adult children. You must become willing to let go—to release your children. If the kids being on their own makes you feel needy or insecure, lean on your mate for strength and support.

Once you let go of your kids, it's time to reconnect with them on an adult level. Your home may be emptied of children, but your love and concern for them never empties. And when they marry, you'll need to work at expanding the family circle. Healthy relationships with your adult children, their spouses, and your grandchildren will enrich the second half of your marriage. At the same time, you need a life together that is separate from outsiders.

Become close companions. With fewer responsibilities to your kids, your marriage can become more personal and more fulfilling. At this time of life a gender shift begins to occur that can increase your potential for building an even closer relationship. Many women become more focused and assertive, and are eager to try their professional wings—especially if they dedicated the first half of their adult life to nurturing and parenting their children. Simultaneously, many husbands decide to slow down and enjoy life more. For men over 50, work may not be so important. These changes, when handled wisely, can produce new creativity, deeper meaning and renewed playfulness to help you become closer companions.

Keep seeking what is best. Every day brings a new opportunity to build your marriage. As you live out your marriage, concentrate on these relationship enhancers:

- Accept each other. Let go of past disappointments, choose to forgive each other and commit to making the rest of your marriage the best of your marriage. Holding on to grudges will prevent you from developing a new, more loving marriage.
- Become best friends. Stretch your boundaries and grow together. The greatest indicator of successful marriage is the couple's friendship.
- Have some fun! You got married in the first place because you enjoyed being together. Friendship, humor and fun are serious business! So wherever you are in your marriage journey, take time to enjoy each other and celebrate your partnership.

When you look ahead to your 50th anniversary, what do you want your marriage to look like? At our 50th, we hope others will notice how much we enjoy each other, are intimate friends, and are still growing, changing and adapting to each other.

David and Claudia Arp

CHAPTER 7

MAKING SENSE OF MONEY MATTERS

MAKING SENSE OF
MONEY
MATTERS

"Money is that something which buys everything but happiness, and takes a man everywhere but heaven" (John Woodbridge Patten).

In an affluent age it is important to remember that Jesus viewed money as a spiritual liability. Jesus says, "I tell you, it is easier for a camel to go through the eye of a needle than for a rich person to enter the kingdom of God" (Mt. 19:24). And again: "Where your treasure is, there your heart will be also (Mt. 6:21).

God created us for His glory, and His desire is that we have Him as our treasure, not money. We can't have it both ways. "No one can be a slave of two masters, since either he will hate one and love the other, or be devoted to one and despise the other. You cannot be slaves of God and of money" (Mt. 6:24). The first and last commandment make it clear that we are to have no other gods before us, including money (Ex. 20: 3, 17). Loving money is coveting and coveting is idolatry (Col. 3:5).

God owns all things, including the cattle on a thousand hills (Ps. 50:15). Solomon said, "Wealth and honor come from you . . . everything comes from you, and we have given you only what comes from your hand" (1 Ch. 29:12, 14, NIV). Consequently, a loose grip is required as we handle our money and possessions because "the love of money is a root of all kinds of evil" (1 Tm. 6:10). Like a trap or snare, money lures us into thinking that true happiness and success are measured by what we have. Remember, "one's life is not in the abundance of his possessions" (Lk. 12:15). The one with the most toys does not win! Rather it is godliness with contentment that is great gain (1 Tm. 6:6).

For those wanting to get rich

First Timothy 6 gives us important warnings and instruction about the use of money:

1. Remember, you can't take it with you (cf. 1 Tm. 6: 7; Ps. 49:17).
2. Remember, the essentials of food, clothing and shelter (implied in the word clothing) is all that is required to be content (v. 8, cf. Php. 4:11-13). (Keeping up with the Joneses is buying things we don't need with money we don't have to impress people we don't like!)
3. Remember, the love of money destroys people's lives and their souls (vv. 9-10).
4. Flee the love of money and pursue righteousness (v. 11)—seek first God's kingdom (cf. Mt. 6:33).
5. Fight the good fight of faith (v. 12). Empty your hands of the things of this world so that you might take hold of the riches that are ours in Christ waiting for us in heaven (v. 12).

And for those who are rich (vv. 17-19)

1. Don't be arrogant—your wealth comes from God. You are not superior because of your wealth (cf. 1 Ch. 29:12; Jms. 2:5).
2. Don't put your hope in your wealth—place it in God, in his ability to supply all your needs (cf. Pr. 11:2; 23:5; 27:24; Php. 4:19).
3. Do good—be rich in good deeds, generous and willing to share. We are called to be rich toward God (cf. Lk. 12:21). We do this by meeting the needs of other Christians (cf. Ac. 4:34; 1 Co. 16:2).

PRAYER: Lord, keep our lives free from the love of money and help us to be content with what we have (cf. Heb. 13:5). Forgive us for coveting. May we only and always find our true satisfaction in You. Increase our appetite for You. Strengthen our faith so that we will seek first Your kingdom over and above the things of this world. Thank You for the opportunity to use our money for Your glory. Open our eyes to the needs around us. Make us eager to give and eager to be generous. Keep our eyes on You so that we will not be tempted by the deceitfulness of wealth. Deliver our souls from this deadly trap. Amen.

7.1 WHEN A WIFE EARNS MORE THAN HER HUSBAND

I'm having a problem with my ego. My wife and I both work, but her salary is almost double what I'm making. At first I thought it was great that she had been offered a job with such a good salary. However, the fact she's the main breadwinner in our family is starting to get to me. Why am I now struggling with something that a year ago wasn't a problem?

> *Even though we understand something rationally, we may still have a deep psychological struggle with it.*

If the old saying is true—"understanding the problem is nine-tenths of the solution"—then you are well on your way toward working this out. However, even though we understand something rationally, we may still have a deep psychological struggle with it. I suspect that's at least part of what is happening to you. You want to be supportive of your wife, her talents, and her job. You're no doubt proud of her abilities. So you know, in your mind, that you ought to feel good about her work and her earnings. And yet on the emotional level you don't feel good about the situation. You have pinpointed it as an ego problem. Perhaps it is. Then again, you may be making half the salary your wife is because of a past commitment. If a man goes into a career in the arts, for example, or into a people-helping profession such as teaching, social work, or the ministry, he may never earn enough to support his family in the way he would like. If that's the case, talking about your feelings may help you recommit yourselves to that earlier decision.

On the other hand, if your wife is working only to maintain a lifestyle that she or both of you want, you may decide that this desire is in conflict with your commitment.

You mention that you wife "really enjoys" her job. Could part of the problem be that you don't enjoy your work? That's something you ought to talk about, too. Maybe you should look for a job you find more fulfilling. Talking together should help you examine a wide variety of options.

Let me also offer a warning. Ego problems that begin as "feelings" can become even more troublesome if little "actions" result. There's a temptation when we're not feeling like we measure up to try to bring other people down to our level. I've seen many men in your situation do little things to depreciate their wives. Sometimes it's deliberate, but a lot of times it's an unconscious response—complaints about the way she keeps the house or that she isn't meeting his sexual needs. This sort of thing is far more damaging to a marriage than the feelings you have, so watch out for signs of a critical spirit. If you make certain those feelings don't turn into unloving actions, you'll be able to work things out by talking with your wife.

Jay Kesler

7.2 GETTING OUT OF DEBT

We made some poor money decisions the first few years of our marriage and now we have $12,000 in consumer debt. We realize that our excessive spending was wrong and we're determined to change our ways. How can we reduce our debt?

The following suggestions should help you pay off your debt. Choose the ones that work best for you and your spouse, then start erasing your debt today.

Do you have any assets that can be sold? Even small things sold through a garage sale can help you pay off smaller debts. But the sale of bigger items such as cars, boats, investments and perhaps even homes should also be considered.

Consider using savings accounts. Using a low-yielding savings account to reduce high-cost debt such as credit card debt or an installment loan is a guaranteed high-yield investment. But don't tap into the emergency fund that you have set aside to protect you and your family against unexpected bills.

Try to double up on payments. By doubling up on credit payments and cutting expenses in other areas, it's possible to pay off debt much more quickly. There are also benefits to paying home mortgages on a bimonthly schedule, or even making just one extra payment per year. Either approach has a dramatic impact on the number of payments needed to pay off the mortgage.

Keep constant the total amount of payments you're making each month. Pay off your smallest debt first. When that is gone, apply that payment to your next-smallest debt. For example, if you have several credit card and installment payments totaling $500 per month, instead of reducing the amount paid each month as the debts are eliminated, continue to spend a total of $500 a month on repayments.

Review your living expense summary and decide where you can cut expenses. You might cut down on entertainment, clothing, food, or your home-maintenance budget. In almost every family, as much as 40 percent of the budget could be used to repay debt, but it requires a change in lifestyle. Then, apply that amount to paying off specific debts.

Review your income-tax withholdings. If you receive an income-tax refund, consider reducing your withholdings to the amount of your projected tax liability. Then apply the increase in your take-home pay to your debt repayment. Determine your tax liability for next year by looking at last year's income tax return to see how much you paid. Then calculate the effect of any pay raises, the birth of a child, having an older child leave home, and so on. After you have determined what you're likely to owe, fill out a new W-4 form. But don't reduce your income tax withholding below your projected tax liability. If you do, you're borrowing from the government to pay someone else. The day of reckoning is merely postponed to April 15.

Don't decrease your charitable giving. Giving should be the first priority use of money, because it is recognition of God's ownership of everything. And in most cases, avoid debt-consolidation loans. Such loans don't solve the basic problem of overspending.

> *Be careful about seeking a second full-time income.*

Be careful about seeking a second full-time income. If your family can cover expenses with one income, you shouldn't seek a second income merely to increase revenues. When you consider the additional expenses of tithing, taxes, childcare, transportation and so on, the economic benefit of a fulltime homemaker getting a job is often almost nonexistent.

There are exceptions, however. A family may face unexpected medical bills or desire to send their children to a private school. In such cases, a second family income may be the means of providing the extra money. Another possible exception is if a wife takes a part-time or temporary job to help pay off debt.

Ron Blue

7.3 RUNAWAY HOLIDAY SPENDING

I was staggered at the bills that came in last January. It's obvious our holiday spending is out of hand. We both know in our hearts that gift giving isn't what Christmas is all about, yet the pressure to give and give generously is amazing. How can we make it through the holidays without going broke?

For most families, Christmas itself is the ultimate big-ticket item. Some conscientious souls dutifully put aside money during the year so they'll be able to afford all that holiday cheer. Others activate the plastic card and try not to think about the January bills.

A lot of us feel guilty about being swept along with the tide of excess, and some of us have actually done something about it. Here are some starting points.

Throw away the catalogues. My husband has jokingly said, "Catalogues are from the devil." I used to laugh; now I don't think it's so funny. The more of these tempters I look at, the more I want, and the more I think I need. The same is true with my children. It's a hard discipline, but now, with a couple of exceptions, the catalogues go in the trash.

Don't go in the mall after Thanksgiving. The commercialism of malls is the real Grinch, robbing us of our joy and belief in the deeper meaning of Christmas.

Withdraw from commercial TV. Or at least consider cutting back. Instead, videotape good Christmas specials and fast-forward through the advertisements.

Encourage joyful giving in your kids (and yourself). Let your children drop the coins into the Salvation Army kettles. Plan a family service project. Buy gifts for a needy family and let the kids help pick them out. Young children have naturally generous impulses. The other day our three-year-old came running downstairs with a fistful of coins. As I tried to pry them out of her hand she exclaimed, "But Mommy, I get to give these to the poor people!" Get to give—what a reminder!

Laura Crosby

7.4 WHY COUPLES FIGHT ABOUT MONEY

I never dreamed we'd argue so much and so often about finances. We seem to agree on so many other things with minimal negotiations and compromises but money remains a real issue. Why do couples have so much difficulty with finances?

Money is the reason given in 50 percent of the divorce cases, but I believe money problems are symptoms of an inability to relate on other levels. How you use money reflects your priorities. For example, one spouse may want to furnish the house, while the other wants to take a vacation. They call it a money problem, but it's really a priority problem, or a problem of communicating about their priorities.

When we talk about priorities, there are bound to be disagreements.

Couples come up with lots of excuses for not discussing money. The problem is that when we talk about priorities, there are bound to be disagreements. So usually, to keep peace, we don't talk about it.

However, couples can improve their communication about finances by beginning with a commitment. Unless a couple has a mutual commitment to work together on their finances, they will probably stop doing it when the going gets tough. Every year, a couple should set aside an hour or two, and each should write on a sheet of paper every financial goal he or she can think of. Next, they should set those goals in priority order.

Then they can get together and compare their lists. It's important that they develop a third list of *"our* goals." That's where a couple works through the priorities of life. They need to do it on paper because both spouses can see it, agree to it, and avoid misunderstandings later on.

Ron Blue, with Ken Sidey

7.5 BECOMING ONE—FINANCIALLY

Several couples we know have a strong his/her mentality when it comes to finances. We'd like to be more unified in our approach, but how do we successfully move from two financial approaches to one?

Learning to listen to and respect your mate's money perspective is one way to invest in a valuable commodity—your marriage. Here's how to get a head start in an area where most couples flounder.

Without self-criticism or self-justification, identify your own relationship with money. What does money mean to you? Does it make you feel powerful, anxious, guilty, loved, responsible or secure? What assumptions and values about money did you develop while you were growing up? *Avoid labeling your spouse's attitudes as right or wrong.* Try to understand one another's money history. Listen for the hurts, fears, wishes and hopes that get funneled into money. Try to empathize rather than criticize. Honoring each other's needs can help you respectfully negotiate your financial decisions. Remember: respect breeds trust.

Avoid labeling your spouse's attitudes as right or wrong.

Learn from each other. Temporarily suspend your own beliefs and see what your spouse has to teach you. A saver can learn a new kind of security when stretched by a spouse who exchanges money for present enjoyment, or who finds satisfaction in giving.

Together, list your priorities. What is valuable to you? Identify the top priorities you share and what this means to your budget. In my husband's family, the adventure of traveling around the United States was a high priority, and their budget was geared toward that. They did without some things, but family gatherings today are enlivened by stories of being "chased down a mountain by a snowstorm" and the potholes on the old Alaska Highway.

Get sound advice. Some conflicts over money come from simply not being aware of your options. Ask someone you trust to refer you to a qualified financial adviser who will respect your particular priorities.

Beverly J. Burch

7.6 SAVING MADE EASY

With our tight budget it seems impossible to save. But I read about others who live on less than we do and still manage to build a significant nest egg. What are some painless ways to save a few dollars?

Financial whiz kids tell us most money messes have more to do with spending than with income. Most of us probably know this, but in the hectic pace of life we're too weary to shop wisely and spend less. Here are a few ways to put extra change in your pocket by first changing your perspective. Your goal is not deprivation, but replacing old shopping habits with new, wiser approaches.

Nix shopping for fun. It's a fact that if you go shopping, you'll most likely spend money. Our culture has turned shopping into recreation, even a form of therapy. Merchants know this better than anyone: that's why they entice us with music and espresso bars. To fight back, *put yourself on a two-week moratorium from shopping for fun.* Instead, visit a friend or take a power walk around the neighborhood and pocket the cash.

Skip a week at the grocery store. Take an inventory of your cupboards and freezer. Is food going to waste? Use it up before it's too late. With the exception of milk, bread and eggs, most of us could feed our families for weeks using the food we already have on hand. By using up the food on hand you can drastically limit what you spend on groceries.

Use things up. Take the grocery-shopping principle one step further by considering all the items that are languishing in closets or on shelves throughout your home. Train yourself to use the things you have already purchased. Not only will you begin to get your money's worth, you'll be less inclined to purchase other items that don't have a clear purpose.

Shop with a list. Whether you're shopping for nuts and bolts or pet food, try to stick to your list. Allow for an occasional impulse item, within reason. Being frugal means shopping smart, not being a tight-fisted grump.

Shop with a list.

Say "no"—half the time. There's no need to deprive yourself completely. Even small changes in daily routines will save money. For instance, bring a sack lunch to work two or three days a week.

Turn shopping into "an adventure in saving." Team up for that next journey to the home improvement center or grocery store. Depend on each other to be the "strong one" when one of you is tempted to make an impulsive purchase.

Outfox the merchandisers. Impulse items are displayed up front. Simply walk to the back of the store to find the closeout sales. Also, nearly all items at eye- or arm-level are more expensive. So bend over or reach up to save significant amounts of cash.

Make it a family affair. Teach your kids to spend wisely. Show them the actual difference, using real money, between Sugar-Frosted Fluffy O's and a generic brand. And discuss other ways to save money, like not allowing the water to run while brushing teeth.

Cynthia G. Yates

7.7 CREATING THE "I HATE TO BUDGET" BUDGET

We've been married six years and have yet to develop a budget. We have a general idea of what we should or shouldn't spend, but nothing that is as elaborate as all the money experts recommend. Both my wife and I hate the word "budget" and feel like financial failures since we can't seem to come up with one that works. Is there some way that we can finally create a budget that is realistic and user-friendly?

That's a good question. How do you go about designing a budget you can live with? I polled several financial planners and came up with a basic format for any couple getting down to business with their money.

First, answer three basic questions:

1. What is our total income after taxes?
2. What do we need to spend? (Rent, groceries, bills and so on.)
3. What's left over? (If your answer is "nothing," rework #2.)

Next take the leftover money and divide it into "yours, mine and ours." The "ours" money is for family luxuries like a vacation and family goals like college educations or a larger home.

Divide the rest between the two of you. Both of you should have a monthly sum of money you call your own and spend however you choose. Make it a small amount if money is tight, but find money for yourselves to assuage the budget blues. Set a date to re-evaluate your budget, and tinker with it until it suits both of you.

Talk about everything: your hopes for the future, your feelings about debt and savings, your need for insurance, and your personal attitudes about money. Don't try to change each other, though. Work toward compromise. If you're a saver and your spouse is a spender, allot equal amounts for both.

Such honesty will almost invariably create conflict. If you find yourselves at a stalemate—fighting more and compromising less—consider consulting an objective third party trained in dealing with financial and communication issues in marriage.

Lynda Rutledge Stephenson

7.8 SQUABBLES THAT MASQUERADE AS MONEY FIGHTS

We sometimes fight about money, but later I can't help but wonder if we're really arguing about something else. Is there such a thing as a "fake" money fight?

Fake money fights can be easily spotted.

There certainly is and fake money fights can be easily spotted. They're usually bogus when:

1. *You keep having the same fight over and over.* You get that "deja vu" feeling, and you know you've actually got something else on your mind. For a real money question, you should come to some decision after only a few discussions. Stop and try to understand what the *real* agenda is.

2. *Your money talks create highly emotional responses.* Usually this is a sign that your hidden agenda is rearing its ugly head again. For instance, when power is the problem, you may find yourself saying, "So you think I'm too dumb to understand about our money. You always thought you were better than me!" Money discussions shouldn't disintegrate into personal attacks. When you see that happening, ask yourself, "Are we still talking about money?"

Lynda Rutledge Stephenson

7.9 AGREEING ON CHARITABLE GIVING

I've been thinking we should increase the amount we give to a relief organization, but my wife gets upset when I bring up the topic. She feels that giving more would threaten our family's welfare. I feel sure that our family's finances will remain intact, and that God will continue to provide for us. Where do spouses draw the line between financial security and giving in faith?

The answer to the question "How much should we give?" is between you, your spouse, and God. In some ways it would be nice if the Bible told us an exact amount (or percentage) to give. That would allow us to feel that a certain portion of our income is God's and the rest is ours to do with as we please. But the truth is that God owns it all, and part of our training in obedience is learning to let Him lead us in this area.

Taken together, the tithes and other gifts that are commanded in the Old Testament actually total 23 percent—not 10 percent (Nm. 18:21). The New Testament sets a higher standard for giving—the example of Christ—and mentions tithing only in connection with the old covenant. The new guideline for giving is found in 2 Corinthians 9:6-7: "The person who sows sparingly will also reap sparingly, and the person who sows generously will also reap generously. Each person should do as he has decided in his heart—not out of regret or out of necessity, for God loves a cheerful giver." And 2 Corinthians 8:12 instructs us to give in relation to our prosperity.

The tithes and other gifts that are commanded in the Old Testament actually total 23 percent—not 10 percent.

Since the question "how much?" does not have a black-and-white answer, couples must discuss this issue and then create their own financial plan—including a family budget and a plan for giving. Once a couple gets their living expenses under control, they are often surprised to discover that they *do* have the wherewithal to give.

In one consulting appointment with a married couple, I discovered a tremendous lack of harmony in the area of charitable giving. The wife wanted to give, and the husband didn't. Although they had adequate means, the husband had strong feelings about providing amply for his family. After creating a financial plan for them, I showed how various levels of giving would affect their current cash flow and the long-term growth of their net worth. At that point, the husband became more comfortable with giving. It has been exciting to see the increased harmony in their marriage, not to mention their significant giving. They have increased their annual giving ten times. Creating a plan put an end to their conflict and increased their satisfaction about giving—and about their marriage.

Giving is good when it is done prayerfully and in harmony with your spouse; when it does not cause a stumbling block for the recipient or for your spouse; and when it is done with the right attitude. But giving is *not* good if it drives a wedge between the two of you. Remember: God doesn't need your money. Giving is for *your* benefit.

Ron Blue

7.10 CREATING A BUDGET WITHOUT A STEADY SALARY

My husband works in sales, and is paid solely by commission. He's a hard worker and usually brings home a good paycheck. However, some weeks are slow and we sometimes go as long as a month or more with very little income. This makes it difficult to budget our money to cover monthly bills, as well as setting aside money for long-range expenses such as insurance premiums, auto maintenance and real estate taxes. How can we budget our money when we never know how much we'll have, or when it will be coming in?

Although it's difficult to control your cash flow while working on commission, it isn't impossible. And it's really not unlike the system that applies to a couple earning a steady salary. The process can be broken down to two essential items: 1) Set up a budget that allocates your funds to meet expenses at predetermined levels; and 2) know the amount of cash you have on hand at all times relative to your predetermined level of spending.

> *You need a cash-flow system that has the same effect as an "envelope system."*

To meet these objectives, you need a cash-flow system that has the same effect as an "envelope system." In the envelope system, you divide a predetermined portion of your paycheck into envelopes that cover various living expenses. The envelopes are marked mortgage, groceries, utilities, giving, recreation, and so forth. When the money in a particular envelope is used up, you stop spending on that item until the next pay period. Actually, putting money into envelopes is a good way to implement a cash-flow system until your spending habits are established.

Keep in mind that only a fixed amount of money is allocated to living expenses each month. During periods when your husband is earning high commissions, allow the surplus funds to build up in your checking account. That money will cover any shortages in income during times of low (or no) commissions.

Obviously the best way to start the budget is during the high-income period—when your income exceeds your expenses. If that isn't possible, it may be necessary to delay allocating funds to annual expenses (such as saving for a vacation or setting aside money to cover life insurance premiums) and concentrate instead on allocating money only for current living expenses until the commissions improve.

The best way for a commissioned salesperson to be on a budget and not overspend is to set your living expenses equal to the lowest level your income might drop to, and then consider anything over that as extra, to be saved for long-term needs, emergencies or luxuries you agree to purchase. This may be difficult, especially if you work on a straight commission basis. But try to be as conservative as possible, and save money during high commission times so you'll have the extra money you need for expenses that come only once or twice a year.

Set your living expenses equal to the lowest level your income might drop to.

Ron Blue

7.11 LIVING ON ONE INCOME

We hope to have our first child within the next two years, and when that times comes my wife plans to quit her job. We'll be shifting from two incomes that support two people to one income that will support three people, and frankly I'm worried. How can we make my salary stretch to support three people?

You are already ahead of the game. By preparing a couple of years in advance, you will be able to ease into your transition.

The first plan of action is to find time for you and your wife to set short- and long-term goals—in many areas of your marriage, not just finances. By setting spiritual, emotional, mental, physical, family and career goals now, you will be able to have a clear view of where you are headed and a better understanding of why you are going there.

When you have established basic goals, prepare a cash-flow analysis. Purchase a budget book to keep track of where and how your money is being spent. Analyze your spending habits for a couple of months so you can determine where to make cuts. If you are paying off credit cards, car loans, or other consumer debt, you should start using your wife's salary to pay off those debts more aggressively.

Once you're out of debt, start putting your wife's income into savings and live solely on your income, based on the budget you have created. When spending problems arise, the flexibility you have built into your budget will accommodate unexpected needs.

It typically takes two years before a couple can come up with a workable budget, so be patient. You have plenty of time to get it all worked out. You are right on target for reaching your goal.

Ron Blue

7.12 LENDING MONEY TO RELATIVES

What are the dos and don'ts of lending money to and borrowing from relatives? Should we insist that we all sign a binding agreement outlining the terms of repayment, the interest rate, and the timetable for repayment? Are there tax penalties against personal loans among family members?

As a general rule, I don't recommend that you lend or borrow money from family members because of the financial and relational risks involved. The financial risk—losing your money—is obvious, and it's a risk you take when borrowing or lending money to anyone.

An additional risk you take in borrowing from relatives is the risk of changing your relationship with them. You might feel an obligation toward your relatives for helping you out. Or you may begin to resent them because you were put in a position to need their financial resources and now they have some power over you because you owe them money.

You also run a relational risk if you loan money to family members. You may begin to feel that you have some power over them, and therefore have some control over their behavior. Or you may not like the way your relatives are using the money, and this can become a stumbling block in your relationship.

Given these precautions, if you decide to lend money to or borrow from relatives, I advise you *always* to have a written agreement so that both parties will be well aware of what is expected of them and there won't be unrealistic expectations regarding interest rate, frequency or amount of payments, and the length of time of the loan.

One final warning: When you are lending money to or borrowing from a relative, there may be tax consequences. If you loan money to anyone, whether a relative or not, and the amount is greater than $10,000, you must charge interest. If you do not, the IRS will make you pay tax on a fair rate of interest on the amount that you loaned, even if you did not receive the interest. Before you loan money to a relative, consult your tax adviser to make sure you are following the tax laws, since these situations can become rather complex.

Ron Blue

When you are lending money to or borrowing from a relative, there may be tax consequences.

7.13 MAKING SENSE OF INSURANCE OPTIONS

My wife and I are in our mid-twenties, and recently we've been besieged by insurance agents. I understand the need for adequate life insurance, but the different types of insurance available confuse me. I have no idea which one is best for us. Can you offer any suggestions?

There are basically four different types of life insurance: term; traditional whole life; the hybrid product (a combination of whole life and term); and universal life.

In general, term insurance can meet most of a young family's insurance needs. At your age, you could begin with an annual renewable term policy, which provides maximum coverage for the lowest initial cost. However, the cost of the premiums will increase annually, making it difficult to maintain this type of policy beyond, say, age 60.

In contrast, the initial premiums on a traditional whole-life policy are more expensive than a term policy. But they don't increase from one year to the next, and a whole-life policy also has the advantage of building up a cash value. While many people say they don't need this "forced savings" plan, experience has shown me that most people do a poor job of saving for the future. So I consider the cash value aspect of a whole-life policy to be helpful.

The hybrid product has some characteristics of both whole-life and term insurance. The premiums are typically lower than a traditional whole-life policy but higher than a term policy. There is a buildup of cash value, but at a lower rate than the pure whole-life policies. The percentage of whole-life versus term insurance initially purchased will dictate the amount of the premiums and the number of years you have to pay.

A universal life policy is essentially a combination of an investment vehicle and term life insurance. The primary advantages are flexibility with regard to the premium you pay, as well as the death benefit that the policy will pay out. There is also flexibility in withdrawing cash from the policy. However, a policyholder needs to realize that varying the premium payments may under-fund the contract in later years, causing the insurance coverage to expire.

For long-term needs, I recommend that couples go with a strong mutual company with a good agent who will be around to service the product 15 to 20 years down the road. The product type will depend on your available cash, but the traditional whole-life policy may be the best choice for most couples.

Ron Blue

7.14 LIVING WITH A CARELESS SPENDER

Since my husband often spends money we don't have, we decided to create a budget that allows for individual allowances. Yet, even with this arrangement, he continues to spend more than the amount that is allocated to him. We're struggling to meet our basic financial obligations and his careless spending makes our financial situation even more tenuous. Besides feeling betrayed by his irresponsible behavior, I'm tired of playing the heavy who must enforce the rules. What other options do I have that would improve the situation?

Statistics indicate that money is one of the leading causes of divorce, but that's because money is symbolic of so many things—effort, self-worth, and status, to name a few. It's also a symbol of your unity as a couple. But perhaps you can also see your situation as a manifestation of complementary personalities, which are usually considered a strength in a marriage. You are the responsible one, balancing your husband's more laissez-faire attitude toward money.

If one person doesn't take responsibility, the family can fall into debt to the point of ruin.

Though it's understandable that you're tired of playing the "heavy," consider your other options. You can leave the situation as it is, and endure a chronic emotional headache. You can give up and dodge creditors for the rest of your life. Or you can suffer serious marital problems over it. The option you've chosen, to try to confront the situation and work out a solution, really is the best way. In financial matters, if one person doesn't take responsibility, the family can fall into debt to the point of ruin.

So I urge you to confront your husband. But see it as a challenge brought on by your complementary personalities, not just as his problem. Say, "We as a family have a problem. The problem is we don't have enough money to go around. Together we need to decide on a way to solve this dilemma." Let your husband know how serious this is to you and how much you fear for your future. Then suggest any or all of the following.

Many people who experience this problem go to a financial counselor. In effect, the counselor becomes the "heavy" to which you are both accountable. He or she sets up a system for you to follow. Because you've paid someone to help you, and because it's more embarrassing to lose face in front of someone outside the family, this method often works. Of course, your husband would have to be willing to meet with this person.

Another option, if you decide to try it on your own, is to move to a cash-only system. It sounds like you've attempted at least some version of this; you may need to take it a bit further. I'm amazed at the number of people from all economic and educational levels who work this way, simply because their credit card was too tempting and they got into trouble. Basically what you do is destroy your credit cards (or, if you'd rather, agree that you alone will keep them for emergency use only). You, as the spouse who finds it easier not to spend money, would keep the checkbook. Together you divide up cash in envelopes marked for certain purposes. Then you each live off the money in your envelopes for the week.

If, say, by Wednesday your husband's money is gone and he has no access to the checkbook or credit cards, he's going to have to come to you and say he's out of money. Then the two of you can rationally decide why that happened: did you not allow enough money, did he spend too much on lunch, did he buy something else that wasn't in the budget? He may have to make some tough choices, such as not eating much for lunch at the end of the week. It's possible that this may be the first time in his life that he confronts the consequences of his spending choices.

There are also a number of books written by Christians that deal with this issue. Visit the bookstore together and select a book you both can agree on. Then work together to follow the author's advice. Whatever you do, don't give up and allow your family to fall into massive debt. You're on the right track—don't give up.

Jay Kesler

7.15 KEEPING CHURCH GIVING A PRIORITY

As Christians, we know that we're to give to our church. But on some Sundays doing so is a real financial stretch, and we either give less or don't give at all. Of course, we feel guilty and try to do better; but within a few months the cycle repeats itself. What are we doing wrong when it comes to regular, consistent church giving?

Giving to help meet the needs of the church or to feed the hungry can, more often than not, seem financially impossible—especially when more immediate needs are sitting at your own dinner table! Still, Christ's expectations in this regard seem all too clear—leaving us, His followers, with the challenge of being obedient while still finding a way to pay our bills.

Over the years I have discovered three basic issues that make it difficult for Christians to be obedient in the area of charitable giving.

First, people don't give because they don't know how much money they actually have. In other words, they don't manage their money based on an established family budget.

Second, they don't give because they don't know how or where to give. Many couples don't realize there are ways to give without disrupting their cash flow, such as establishing trusts, giving away appreciated property, using private foundations and community foundations. (Making use of these options often requires expert advice.)

And finally, they don't give because they fail to plan ahead. Rather than establishing long-term giving goals, many couples wait until specific needs are presented and then react to them. Without a plan, priorities are nonexistent.

All of us need to make a concerted—and conscientious—effort to develop a plan that is consistent with the financial priorities set forth in the Bible. If we don't, then life's inevitable surprises—car repairs or medical bills—will consistently interfere with our desire and our ability to give.

Each of us is responsible to prioritize the use of our income. To help us do that, the Bible provides four financial priorities. First, God calls us to give back to Him what is His in the first place (Pr. 3:9, 1 Co. 16:2); to pay taxes (Rm. 13:7, Mt. 22:21); to repay our debts (Ps. 37:21); and to provide for our family's needs (1 Tm. 5:8). Any money remaining after these obligations have been met is the amount available for us to set aside for the future, or to fund the lifestyle we believe God would have us live. In too many cases, however, our lifestyles are the top priority, with giving relegated to a fourth or even fifth priority.

God calls us to give back to Him what is His in the first place.

Most of the time, our giving is done with discretionary dollars—that is, the dollars left over after the bills are paid and our family is supplied with food, housing and clothing. The problem, of course, is that for many couples there simply isn't much money left over; and we feel frustrated and guilty that we aren't able to give more. As a result, let me suggest that you avoid leaving the amount of your gift to whatever cash is left over at the end of the month. Instead, set aside a certain amount every week, perhaps in a separate bank account. It may be that you don't give your full tithe amount weekly, but leave some reserve funds in the "giving account" to meet unexpected giving opportunities that come throughout the year. When you do this, you are setting aside money—as a first priority—to be given away. And you are removing some of the temptation to regard those "giving dollars" as discretionary funds to be used for family or personal expenses.

When unexpected expenses arise and it appears that the only possible way to meet them is to use money designated for charitable giving, you should seek counsel from your pastor or a friend who will hold you accountable. The two of you may determine that you'll have to give less for a while, or you may decide not to give anything until the debt is paid off. Whatever the decision, the caring counsel of a friend or pastor will help you think through the right strategy—not to mention hold you accountable for getting back on track once the unexpected expenses are paid off.

Ron Blue

7.16 CONFUSED ABOUT TITHING

My wife grew up in a church that stressed giving a ten-percent tithe. My church background stressed an approach to giving that was tied to obedience, not to a definite percentage. What does the Bible really teach about tithing?

People often ask me, "What is the correct amount to tithe?" I don't believe there is one single "right" level of giving, either in terms of a percentage of your income or a set dollar amount. But there *are* some helpful guidelines, as well as the convictions of your heart.

I advise couples first to avoid the trap of assuming that the financial resources entrusted to them are part theirs and part God's. A couple's income is *all* God's, and the giving that you do should come from a personal conviction that recognizes His ownership of everything. By thinking and acting in that way, you and your spouse can eliminate some of the legalistic thoughts—and accompanying guilt—related to giving based on a set percentage of your income.

> *I personally view ten percent as a bare minimum.*

I personally view ten percent as a bare minimum, a goal upon which we can build and increase our giving over time. However, God doesn't call us to be slaves to a set percentage, but to freely give back to Him what our grateful hearts demand. Giving from the heart breaks the power of money, because the giver must first acknowledge the true Owner of the money and see himself or herself as merely a manager of those finances.

In serving God with our money, our motives—and ultimately our actions—will be different than if our lifestyle and material wants superseded all other priorities. The difficulty most of us feel in this critical area is exacerbated by a culture that reserves high praise for the men and women "with all the toys." But in direct contrast to the world's values, the Bible calls us to "profane" the god of money by giving it away. And to do that, we must take Christ's famous exhortation and apply it to our checkbooks: "For where your treasure is," Jesus said, "there your heart will be also" (Mt. 6:21).

Ron Blue

7.17 SETTING REALISTIC FINANCIAL GOALS

We've only been married six months and already my husband is talking about buying a house and setting up several retirement funds. While he's dreaming big, I'm thinking, "How are we going to pay our rent and buy groceries this month?" I'm pleased he's considering our future, but I question whether he's being realistic. What are some realistic financial expectations for newlyweds to have for their first two or three years of marriage?

Several years ago, my wife and I taught a young marrieds' Sunday school class at our church. This was a group of sharp couples who had been married anywhere from a few weeks to five years. The first Sunday, we asked each person in the class to identify their biggest adjustment in marriage thus far. Not surprisingly, they pinpointed financial tensions and expectations.

These couples had entered marriage thinking they could start where their parents left off.

These couples had entered marriage thinking they could start where their parents left off: a house full of furniture, two cars, resort vacations, all the clothes they needed, and all the toys they wanted—DVDs, lawn equipment, boats and so on. Never mind that their parents had worked years and years to reach that point.

The gap between expectation and reality—the "coping gap"—needs to be bridged if a marriage is to prosper spiritually, emotionally and financially. Indeed, a marriage will begin on a much sounder foundation, financially speaking, if you follow a few general principles.

First, as the wedding vows indicate, becoming husband and wife means money and possessions are no longer "yours" and "mine," but "ours." The two of you have become one. It isn't your income, your savings account, your home, your car, your debt, or your anything. A selfish attitude regarding money or possessions will most certainly undermine the relationship.

Second, make sure you're both working on establishing good financial habits. For example, don't spend what you don't have. The credit crunch is waiting to devour anyone—including you—and it will unless you jointly determine to delay gratification until the hard cash is in hand. These days, such an attitude is definitely countercultural. But rest assured, it will serve you in good stead throughout your married life.

Developing good financial habits will be much easier if you work together on the following:

1. Jointly commit your goals to paper.
2. Draft your first will.
3. Establish charitable giving as a priority.
4. Follow the sequential strategy for building financial resources (see 7.27 in this section).
5. Avoid foolish tax-planning decisions.
6. Establish a life insurance program.
7. Decide wisely about purchasing your first home.

Third, you need to commit yourselves to constant communication. The two of you may have been raised in families where money matters were handled completely differently. If so, you need to talk about those differences now so you can understand each other and, in turn, build a foundation for mutual understandings about when and how money should be spent. If you start out right, you can avoid a lot of pain and frustration down the road and be miles ahead of most other couples.

It takes roughly two years to set up a workable budget.

Finally, you need to create a budget. It takes roughly two years to set up a workable budget: one year to figure out how much you are spending and what you'd like to spend, and a second year to live according to a first-draft budget to see if it is reasonable. The third year is when a couple can actually begin to live within a realistic budget.

A budget can be the most freeing thing any couple can do financially. It gives you a realistic picture of your financial health and, consequently, gives you a better handle on your decision making.

Ron Blue

7.18 PREPARING FOR RETIREMENT

How can my wife and I prepare for retirement when our employment history has been sporadic at best? We're both in our late 30s and I figure we have another 30 or so years of work ahead of us. But what can we do right now to build a nest egg for our future?

One of the best ways to save for retirement is through an employer-sponsored retirement plan, such as a 401(k). Many employers offer programs in which they "match" employee contributions to the retirement plan, up to a certain percentage. By taking advantage of an employer's matching program, you can get a 100 percent rate of return on your investment right from the start.

One of the best ways to save for retirement is through an employer-sponsored retirement plan.

If you have access to an employer-sponsored retirement plan, contribute the maximum amount each year before looking at other retirement savings options. If you don't have this option through your employer, you can reap many of the same benefits by opening an Individual Retirement Account (IRA). Both traditional IRAs and new Roth IRAs have specific advantages that make them attractive vehicles for retirement savings.

Traditional IRAs offer investors the opportunity to defer taxes and potentially to receive a tax deduction for the funds contributed into an IRA account. You may be able to deduct all or part of your contributions to a traditional IRA, depending on your income level and whether you have access to an employer-sponsored retirement plan. You don't pay taxes on the contributions (or the earnings) until you take the money out—ideally, when you retire and are in a lower tax bracket.

In contrast, contributions to a Roth IRA are not tax deductible. But the advantage to this type of IRA is that the earnings accumulate tax-free, rather than tax-deferred. You won't have to pay any taxes on the money when you take a distribution, provided you meet certain requirements.

Withdrawal policies for both traditional IRAs and Roth IRAs are less stringent than they used to be. For example, penalty-free distributions can be taken from both types of accounts prior to age 59½ for several reasons, including the purchase of a first home. Also, a traditional IRA will allow distributions to fund eligible higher-education expenses. (Note: In order to take money out of a Roth IRA penalty-free, it must have been in the account for at least five years.)

While both types of IRAs are attractive, they have some distinct differences. The Roth IRA, for instance, has no minimum distribution requirements or cut-off dates for contributions. Traditional IRAs require investors to stop contributing and begin taking minimum distributions—and paying the taxes on them—at age 70-1/2. With the Roth IRA, on the other hand, you never have to withdraw your money and you can keep adding to the account even after you pass the 70½ mark.

> *Thirty years is a long time to let the "magic" of compounding work on your behalf!*

Talk with a qualified financial advisor to find out which type of IRA would work best for you. Also, many financial institutions publish excellent guides to help you navigate your way through the IRA maze. Don't forget to start with your employer and remember, no matter which option you choose, the sooner you start saving, the better. Thirty years is a long time to let the "magic" of compounding work on your behalf!

Ron Blue

7.19 WHEN TO PURCHASE A HOME

My wife and I feel like we're throwing our money away on rent every month. We have saved enough to cover the down payment on a house, but it would wipe out all our savings. Is the real estate investment worth it, or should we wait until we can buy a home without eliminating our contingency fund and retirement savings?

One of the most common financial misconceptions is that it is always better to buy a home than to rent. In truth, real estate is not the investment it used to be. Depending on inflation, interest rates and local economic conditions, a home may not appreciate in value as much as some other investments over the same period of time. And unless you plan to stay in your house for at least two years, it's better to rent. The buying and selling costs associated with home ownership can more than offset any appreciation value.

As a renter, you are not throwing your money away. Renting is a means to an end: it enables you to save surplus cash toward an eventual down payment on a home of your own.

Before you buy a home, however, you should achieve several intermediate goals. First, pay off all high-interest debt. Next, set aside one month's living expenses in an interest-bearing checking account. Use this surplus as a budget stabilizer if, for example, your car needs a major repair or a utility bill is unusually high. Finally, keep three- to six-months living expenses in a money market fund or savings account for major purchases and emergencies.

It would be presumptuous to wipe out your contingency fund in order to purchase a home. As James 4:14 puts it, "You don't even know what tomorrow will bring." So keep your emergency savings intact.

As you continue to save toward the down payment on a home, take a long-term perspective. By putting down twenty percent of the purchase price, instead of five or ten percent, you can lower your monthly payments and avoid additional costs such as mortgage insurance. This will ultimately put you in a better financial position.

Ron Blue

7.20 SETTING A CHILD'S ALLOWANCE

Our kids, who are 10, 13, and 15, claim their allowance is far smaller than that of their friends. We provide their clothes and food and pay for any special expenses, like a church retreat or camp. How much money should kids their age be receiving for spending on fast food and fun with their friends?

Many parents struggle with this common family dilemma. I can picture your kids, who are on a set budget, meeting other kids at the mall. These kids have fists full of credit cards—which *maybe* their parents gave them—and seem to have no limit on spending. Your kids naturally feel the difference.

But it is difficult to give an answer regarding how much allowance a child should be given. There are several pertinent factors: the age of the child, the child's maturity level, what your child is expected to pay for, and how much your family can afford.

Start by talking about the large picture with your children. They are experiencing something that each of us deals with every day of our lives. There will always be

Spending because others spend is never wise.

others with more money and less discipline. Succumbing to the pressure of what others do is not a money problem but rather a values and self-discipline problem. Your family has certain values that are reflected in the way you spend money. Just because someone else has "different" values does not make the "different" values right. So it is important to be firm in your decisions. Spending because others spend is never wise.

Another part of the solution is to involve your children in the allowance decision process. First, gather facts. Do the kids down the street really receive more money? Are your children telling you the whole story about their friends' allowances? This may require some phone calls to other parents or having your children verify the information.

Second, if possible, re-evaluate the budget amount that you are giving your children. If you as a family are having trouble keeping up with monthly bills, your kids will learn that avoiding debt sometimes means not buying every item we'd like to have.

Third, make your children part of the process of evaluation, especially discussing the money already spent on food, clothes and special events, and their own maturity.

Finally, if you still feel you are doing exactly as you should after gathering the facts and re-evaluating the budget, be firm in your decision. Dealing with the "keeping up" dilemma may be one of your greatest teaching opportunities. Don't miss this one by caving in to the pressure—or the pressure you feel yourself to "keep up" with others.

Ron Blue

Dealing with the "keeping up" dilemma may be one of your greatest teaching opportunities.

7.21 TEACHING KIDS ABOUT MONEY

Our ten-year-old son is a good student and generally a conscientious kid. But he lost two wallets—and about $20—in the past few months. The loss didn't faze him in the least! Besides being careless with money, he can't seem to grasp the concept that *he needs to save his allowance for several months to buy a new baseball glove. How can we teach him to use his money responsibly?*

First, let me assure you that you are not alone. While doing research for my book *Stress and the Healthy Family* (Winston), the role of money and children ranked high on the list of family money stresses. We parents need help in the troubling area of teaching children how to use money responsibly.

Most crucial is how we ourselves view money and its uses. Money is merely a tool to help simplify life—who wants to go back to bartering? But if we view the acquisition and use of money as a *goal* rather than as a tool, it takes on an importance beyond practicality and interferes with higher values like relationships, good stewardship, and spirituality.

Sadly, most Americans view money as a goal in life, if not the goal. Your son swings to the other end of the continuum. He uses the tool of money carelessly. In one sense, it's good that he isn't obsessed with money. But if losing $20 is no big deal to him, he has to suffer loss so he will learn to care for this tool. Part of your job as a parent is to see that he experiences a bit more suffering until he learns to be responsible.

For instance, make losing $20 a bigger deal by telling him you realize he doesn't need as much allowance as he has been getting; that it was your error in giving him too much; and that you will help him handle money responsibly by giving him a more realistic allowance. Stick to this idea. Don't bail him out when he is careless, even if it means he has to play ball without a glove or has no money to play video games.

Parents often rescue their kids when they are careless, depriving them of lessons in responsibility. One boy lost three jackets in one winter and each time his parents drove him to the mall to get another. When, in frustration, they asked my counsel, I suggested they go to a second-hand shop and buy the shabbiest warm jacket they could find for him. But they couldn't do it. Pride took precedence over good parenting.

Parents often rescue their kids when they are careless, depriving them of lessons in responsibility.

As a general rule, I suggest parents set a reasonable allowance with certain conditions: a portion for church and other charitable giving, a portion to be saved and the rest to cover simple pleasures. If children want a luxury item, they must, like us, give up some simple pleasures to save up for it. This teaches responsible use of money, takes parental nagging out of the picture and teaches children that delayed gratification is part of life.

Dolores Curran

7.22 RESISTING BECOMING A TWO-INCOME FAMILY

My wife and I are strapped for cash, and to help ease the burden I'd like her to go back to work. But she prefers to stay home with our kids, saying we should economize more and make do on one income. I don't want a life of luxury, but I would like to be able to pay our bills on time. We can't do that unless my wife gets a part-time job. She's resisting it, and we're arguing about it more and more. What should we do?

Your conflict revolves around the opposite ways the two of you have analyzed your financial situation. You have calculated that you can't make it on one income; your wife feels you can. Apparently, you have already discussed this difference of opinion. So perhaps it's time to bring in a third viewpoint. A financial counselor could help each of you evaluate spending patterns, budgets and savings. The counselor may even help you make your current income go farther.

> *Sometimes a financial counselor can bring spending patterns to light that you are not aware of.*

Sometimes a financial counselor can bring spending patterns to light that you are not aware of, and then suggest ways to cut back. For example, a wife with a generous clothing budget may have to re-evaluate her desire to dress fashionably against her desire not to work outside the home. Or a husband who regularly attends sporting events may be spending $100 a month on that pastime. He will have to weigh his recreational spending against his wife's desire not to work.

Your real goal is to make things work financially—to pay your bills on time and reduce your debt—not to "win" the argument with your wife. Let a financial counselor help you meet your goal. After working through your finances, the adviser may agree that your family needs a second income. In that case, he or she may help your wife accept the idea of taking on part of the financial load. Or the counselor may help you come up with money-saving solutions to help you meet your financial obligations without a second income.

Jay Kesler

7.23 RISKS OF HOME EQUITY LOANS

We've really been tempted to get a home equity loan to help pay off some old credit card debt. But before we sign on a dotted line, I'd like to know the primary dangers of borrowing money against the value of our house. If we do opt for a home-equity loan, could we actually lose our home if we missed a payment?

When you take out a home-equity loan, you use the equity you have built up in your house as the collateral for the loan. Should you default on your payments, the bank would use the collateral—in this case, your home—to satisfy the terms of the loan.

Couples can get into trouble in these situations due to a lack of careful planning. Home-equity loans often begin with fixed monthly payments over several years, and then require a large balloon payment at the end of the loan period. Let's say for five years a couple makes monthly payments on their loan, and then all of a sudden they receive a final bill for $20,000. If they haven't planned ahead to prepare for this balloon payment, they could lose their house. These details are negotiated and spelled out in the original loan agreement, but couples often file that information away and forget the actual terms. Beyond that, unforeseen circumstances, such as the loss of a job or the death of a spouse, could prevent a person from being able to repay the loan.

Some lending institutions widely advertise home-equity loans, describing them as a viable, quick cure for a family's cash-flow problems. But in my opinion, the benefits of home-equity loans are slight compared to the risks and drawbacks. Many people rationalize that a home-equity loan involves a lower interest rate than a regular bank loan, and that the interest on the loan is tax deductible. Perhaps in some cases those are good

In my opinion, the benefits of home-equity loans are slight compared to the risks and drawbacks.

reasons to use this type of loan. But should you decide to take out a home-equity loan, make sure you are aware of all the terms of your agreement and then prepare and plan accordingly.

Ron Blue

7.24 WHEN TO GET HELP WITH INVESTING

My husband and I have a middle-range income and a few small investments, and we've been wondering if it's time to seek out a financial adviser. At what point does a couple really need outside help in making wise investments?

Many people *never* reach the stage where they need a financial adviser to handle their finances, and if they do it's usually later in life. At our firm, we have a six-step Sequential Accumulation Strategy that allows couples to function as their own banker and investor while maintaining a high level of liquidity. You may find yourself working on some of the steps simultaneously; however, you want to make sure you don't skip any of the steps in the process:

1. Eliminate all high-interest or short-term debt.
2. Keep one month's living expenses in an interest-bearing checking account.
3. Keep three to six months' living expenses in a money market fund or savings account.
4. Save for major purchases in a bank CD, a government-security mutual fund or treasury bill.
5. Invest to meet long-term goals.
6. Speculate in higher-risk investments.

Eliminate all high-interest or short-term debt.

(Only after the previous five steps have been completed.)

It's important to lay an adequate foundation before using a financial adviser or investment firm. When following this strategy, you would not need a financial adviser to help with the investment and management of your assets until you have completed the first four steps. Up to this point you can handle your finances on your own.

Ron Blue

7.25 WHY WILLS MATTER

My husband and I are expecting our first child, but we haven't gotten around to making out a will. We still live in an apartment and our possessions don't add up to much. Do we really need a will or is it an expense we can hold off on for a few more years?

When considering your own mortality, the primary issue is where you and your family will spend eternity. Once you have settled that, the second most significant issue is avoiding unnecessary financial problems when you or your husband dies.

The second most significant issue is avoiding unnecessary financial problems when you or your husband dies.

Every couple should have a will—even if they don't have children. However, a couple with children needs to make additional provisions such as appointing a guardian.

Estate planning is similar to other kinds of financial planning. It requires goal setting, establishing a specific plan and committing yourselves to your plan. Many think estate planning is simply allocating dollar amounts: "John gets $5,000, Susan gets $5,000, and Aunt Mary gets whatever is left over." But my definition is more comprehensive. Estate planning insures that your financial resources are distributed—and your family is cared for—in accordance with your objectives.

To begin, think through these issues:

1. Determine the scope of your family, including your immediate family, extended family, spiritual family and close friends.

2. Evaluate your financial resources. This includes assets, business interests, life insurance, retirement programs and government programs such as Social Security benefits paid to an underage child whose parents die. These resources are broader in scope than those you include on a statement of net worth.

3. Know your distribution choices. Four distribution alternatives are available: family and friends, charitable organizations, the government and whoever incurs estate expenses. Without estate planning, taxes and final expenses can siphon off as much as 70 percent of your estate to pay for

probating the will, estate and inheritance taxes, attorney's fees, funeral expenses and so forth. You can determine now what dollar amounts or percentages of your resources you want to go to each of these categories.

4. Rethink your level of care. The mental, physical, spiritual and emotional needs of your family and friends can, to the best of your ability, be planned for in order to minimize their problems as they face life without you.

5. Contemplate your objectives. Setting your objectives is the most difficult step. This can only be accomplished effectively through time and prayer.

Young couples often believe that writing a will and doing a thorough job of estate planning is too expensive. But the costs may be quite reasonable. Ask friends for recommendations, and get several cost estimates from people who are qualified to prepare the necessary documents. It's worth the cost to make it easier on your children and their guardians in the event you should die.

Ron Blue

7.26 WHEN TO REVIEW YOUR FINANCIAL PICTURE

We've read that a couple should review their family finances together on a regular basis. Is a monthly review necessary, or should we do it on an annual basis? Also, how often should we review our insurance policies, investments and long-term financial plans?

I agree that couples should regularly discuss their financial picture, their goals and their plans for the future. However, the frequency of these discussions is less relevant than the reason behind them. If you and your spouse are communicating for the right reasons, then you will naturally communicate frequently enough.

A couple should discuss their finances for several reasons. First, so they both will be aware of their family's financial picture. Two people can't work toward the same goals without knowing where they are, what resources are available, and what choices are being made.

The second reason is unity. I often hear couples explain that they don't communicate because "my wife [or husband] just doesn't understand." It's true that men and women tend to perceive things differently. This can cause frustration in communication, but it doesn't mean communication is not needed. My best financial decisions are made jointly with my wife.

My best financial decisions are made jointly with my wife.

The third reason is to enhance understanding. Not only are men and women different in their communication styles, they are also different in their needs. Women tend to need security in contrast to men, who need significance. This is why a woman might be risk-averse while a man might be risk-tolerant. A woman is more likely to want to hold on to what she has, while a man is more willing to risk it to achieve more. Communication allows a couple to formulate a plan that addresses both person's needs.

Not only will regular financial discussions and planning help you achieve financial success, your marriage will reap mutual honor, respect, and submission. When a couple achieves a satisfying level of communication about their finances, they are usually communicating well about other areas of their marriage.

A financial plan (which includes your budget) should be reviewed at least once a year. This allows you to adjust for changes in your income, taxes, and other expenses. It also serves as a reminder of where you are and where you want to be going.

You should seriously reconsider your insurance, wills, investments and retirement planning if significant changes occur in your family or in the economy. As a home fills with children or empties of children, adjustments are needed. A new home, one spouse entering or leaving the work force, serious health changes, or taking on the responsibility for an aging parent are typical life events that signal the need for a financial review. Economic changes such as higher inflation, new tax laws, and higher (or lower) interest rates are also factors to watch.

Ron Blue

7.27 WHERE TO PUT A MODEST INVESTMENT

My wife and I have only about $2,000 to invest, but we want to get started in some type of savings program. What are the best options for investing a modest amount of cash?

Your decision should be made in light of where you are in a comprehensive strategy for financial freedom. This strategy begins with having a positive cash-flow margin, which means that on a regular basis you and your spouse have money left over once all your expenses are paid.

When that is achieved, I recommend a sequential strategy for building financial resources. Each step builds toward the next.

Step One: Eliminate all high-interest or short-term debt. Before you start thinking about buying stocks or CDs, "invest" by paying off debt. Paying off credit cards is a risk-free investment and can pay high returns.

Step Two: Keep one month's living expenses in an interest-bearing checking account. Once you have repaid all high-interest debt, start funneling your extra cash into an interest-bearing checking account to handle minor emergencies.

Step Three: Keep three to six months' living expenses in a money-market fund or savings account. With a healthy money-market fund, you can "borrow" from yourself instead of the bank if you need extra funds. Remember to replace the money you use and resist the temptation to use the fund for undisciplined spending.

Step Four: Save for major purchases with a bank CD, a government-security mutual fund or treasury bill. Certificates of deposit, government funds and T-bills are conservative, low-risk investments that make ideal saving vehicles for major purchases.

Step Five: Invest to meet long-term goals. Investing for long-term goals calls for a diversified investment portfolio. Money market funds, mutual funds, real estate, bonds and international equities may all be part of the picture.

Step Six: Speculate. Speculation carries a significant amount of risk. Speculations demand time and willingness to research and become actively involved in the investments themselves. Speculate only if and when you've effectively completed steps one through five and you have a temperament that allows you to take risks.

I would recommend the *Sound Mind Investing* newsletter written by Austin Pryor as a guide for working through each of these steps. He relies on a biblical philosophy of finances to make recommendations for each step. The newsletter also provides economic updates and information about other issues such as insurance and estate planning. For more information write to *Sound Mind Investing*, P.O. Box 22128, Louisville, KY 40252-0128 or visit their web site at www.soundmindinvesting.com.

Ron Blue

7.28 IS DEBT EVER ACCEPTABLE?

Not a week goes by without our mailbox being stuffed full of solicitations for credit cards. The world today runs on debt, or so it seems. We never thought we'd need to borrow money, but some recent needs have made us seriously consider taking on debt. Is it ever acceptable to go into debt?

If you're considering any type of debt—whether it's credit cards, consumer debt, a mortgage, or business and investment debt—these four criteria can help you make the right decision.

Spiritual criteria. Do you have a freedom before God to take on the debt? It's really between you and the Lord. Take each of your debt decisions to him.

Economic criteria. Does the debt make financial sense? Two rules will help you answer this question. First, the return you get from your purchase must be greater than the cost of the purchase. For example, is the house you want to buy likely to appreciate faster than the mortgage loan rate? Second, you must have a guaranteed way to repay the debt.

> *Do you have a freedom before God to take on the debt?*

Psychological criteria. How much debt can you handle psychologically? Debt causes stress, and the greater the amount of debt, the higher the stress level. We rarely ask ourselves how much debt we can handle emotionally.

Personal-goals criteria. What goals can be met through debt? For example, if a particular vehicle will make transporting your handicapped child much easier and quicker, that's a significant personal goal. Even though the vehicle may depreciate, you would place a higher value on the personal goal.

Ron Blue

ACKNOWLEDGEMENTS

ACKNOWLEDGEMENTS

CHAPTER 1:
COMMUNICATING WITH CONFIDENCE

1.1   From the "Q & A" column by Jay Kesler that appeared in the Summer 1988 issue of *Marriage Partnership* magazine. Used by permission of the author.

1.2   From the "Q & A" column by Jay Kesler that appeared in the Winter 1989 issue of *Marriage Partnership* magazine. Used by permission of the author.

1.3   From the article, "You're Talking So Much I Can't Hear You," by Karen L. Maudlin that appeared in the Spring 1996 issue of *Marriage Partnership* magazine. Used by permission of the author.

1.4   From the article, "What to Do When Your Marriage Hits a Dry Spell," by H. Norman Wright that appeared in the Winter 1989 issue of *Marriage Partnership* magazine. Adapted from *Romancing Your Marriage*, by H. Norman Wright, 1987. Used by permission of Regal Books, Ventura, California.

1.5   From the "Q & A" column by Jay Kesler that appeared in the Fall 1989 issue of *Marriage Partnership* magazine. Used by permission of the author.

1.6   From the article, "Do You Still Play Hide and Seek?" by Jeanette C. and Robert H. Lauer that appeared in the Spring 1994 issue of *Marriage Partnership* magazine. Used by permission of the authors.

1.7   From the "Q & A" column by Jay Kesler that appeared in the Summer 1995 issue of *Marriage Partnership* magazine. Used by permission of the author.

1.8　From the article, "Public Disclosures," by Janis Long Harris that appeared in the Winter 1997 issue of *Marriage Partnership* magazine. Used by permission of the author.

1.9　From the article, "How Much Honesty Can Your Marriage Take?" by Jeanette C. and Robert H. Lauer that appeared in the Summer 1991 issue of *Marriage Partnership* magazine. Used by permission of the authors.

1.10　From the article, "You're Talking So Much I Can't Hear You," by Karen L. Maudlin that appeared in the Spring 1996 issue of *Marriage Partnership* magazine. Used by permission of the author.

1.11　From the article, "Too Much 'Home Improvement'?" by Tim Sutherland that appeared in the Summer 1996 issue of *Marriage Partnership* magazine. Used by permission of the author.

1.12　From the "Q & A" column by Jay Kesler that appeared in the Spring 1996 issue of *Marriage Partnership* magazine. Used by permission of the author.

1.13　From the article, "Are Men Bad Listeners?" by Kevin A. Miller that appeared in the Winter 1995 issue of *Marriage Partnership* magazine. Used by permission of the author.

1.14　From the "Q & A" column by Jay Kesler that appeared in the Winter 1996 issue of *Marriage Partnership* magazine. Used by permission of the author.

1.15　From the "Early Years" column by Archibald Hart that appeared in the Fall 1991 issue of *Marriage Partnership* magazine. Used by permission of the author.

1.16　From the "Early Years" column by Archibald Hart that appeared in the Fall 1991 issue of *Marriage Partnership* magazine. Used by permission of the author.

1.17　From the article, "Too Much 'Home Improvement'?" by Tim Sutherland that appeared in the Summer 1996 issue of *Marriage Partnership* magazine. Used by permission of the author.

1.18　From the "Q & A" column by Jay Kesler that appeared in the Spring 1990 issue of *Marriage Partnership* magazine. Used by permission of the author.

1.19 From the article, "Stand by Me," by Alicia Howe that appeared in the Winter 1997 issue of *Marriage Partnership* magazine. Used by permission of the author.

1.20 From the article, "When to Put the Brakes on Your Spouse's Dreams," by Louis McBurney, M.D., that appeared in the Winter 1992 issue of *Marriage Partnership* magazine. Used by permission of the author.

1.21 From the article, "How Can You Find the Perfect Gift?" by Eileen Silva Kindig that appeared in the Fall 1992 issue of *Marriage Partnership* magazine. Used by permission of the author.

1.22 From the article, "Time for a Change?" by Jeanette C. and Robert H. Lauer that appeared in the Fall 1992 issue of *Marriage Partnership* magazine. Used by permission of the authors.

1.23 From the "Q & A" column by Jay Kesler that appeared in the Fall 1992 issue of *Marriage Partnership* magazine. Used by permission of the author.

1.24 From the article, "Talk, Talk, Talk," by Robert and Rosemary Barnes that appeared in the Fall 1994 issue of *Marriage Partnership* magazine. Adapted from *Rock Solid Marriage*, 1993, by Robert and Rosemary Barnes. Used by permission of Zondervan Publishing House.

CHAPTER 2:
WORKING THROUGH CONFLICT

2.1 From the article, "Go Ahead and Fight...but Keep It Clean," by Charles R. Swindoll that appeared in the Summer 1988 issue of *Marriage Partnership* magazine. Adapted from *Strike the Original Match*, 1980, by Charles R. Swindoll, Inc. Used by permission of Zondervan Publishing House.

2.2 From the article, "Living with a Screamer," by Carol DeChant that appeared in the Summer 1989 issue of *Marriage Partnership* magazine. Used by permission of the author.

2.3 From the article, "There's Nothing like a Good Fight," by Paige Jaeger that appeared in the Summer 1990 issue of *Marriage Partnership* magazine. Used by permission of the author.

2.4 From the article, "When Push Comes to Shove," by Janis Long Harris that appeared in the Summer 1989 issue of *Marriage Partnership* magazine. Used by permission of the author.

2.5 From the article, "Dr. Jekyll & Mr. Saturday," by Kevin A. Miller that appeared in the Spring 1989 issue of *Marriage Partnership* magazine. Used by permission of the author.

2.6 From the article, "How to Keep Anger in Its Place," by Diana and David Garland that appeared in the Winter 1991 issue of *Marriage Partnership* magazine. Adapted from *Marriage: For Better or for Worse?*, 1991, by Diana and David Garland. Used by permission of the authors.

2.7 From the article, "How to Keep Anger in Its Place," by Diana and David Garland that appeared in the Winter 1991 issue of *Marriage Partnership* magazine. Adapted from *Marriage: For Better or for Worse?*, 1991, by Diana and David Garland. Used by permission of the authors.

2.8 From the "Q & A" column by Jay Kesler that appeared in the Winter 1991 issue of *Marriage Partnership* magazine. Used by permission of the author.

2.9 From the article, "When to Call Foul!" by Dan Benson that appeared in the Fall 1991 issue of *Marriage Partnership* magazine. Adapted from *Man Talk*, 1991, by Dan Benson. Used by permission of the author.

2.10 From the article, "How to Solve a Problem Once and for All," by Janis Long Harris that appeared in the Spring 1991 issue of *Marriage Partnership* magazine. Used by permission of the author.

2.11 From the "Q & A" column by Jay Kesler that appeared in the Summer 1990 issue of *Marriage Partnership* magazine. Used by permission of the author.

2.12 From the "Q & A" column by Jay Kesler that appeared in the Summer 1993 issue of *Marriage Partnership* magazine. Used by permission of the author.

2.13 From the article, "What's the Best Way to Handle Conflict?" by Wes and Judy Roberts and H. Norman Wright that appeared in the Spring 1992 issue of *Marriage Partnership* magazine. Adapted from *After You Say "I Do,"* 1979, by Harvest House Publishers. Used by permission.

2.14 From the "Q & A" column by Jay Kesler that appeared in the Summer 1992 issue of *Marriage Partnership* magazine. Used by permission of the author.

2.15 From the "Q & A" column by Jay Kesler that appeared in the Winter 1990 issue of *Marriage Partnership* magazine. Used by permission of the author.

2.16 From the "Q & A" column by Jay Kesler that appeared in the Fall 1990 issue of *Marriage Partnership* magazine. Used by permission of the author.

2.17 From the article, "Do You Need Counseling?" by Louis McBurney, M.D., that appeared in the Spring 1990 issue of *Marriage Partnership* magazine. Used by permission of the author.

2.18 From the article, "What to Do When Careers—and Housework—Collide," by Judith Balswick that appeared in the Spring 1992 issue of *Marriage Partnership* magazine. Used by permission of the author.

2.19 From the "Q & A" column by Jay Kesler that appeared in the Spring 1995 issue of *Marriage Partnership* magazine. Used by permission of the author.

2.20 From the "Q & A" column by Jay Kesler that appeared in the Summer 1994 issue of *Marriage Partnership* magazine. Used by permission of the author.

2.21 From the article, "What to Do When Your Spouse Bugs You," by Jeanette C. and Robert H. Lauer that appeared in the Summer 1994 issue of *Marriage Partnership* magazine. Used by permission of the authors.

2.22 From the article, "Do You Need Marriage Counseling?" by Everett L. Worthington, Jr., that appeared in the Summer 1994 issue of *Marriage Partnership* magazine. Adapted from *Hope for Troubled Marriages*, 1993, by Everett L. Worthington, Jr. Used by permission of the author.

2.23 From the article, "Do You Need Marriage Counseling?" by Everett L. Worthington, Jr., that appeared in the Summer 1994 issue of *Marriage Partnership* magazine. Adapted from *Hope for Troubled Marriages*, 1993, by Everett L. Worthington, Jr. Used by permission of the author.

2.24 From the article, "Do You Need Marriage Counseling?" by Everett L. Worthington, Jr., that appeared in the Summer 1994 issue of *Marriage Partnership* magazine. Adapted from *Hope for Troubled Marriages*, 1993, by Everett L. Worthington, Jr. Used by permission of the author.

CHAPTER 3:
SEX: THE WAY GOD DESIGNED IT

3.1 From the article, "Sexual Fidelity," by Harold B. Smith that appeared in the Fall 1994 issue of *Marriage Partnership* magazine, by Christianity Today International Used by permission.

3.2 From the article, "The Secret to Great Sex," by Robert L. Moeller that appeared in the Fall 1994 issue of *Marriage Partnership* magazine. Adapted from *For Better, for Worse, for Keeps*, 1993, by Robert L. Moeller. Used by permission of Multnomah Publishers, Inc.

3.3 From the "Real Sex" column by Clifford L. and Joyce J. Penner that appeared in the Fall 1995 issue of *Marriage Partnership* magazine. Used by permission of the authors.

3.4 From the "Real Sex" column by Clifford L. and Joyce J. Penner that appeared in the Fall 1994 issue of *Marriage Partnership* magazine. Used by permission of the authors.

3.5 From the "Real Sex" column by Clifford L. and Joyce J. Penner that appeared in the Summer 1994 issue of *Marriage Partnership* magazine. Used by permission of the authors.

3.6 From the article, "Was It Good for You?" by Louis McBurney, M.D., that appeared in the Winter 1995 issue of *Marriage Partnership* magazine. Used by permission of the author.

3.7 From the article, "Was It Good for You?" by Louis McBurney, M.D., that appeared in the Winter 1995 issue of *Marriage Partnership* magazine. Used by permission of the author.

3.8 From the article, "Unsafe Sex," by Douglas B. DeMerchant that appeared in the Winter 1991 issue of *Marriage Partnership* magazine. Used by permission of the author.

3.9 From the "Real Sex" column by Clifford L. and Joyce J. Penner that appeared in the Spring 1994 issue of *Marriage Partnership* magazine. Used by permission of the authors.

3.10 From the "Real Sex" column by Clifford L. and Joyce J. Penner that appeared in the Summer 1990 issue of *Marriage Partnership* magazine. Used by permission of the authors.

3.11 From the article, "How to Love Your Marriage Enough to Protect It," by Jerry B. Jenkins that appeared in the Summer 1990 issue of *Marriage Partnership* magazine. Adapted from *Loving Your Marriage Enough to Protect It*, 1989, by Jerry B. Jenkins. Used by permission of Moody Press.

3.12 From the "Q & A" column by Jay Kesler that appeared in the Spring 1990 issue of *Marriage Partnership* magazine. Used by permission of the author.

3.13 From the "Real Sex" column by Clifford L. and Joyce J. Penner that appeared in the Spring 1995 issue of *Marriage Partnership* magazine. Used by permission of the authors.

3.14 From the "Real Sex" column by Clifford L. and Joyce J. Penner that appeared in the Winter 1994 issue of *Marriage Partnership* magazine. Used by permission of the authors.

3.15 From the "Real Sex" column by Clifford L. and Joyce J. Penner that appeared in the Summer 1993 issue of *Marriage Partnership* magazine. Used by permission of the authors.

3.16 From the "Real Sex" column by Clifford L. and Joyce J. Penner that appeared in the Winter 1993 issue of *Marriage Partnership* magazine. Used by permission of the authors.

3.17 From the "Real Sex" column by Clifford L. and Joyce J. Penner that appeared in the Spring 1992 issue of *Marriage Partnership* magazine. Used by permission of the authors.

3.18 From the "Real Sex" column by Clifford L. and Joyce J. Penner that appeared in the Spring 1992 issue of *Marriage Partnership* magazine. Used by permission of the authors.

3.19 From the article, "How to Guard Against an Affair," by the late Jim Smith that appeared in the Summer 1992 issue of *Marriage Partnership* magazine. Used by permission of Mrs. Jim Smith.

3.20 From the article, "How to Guard Against an Affair," by the late Jim Smith that appeared in the Summer 1992 issue of *Marriage Partnership* magazine. Used by permission of Mrs. Jim Smith.

3.21 From the "Real Sex" column by Clifford L. and Joyce J. Penner that appeared in the Winter 1994 issue of *Marriage Partnership* magazine. Used by permission of the authors.

3.22 From the "Real Sex" column by Clifford L. and Joyce J. Penner that appeared in the Summer 1992 issue of *Marriage Partnership* magazine. Used by permission of the authors.

3.23 From the "Real Sex" column by Clifford L. and Joyce J. Penner that appeared in the Winter 1992 issue of *Marriage Partnership* magazine. Used by permission of the authors.

3.24 From the "Real Sex" column by Clifford L. and Joyce J. Penner that appeared in the Fall 1992 issue of *Marriage Partnership* magazine. Used by permission of the authors.

3.25 From the "Real Sex" column by Clifford L. and Joyce J. Penner that appeared in the Fall 1992 issue of *Marriage Partnership* magazine. Used by permission of the authors.

3.26 From the "Real Sex" column by Clifford L. and Joyce J. Penner that appeared in the Fall 1993 issue of *Marriage Partnership* magazine. Used by permission of the authors.

3.27 From the "Real Sex" column by Clifford L. and Joyce J. Penner that appeared in the Spring 1995 issue of *Marriage Partnership* magazine. Used by permission of the authors.

3.28 From the "Real Sex" column by Clifford L. and Joyce J. Penner that appeared in the Summer 1995 issue of *Marriage Partnership* magazine. Used by permission of the authors.

CHAPTER 4:
INTIMACY: GROWING CLOSER TOGETHER

4.1 From the article, "Caring & Commitment: Learning to Live the Love We Promise," by Lewis B. Smedes that appeared in the Fall 1988 issue of *Marriage Partnership* magazine. Adapted from *Caring & Commitment,* 1988, by Lewis B. Smedes. Used by permission of HarperCollins Publishers.

4.2 From the article, "Secrets for Finding Extra Hours in Your Day," by Dolores Curran that appeared in the Winter 1989 issue of *Marriage Partnership* magazine. Adapted from *Stress and the Healthy Family,* 1985, by Dolores Curran. Used by permission of the author.

4.3 From the article, "Married and Miserable," by Ed Wheat, M.D., with Gloria Okes Perkins, that appeared in the Summer 1989 issue of *Marriage Partnership* magazine. Adapted from *Love Life for Every Married Couple*, 1980, 1987, by Ed Wheat, M.D. Used by permission of Zondervan Publishing House.

4.4 From the article, "Escape from Togetherness," by Lyn Cryderman that appeared in the Fall 1989 issue of *Marriage Partnership* magazine. Used by permission of the author.

4.5 From the article, "What to Do When Your Marriage Hits a Dry Spell," by H. Norman Wright that appeared in the Winter 1989 issue of *Marriage Partnership* magazine. Adapted from *Romancing Your Marriage*, by H. Norman Wright, 1987. Used by permission of Regal Books, Ventura, California.

4.6 From the article, "What Makes a Forever Relationship?" by Ed Wheat, M.D., with Gloria Okes Perkins, that appeared in the Spring 1989 issue of *Marriage Partnership* magazine. Adapted from *The First Years of Forever*, 1988, by Ed Wheat, M.D. Used by permission of Zondervan Publishing House.

4.7 From the "Q & A" column by Jay Kesler that appeared in the Summer 1991 issue of *Marriage Partnership* magazine. Used by permission of the author.

4.8 From the "Q & A" column by Jay Kesler that appeared in the Fall 1990 issue of *Marriage Partnership* magazine. Used by permission of the author.

4.9 From the article, "The Hard Truth About Happiness" by Barbara Russell Chesser that appeared in the Fall 1990 issue of *Marriage Partnership* magazine. Adapted from *Twenty-One Myths That Can Wreck Your Marriage*, 1990, by Barbara Russell Chesser. Used by permission of Word Publishing, Nashville, Tennessee. All rights reserved.

4.10 From the article, "Give and Take," by Jim and Sally Conway that appeared in the Fall 1990 issue of *Marriage Partnership* magazine. Adapted from *Your Marriage Can Survive Mid-Life Crisis*, 1987, by Jim and Sally Conway. Used by permission of the author.

4.11   From the article, "You Can Say It with Flowers," by Bill Hybels that appeared in the Spring 1990 issue of *Marriage Partnership* magazine. Adapted from *Honest to God,* 1990, by Bill Hybels. Used by permission of Zondervan Publishing House.

4.12   From the "Q & A" column by Jay Kesler that appeared in the Fall 1993 issue of *Marriage Partnership* magazine. Used by permission of the author.

4.13   From the article, "Are You Afraid to Talk to Each Other?" by Louis McBurney, M.D., that appeared in the Fall 1993 issue of *Marriage Partnership* magazine. Used by permission of the author.

4.14   From the article, "What to Do When Careers—and Housework—Collide," by Judith Balswick that appeared in the Spring 1992 issue of *Marriage Partnership* magazine. Used by permission of the author.

4.15   From the article, "Is Boredom Killing Your Marriage?" by Jeanette C. and Robert H. Lauer that appeared in the Spring 1992 issue of *Marriage Partnership* magazine. Used by permission of the authors.

4.16   From the article, "Don't Stop Growing When You Grow Up," by Jim and Sally Conway that appeared in the Spring 1992 issue of *Marriage Partnership* magazine. Adapted from *Traits of a Lasting Marriage,* 1991, by Jim and Sally Conway. Used by permission of InterVarsity Press, Downers Grove, Illinois.

4.17   From the article, "Do You Still Play Hide and Seek?" by Jeanette C. and Robert H. Lauer that appeared in the Spring 1994 issue of *Marriage Partnership* magazine. Used by permission of the authors.

4.18   From the article, "Danger Zones," by Daniel Green that appeared in the Spring 1994 issue of *Marriage Partnership* magazine. Used by permission of the author.

4.19   From the article, "Do You Need Marriage Counseling?" by Everett L. Worthington, Jr., that appeared in the Summer 1994 issue of *Marriage Partnership* magazine. Adapted from *Hope for Troubled Marriages,* 1993, by Everett L. Worthington, Jr. Used by permission of the author.

4.20   From the article, "Is Marriage a Box of Goodies?" by J. Allan Petersen that appeared in the Spring 1989 issue of *Marriage Partnership* magazine. Used by permission of the author.

4.21 From the article, "It's a Guy Thing," by Leslie Parrott that appeared in the Fall 1996 issue of *Marriage Partnership* magazine. Used by permission of the author.

4.22 From the article, "It's a Guy Thing," by Leslie Parrott that appeared in the Fall 1996 issue of *Marriage Partnership* magazine. Used by permission of the author.

4.23 From the article, "Are You Drifting Apart?" by Louis McBurney, M.D., that appeared in the Fall 1996 issue of *Marriage Partnership* magazine. Used by permission of the author.

4.24 From the article, "Commitment Isn't Everything," by Scott M. Stanley that appeared in the Spring 1996 issue of *Marriage Partnership* magazine. Used by permission of the author.

4.25 From the "Q & A" column by Jay Kesler that appeared in the Summer 1997 issue of *Marriage Partnership* magazine. Used by permission of the author.

4.26 From the "Q & A" column by Jay Kesler that appeared in the Summer 1989 issue of *Marriage Partnership* magazine. Used by permission of the author. Also from the "Q & A" column by Jay Kesler that appeared in the Winter 1993 issue of *Marriage Partnership* magazine. Used by permission of the author.

4.27 From the article, "If Friends Are So Important, Where Are They?" by Janis Long Harris that appeared in the Fall 1988 issue of *Marriage Partnership* magazine. Used by permission of the author.

CHAPTER 5:
GROWING IN SPIRITUAL ONENESS

5.1 From the "Q & A" column by Jay Kesler that appeared in the Winter 1989 issue of *Marriage Partnership* magazine. Used by permission of the author.

5.2 From the "Q & A" column by Jay Kesler that appeared in the Spring 1989 issue of *Marriage Partnership* magazine. Used by permission of the author.

5.3 From the "Q & A" column by Jay Kesler that appeared in the Summer 1988 issue of *Marriage Partnership* magazine. Used by permission of the author.

5.4 From the article, "When It's Better Not to Forgive," by Lewis B. Smedes, with James D. Berkley, that appeared in the Winter 1991 issue of *Marriage Partnership* magazine. Used by permission of the authors.

5.5 From the article, "Am I My Spouse's Keeper?" by Mark Galli that appeared in the Fall 1991 issue of *Marriage Partnership* magazine. Used by permission of the author.

5.6 From the "Q & A" column by Jay Kesler that appeared in the Summer 1991 issue of *Marriage Partnership* magazine. Used by permission of the author.

5.7 From the article, "I've Fallen and I Can Get Up," by Paul Stevens that appeared in the Spring 1991 issue of *Marriage Partnership* magazine. Adapted from *Marriage Spirituality: Ten Disciplines for Couples Who Love God,* 1989, by Paul Stevens. Used by permission of the author.

5.8 From the "Q & A" column by Jay Kesler that appeared in the Summer 1992 issue of *Marriage Partnership* magazine. Used by permission of the author.

5.9 From the "Q & A" column by Jay Kesler that appeared in the Winter 1993 issue of *Marriage Partnership* magazine. Used by permission of the author.

5.10 From the article, "Skimming the Surface?" by Les and Leslie Parrott that appeared in the Winter 1995 issue of *Marriage Partnership* magazine. Adapted from *Saving Your Marriage Before It Starts,* 1995, by Dr. Leslie Parrott and Dr. Les Parrott III. Used by permission of Zondervan Publishing House.

5.11 From the "Q & A" column by Jay Kesler that appeared in the Winter 1995 issue of *Marriage Partnership* magazine. Used by permission of the author.

5.12 From the article, "Sacrificial Love," by Jim and Sally Conway that appeared in the Spring 1995 issue of *Marriage Partnership* magazine. Used by permission of the author.

5.13 From the article, "My Favorite Sin," by Robert L. Moeller that appeared in the Fall 1995 issue of *Marriage Partnership* magazine. Used by permission of the author.

5.14 From the "Q & A" column by Jay Kesler that appeared in the Fall 1995 issue of *Marriage Partnership* magazine. Used by permission of the author.

5.15 From the "Q & A" column by Jay Kesler that appeared in the Winter 1994 issue of *Marriage Partnership* magazine. Used by permission of the author.

5.16 From the "Q & A" column by Jay Kesler that appeared in the Winter 1996 issue of *Marriage Partnership* magazine. Used by permission of the author.

5.17 From the article, "My, Myself and I," by Louis McBurney, M.D., that appeared in the Summer 1994 issue of *Marriage Partnership* magazine. Used by permission of the author.

5.18 From the article, "Coming in Second," by Kevin A. Miller that appeared in the Fall 1996 issue of *Marriage Partnership* magazine, by Christianity Today International Used by permission.

5.19 From the article, "Whatever Happened to the Full-Service Marriage?" by Alicia Howe that appeared in the Fall 1996 issue of *Marriage Partnership* magazine. Used by permission of the author.

5.20 From the article, "Lost and Found," by Les and Leslie Parrott that appeared in the Fall 1997 issue of *Marriage Partnership* magazine. Used by permission of the authors.

5.21 From the "Q & A" column by Jay Kesler that appeared in the Spring 1997 issue of *Marriage Partnership* magazine. Used by permission of the author.

5.22 From the article, "The Touchiest Topic," by Tim Sutherland that appeared in the Spring 1997 issue of *Marriage Partnership* magazine. Used by permission of the author.

5.23 From the article, "The Touchiest Topic," by Tim Sutherland that appeared in the Spring 1997 issue of *Marriage Partnership* magazine. Used by permission of the author.

5.24 From the article, "The Touchiest Topic," by Tim Sutherland that appeared in the Spring 1997 issue of *Marriage Partnership* magazine. Used by permission of the author.

5.25 From the article, "How to Do the Undoable," by Jerry Bridges, with Annette LaPlaca that appeared in the Summer 1996 issue of *Marriage Partnership* magazine. Used by permission of the author.

5.26 From the "Q & A" column by Jay Kesler that appeared in the Summer 1996 issue of *Marriage Partnership* magazine. Used by permission of the author.

5.27 From the article, "Bonds of Steel," by Donald R. Harvey that appeared in the Winter 1996 issue of *Marriage Partnership* magazine. Used by permission of the author.

CHAPTER 6:
PARENTING AS A TEAM

6.1 From the "Q & A" column by Jay Kesler that appeared in the Spring 1988 issue of *Marriage Partnership* magazine. Used by permission of the author.

6.2 From the article, "Secrets for Finding Extra Hours in Your Day," by Dolores Curran that appeared in the Winter 1989 issue of *Marriage Partnership* magazine. Adapted from *Stress and the Healthy Family,* 1985, by Dolores Curran. Used by permission of the author.

6.3 From the article, "Driven to Failure," by Janis Long Harris that appeared in the Winter 1989 issue of *Marriage Partnership* magazine. Used by permission of the author.

6.4 From the "Q & A" column by Jay Kesler that appeared in the Summer 1989 issue of *Marriage Partnership* magazine. Used by permission of the author.

6.5 From the "Q & A" column by Jay Kesler that appeared in the Summer 1989 issue of *Marriage Partnership* magazine. Used by permission of the author.

6.6　From the "Q & A" column by Jay Kesler that appeared in the Winter 1991 issue of *Marriage Partnership* magazine. Used by permission of the author.

6.7　From the article, "Danger Zones," by Daniel Green that appeared in the Spring 1994 issue of *Marriage Partnership* magazine. Used by permission of the author.

6.8　From the "Q & A" column by Jay Kesler that appeared in the Fall 1991 issue of *Marriage Partnership* magazine. Used by permission of the author.

6.9　From the "Kid Talk" column by Dolores Curran that appeared in the Fall 1991 issue of *Marriage Partnership* magazine. Used by permission of the author.

6.10　From the "Kid Talk" column by Dolores Curran that appeared in the Fall 1991 issue of *Marriage Partnership* magazine. Used by permission of the author.

6.11　From the "Kid Talk" column by Dolores Curran that appeared in the Summer 1991 issue of *Marriage Partnership* magazine. Used by permission of the author.

6.12　From the "Q & A" column by Jay Kesler that appeared in the Spring 1991 issue of *Marriage Partnership* magazine. Used by permission of the author.

6.13　From the article, "How Do You Spell Relief?" by Gregg Lewis that appeared in the Winter 1990 issue of *Marriage Partnership* magazine. Adapted from *Motherhood Stress*, 1989, by Deborah Shaw Lewis. Used by permission of the authors.

6.14　From the article, "Nice Kids Finish First," by Dolores Curran that appeared in the Fall 1990 issue of *Marriage Partnership* magazine. Used by permission of the author.

6.15　From the article, "Raising Keds Kids in an Air Jordan World," by James D. Berkley that appeared in the Fall 1990 issue of *Marriage Partnership* magazine. Used by permission of the author.

6.16　From the "Q & A" column by Jay Kesler that appeared in the Spring 1993 issue of *Marriage Partnership* magazine. Used by permission of the author.

6.17 From the "Real Sex" column by Clifford L. and Joyce J. Penner that appeared in the Winter 1993 issue of *Marriage Partnership* magazine. Used by permission of the authors.

6.18 From the "Kid Talk" column by Dolores Curran that appeared in the Winter 1993 issue of *Marriage Partnership* magazine. Used by permission of the author.

6.19 From the "Kid Talk" column by Dolores Curran that appeared in the Winter 1993 issue of *Marriage Partnership* magazine. Used by permission of the author.

6.20 From the "Kid Talk" column by Dolores Curran that appeared in the Summer 1992 issue of *Marriage Partnership* magazine. Used by permission of the author.

6.21 From the "Kid Talk" column by Dolores Curran that appeared in the Winter 1992 issue of *Marriage Partnership* magazine. Used by permission of the author.

6.22 From the special section, "A 90s Kind of Dad," by R. Kent Hughes that appeared in the Fall 1992 issue of *Marriage Partnership* magazine. Adapted from *Disciplines of a Godly Man*, 1991, by R. Kent Hughes. Used by permission of Crossway Books.

6.23 From the "Kid Talk" column by Dolores Curran that appeared in the Fall 1992 issue of *Marriage Partnership* magazine. Used by permission of the author.

6.24 From the article "Is There Marriage After Children?" by Dolores Curran that appeared in the Winter 1995 issue of *Marriage Partnership* magazine. Used by permission of the author.

6.25 From the "Kid Talk" column by Dolores Curran that appeared in the Spring 1995 issue of *Marriage Partnership* magazine. Used by permission of the author.

6.26 From the "Kid Talk" column by Dolores Curran that appeared in the Winter 1994 issue of *Marriage Partnership* magazine. Used by permission of the author.

6.27 From the "Q & A" column by Jay Kesler that appeared in the Spring 1994 issue of *Marriage Partnership* magazine. Used by permission of the author.

6.28 From the "Kid Talk" column by Dolores Curran that appeared in the Summer 1994 issue of *Marriage Partnership* magazine. Used by permission of the author.

6.29 From the "Q & A" column by Jay Kesler that appeared in the Fall 1994 issue of *Marriage Partnership* magazine. Used by permission of the author.

6.30 From the "Kid Talk" column by Dolores Curran that appeared in the Fall 1994 issue of *Marriage Partnership* magazine. Used by permission of the author.

6.31 From the "Q & A" column by Jay Kesler that appeared in the Winter 1994 issue of *Marriage Partnership* magazine. Used by permission of the author.

6.32 From the "Kid Talk" column by Dolores Curran that appeared in the Fall 1993 issue of *Marriage Partnership* magazine. Used by permission of the author.

6.33 From the "Kid Talk" column by Dolores Curran that appeared in the Fall 1993 issue of *Marriage Partnership* magazine. Used by permission of the author.

6.34 From the article, "Life in the Narrow Lane," by Nancy Sommerville Langham that appeared in the Spring 1993 issue of *Marriage Partnership* magazine. Used by permission of the author.

6.35 From the "Now & Forever" column by David and Claudia Arp that appeared in the Fall 1997 issue of *Marriage Partnership* magazine. Used by permission of the authors.

6.36 From the "Now & Forever" column by David and Claudia Arp that appeared in the Fall 1997 issue of *Marriage Partnership* magazine. Used by permission of the authors.

CHAPTER 7:
MAKING SENSE OF MONEY MATTERS

7.1 From the "Q & A" column by Jay Kesler that appeared in the Summer 1989 issue of *Marriage Partnership* magazine. Used by permission of the author.

7.2 From the article, "Debt-Free," by Ron Blue that appeared in the Winter 1991 issue of *Marriage Partnership* magazine. Used by permission of the author.

7.3 From an article, by Laura Crosby that appeared in the "For Women Only" section of the Fall 1991 issue of *Marriage Partnership* magazine. Used by permission of the author.

7.4 From the article, "Money Advice That Works," by Ron Blue, with Ken Sidey, that appeared in the Summer 1991 issue of *Marriage Partnership* magazine. Used by permission of the authors.

7.5 From the article, "Stop the Money Madness," by Beverly J. Burch that appeared in the Spring 1997 issue of *Marriage Partnership* magazine. Used by permission of the author.

7.6 From the article, "Save $100 This Month," by Cynthia G. Yates that appeared in the Winter 1996 issue of *Marriage Partnership* magazine. Used by permission of the author.

7.7 From the article, "Why Couples Argue About Money...and How to Stop," by Lynda Rutledge Stephenson that appeared in the Spring 1988 issue of *Marriage Partnership* magazine. Used by permission of the author.

7.8 From the article, "Why Couples Argue About Money...and How to Stop," by Lynda Rutledge Stephenson that appeared in the Spring 1988 issue of *Marriage Partnership* magazine. Used by permission of the author.

7.9 From the "Your Money" column by Ron Blue that appeared in the Fall 1993 issue of *Marriage Partnership* magazine. Used by permission of the author.

7.10 From the "Your Money" column by Ron Blue that appeared in the Fall 1993 issue of *Marriage Partnership* magazine. Used by permission of the author.

7.11 From the "Your Money" column by Ron Blue that appeared in the Fall 1993 issue of *Marriage Partnership* magazine. Used by permission of the author.

7.12 From the "Your Money" column by Ron Blue that appeared in the Summer 1993 issue of *Marriage Partnership* magazine. Used by permission of the author.

7.13 From the "Your Money" column by Ron Blue that appeared in the Summer 1992 issue of *Marriage Partnership* magazine. Used by permission of the author.

7.14 From the "Q & A" column by Jay Kesler that appeared in the Winter 1992 issue of *Marriage Partnership* magazine. Used by permission of the author.

7.15 From the "Your Money" column by Ron Blue that appeared in the Winter 1992 issue of *Marriage Partnership* magazine. Used by permission of the author.

7.16 From the "Your Money" column by Ron Blue that appeared in the Winter 1992 issue of *Marriage Partnership* magazine. Used by permission of the author.

7.17 From the "Your Money" column by Ron Blue that appeared in the Fall 1992 issue of *Marriage Partnership* magazine. Used by permission of the author.

7.18 From the "Your Money" column by Ron Blue that appeared in the Fall 1992 issue of *Marriage Partnership* magazine. Revised 1998. Used by permission of the author.

7.19 From the "Your Money" column by Ron Blue that appeared in the Spring 1995 issue of *Marriage Partnership* magazine. Used by permission of the author.

7.20 From the "Your Money" column by Ron Blue that appeared in the Spring 1994 issue of *Marriage Partnership* magazine. Used by permission of the author.

7.21 From the "Kid Talk" column by Dolores Curran that appeared in the Spring 1994 issue of *Marriage Partnership* magazine. Used by permission of the author.

7.22 From the "Q & A" column by Jay Kesler that appeared in the Summer 1994 issue of *Marriage Partnership* magazine. Used by permission of the author.

7.23 From the "Your Money" column by Ron Blue that appeared in the Summer 1994 issue of *Marriage Partnership* magazine. Used by permission of the author.

7.24 From the "Your Money" column by Ron Blue that appeared in the Summer 1994 issue of *Marriage Partnership* magazine. Revised 1998. Used by permission of the author.

7.25 From the "Your Money" column by Ron Blue that appeared in the Winter 1994 issue of *Marriage Partnership* magazine. Used by permission of the author.

7.26 From the "Your Money" column by Ron Blue that appeared in the Winter 1994 issue of *Marriage Partnership* magazine. Used by permission of the author.

7.27 From the "Your Money" column by Ron Blue that appeared in the Winter 1994 issue of *Marriage Partnership* magazine. Revised 1998. Used by permission of the author.

7.28 From the "Your Money" column by Ron Blue that appeared in the Spring 1995 issue of *Marriage Partnership* magazine. Used by permission of the author.

TOPICAL INDEX

TOPICAL INDEX

BALANCED LIVING
feeling squeezed out of spouse's schedule 1.14
as it relates to family responsibilities 1.16, 6.2
making time for marriage 4.2

BLAME
ending the habit of blaming spouse for a problem 5.8
as a way to alleviate personal guilt 6.2

BODY IMAGE
accepting physical changes after mastectomy 3.3
inhibited about appearance 3.5
turned off by weight gain 3.13

BOREDOM
hum-drum sex life 3.10
no longer feeling in love 4.3
banishing chronic boredom 4.15

BUDGETING
easy ways to save money 7.6
creating a workable budget 7,7
budgeting without a steady salary 7.10
ways to live on one income 7.11
living with a careless spender 7.14
saving for retirement 7.18

CAREERS/WORK
getting a spouse to talk about work stresses 1.1
living with a workaholic 1.16
at odds over career dreams 2.16
job pressures driving couple apart 4.14
wife who is resistant to working outside the home 7.22

COMMUNICATING

expressing a frustrations in a healthy way 1.1; 2.9

helping a quiet spouse open up 1.2

not feeling understood 1.8

no time to talk 1.16

COMPROMISE

balancing couple time with individual time 4.4

comprising on preferred style of worship 5.3

regarding degree of church involvement 5.19

CONFRONTATION

facing a self-centered spouse 1.12

different styles of confronting conflict 2.13

challenging a careless spender 7.14

CONTENTMENT

understanding what love really is 4.6

wanting more than an "okay" marriage 4.19

ways to develop lasting contentment 5.2

COUNSELING

regarding physical violence 2.15

mate resistant to counseling 2.17

when to consider counseling 2.22

what to expect in counseling 2.23

selecting a counselor 2.24

COUPLE TIME

making it a priority 4.2; 6.35

finding shared interests 4.8

nurturing similar interests 4.16

night owl child who cuts into couple time 6.10

DIVORCE

as it relates to physically abusive spouse 2.22

EMOTIONS/FEELINGS

why husbands shut out wives 1.6; 4.21

using caution when expressing feelings 1.19

why emotional intimacy is difficult 1.24; 4.13

learning a mate's love language 4.11

two-faced spouse 4.17

how to know if a marriage is drifting 4.23

EMPTY NEST

redefining a marriage once children leave home 6.36

ENCOURAGEMENT

how to genuinely encourage a spouse 5.9

supporting a busy mother 6.13

EXPECTATIONS

conflicting expectations about sex 3.20

wanting a spouse to be more independent 4.12

FAITH

spiritually lax spouse 5.5

in-laws who are hostile to Christianity 5.11

FAITHFULNESS

what faithful really means 4.6

FAMILY TIME

keeping family needs balanced with couple needs 4.25

making the most of limited time together 6.1

ending the time-crunched lifestyle 6.2

GOD

understanding spiritual leadership 5.1; 5.2

communicating with God through shared prayer 5.10

building a God-centered marriage 5.20

GUILT

easing motherhood guilt 6.9

HAPPINESS

assuming responsibility for personal happiness 4.10

how blame thwarts sense of happiness 5.13

HOLIDAYS

ending runaway holiday spending 7.3

HOME

fairly dividing household duties 2.18

living with a messy spouse 2.21

when to purchase a home 7.19

HONESTY

how much honesty is good for a marriage 1.9

being open about problems 1.23

HUMILITY

fostering an attitude of humility 5.13

IN-LAWS

interfering or critical relatives 2.8; 2.20

too much time with in-laws 2.11; 2.12

unaccepting in-laws 2.19

who are hostile to Christianity 5.11

grandparents who play favorites with grandchildren 6.21

uninvolved grandparents 6.23

lending money to relatives 7.12

LOVE

finding the right words to communicate love 1.4
lost loving feelings 4.3; 5.25
falling out of love 4.3
doubting a partner's love 4.11; 4.22

LUST

ways to guard against lust 3.18
struggling with lustful thought 5.6

MENOPAUSE

expected changes in sex life 3.25
facing a hysterectomy 3.28

NAGGING

understanding why women nag 1.10
impossible to please mate 1.17
ways to end bickering 2.5

PARENTING

creating privacy for intimacy 3.17; 3.20; 3.26; 6.17
becoming supportive parents 6.3
effectively praising children 6.14
opposite discipline styles 6.20
lacking a role model for good fathering 6.22
nurturing a child's self-esteem 6.25
at odds over how to help child with homework 6.26
adjusting to the demands of parenthood 6.34
making sure a marriage with withstand the pressures of parenting 6.35
teaching children about giving 7.21

CONTRIBUTORS

CONTRIBUTORS

David and Claudia Arp are founders of Marriage Alive International, a marriage and family education ministry. They are the authors of numerous books, including *10 Great Dates* and *The Second Half of Marriage* (both published by Zondervan).

Judith Balswick, Ed.D., is associate professor of Marital and Family Therapy and Director of Clinical Training at Fuller Theological Seminary. She co-authored *Authentic Human Sexuality* (InterVarsity) with her husband, Jack.

Robert Barnes is executive director of Sheridan House Family Ministries, Fort Lauderdale, Florida, and is the author of several books including, *Rock-Solid Marriage* (Word) which he co-wrote with his wife, **Rosemary.**

Dan Benson is senior editor for Multnomah Publishers. He is the author of *21 Days to Financial Freedom* (Zondervan) and *The Total Man* (Tyndale).

James D. Berkley is associate pastor of evangelism and membership development at First Presbyterian Church of Bellevue, Washington, and a contributing editor for *Leadership*.

Ron Blue is a financial adviser with more than 20 years of experience helping people with accounting and financial planning. He is the founder of Ronald Blue & Company, headquartered in Atlanta, and the author of *Master Your Money* (Thomas Nelson).

Jerry Bridges is the former vice president for corporate affairs for The Navigators and is now engaged full-time in a Bible-teaching ministry. He is the author of *Transforming Grace* and *The Pursuit of Holiness* (both published by NavPress).

Beverly J. Burch is a psychotherapist in private practice in the Chicago area.

Barbara Russell Chesser is a human-relations specialist and vice-president of Success Motivation, Inc., in Waco, Texas.

Rodney Clapp is the editorial director of Brazos Press and the author of numerous books.

Jim Conway, Ph.D., and Sally Conway were the founders of Mid-Life Dimensions, a ministry that offers direction and resources for men and women between the ages of 35 and 55. Jim is president and Sally served as vice president of the organization until her death in May 1997.

Laura Crosby is a speaker and author living in Minnesota.

Lyn Cryderman is associate publisher at Zondervan Publishing House in Grand Rapids, Michigan.

Dolores Curran has been a parenting educator for more than 20 years. She is the author of several books, including *Traits of a Healthy Family* (HarperSanFrancisco).

Carol DeChant, former president of a public relations firm in Chicago, is a freelance writer.

Douglas B. DeMerchant, Psy.D., is a licensed clinical psychologist in private practice in suburban Chicago.

Mark Galli is managing editor of *Christianity Today.*

Diana R. Garland, Ph.D., is a professor of social work and director for the social work graduate program at Baylor University. **David E. Garland, Ph.D.,** is professor of Christian Scriptures at the George W. Truett Seminary at Baylor University.

Daniel Green, Ph.D., is a psychologist and clinical director of New Life Resources, Inc., in Waukesha, Wisconsin.

Janis Long Harris is a writer and communications consultant in the Chicago area. She is the co-author of *What If I Married the Wrong Person?* (Bethany).

Archibald Hart, Ph.D., is a clinical psychologist and professor of psychology at Fuller Theological Seminary Graduate School of Psychology. He is the author of numerous books, including *The Sexual Man* (Word).

Donald R. Harvey, Ph.D., is a professor of marriage and family therapy at Trevecca Nazarene University in Nashville, Tennessee, and also practices as a marriage therapist. He is the author of *I Love You—Talk to Me!* (Baker).

Alicia Howe is a public relations consultant and a frequent contributor to *Marriage Partnership*.

R. Kent Hughes is senior pastor of College Church in Wheaton, Illinois.

Bill Hybels is senior pastor of Willow Creek Community Church in South Barrington, Illinois and co-authored *Fit to Be Tied* (Zondervan) with his wife, Lynne.

Paige Jaeger is a New York-based free-lance writer.

Jerry B. Jenkins is the coauthor of the *Left Behind* series and the author of *Loving Your Marriage Enough to Protect It* (Moody).

Jay Kesler is former president and current chancellor of Taylor University in Upland, Indiana. He has been a pastor and also served as president of Youth for Christ.

Eileen Silva Kindig is a freelance writer in Ohio and the author of *A Simply Beautiful Wedding* (InterVarsity).

Nancy Sommerville Langham is publications manager for the Illinois Family Institute in Glen Ellyn, Illinois.

Annettee LaPlaca is a freelance writer in West Chicago, Illinois.

Robert Lauer, Ph.D., and Jeanette C. Lauer, Ph.D., are the authors of several books including *No Secrets? How Much Honesty Is Good for Your Marriage?* (Zondervan) and *Intimacy on the Run* (Dimensions for Living).

Gregg Lewis is a Georgia-based free-lance writer.

Karen L. Maudlin, Psy.D., is a licensed clinical psychologist who specializes in marriage and family therapy. She is in private practice in the Chicago area.

Melissa and Louis McBurney, M.D., are the "Real Sex" columnists for *Marriage Partnership*. They are marriage therapists and co-founders of Marble Retreat in Marble, Colorado, where they counsel clergy couples.

Kevin A. Miller is vice-president of resources for *Christianity Today International*, in Carol Stream, Illinois. He co-authored *More Than You & Me: Touching Others Through the Strength of Your Marriage* (Focus on the Family) with his wife, Karen.

Robert Moeller is pastor of Winnetka Bible Church in Winnetka, Illinois, and author of several books, including *For Better, for Worse, for Keeps* (Multnomah).

Les Parrott, Ph.D., is a professor of clinical psychology and **Leslie Parrott, Ed.D.,** is a marriage and family therapist. They are the authors of *Saving Your Marriage Before It Starts* and *Becoming Soulmates* (both published by Zondervan). Les and Leslie Parrott are co-directors of the Center for Relationship Development at Seattle Pacific University.

Clifford L. Penner, Ph.D., and Joyce J. Penner are the authors of *The Gift of Sex* and *Restoring the Pleasure* (both published by Word). Clifford is a clinical psychologist and Joyce is a clinical nurse specialist. The Penners are sex therapists in private practice in Pasadena, California.

J. Allan Petersen is a family counselor and seminar speaker as well as the founder of Family Concern, Inc., based in Morrison, Colorado. He is the author of *The Myth of Greener Grass* and *For Men Only* (both published by Tyndale).

Wes and Judy Roberts serve as president and vice-president, respectively, of Life Enrichment, a Colorado-based international ministry to Christian leaders.

Lewis B. Smedes, Ph.D., now retired, was a professor of philosophy and integration at the Fuller Theological Seminary Graduate School of Psychology. He is the author of numerous books including, *Forgive and Forget* and *Caring and Commitment* (both published by Harper & Row).

Harold B. Smith is corporate vice-president at *Christianity Today International* and the author of *Hey, Dad! Are We There Yet?* (NavPress).

Jim Smith served as executive director of the Highland Park Presbyterian Church Family Life Center in Dallas until his death in 1993. He is the author of *Learning to Live with the One You Love* (Tyndale).

Scott M. Stanley, Ph.D., is a clinical psychologist specializing in research on marriage. He is the co-director of the Center for Marital and Family Studies at the University of Denver and co-author of *A Lasting Promise: A Christian Guide to Fighting for Your Marriage* (Jossey-Bass).

Lynda Rutledge Stephenson is a professional writer living in Michigan.

Paul Stevens teaches at Regent College/Carey Hall in Vancouver, British Columbia, and is the author of several books including *Marriage Spirituality* (InterVarsity).

Tim Sutherland is in private practice as a licensed marriage and family therapist and also serves as teaching pastor at Community Christian Church in Naperville, Illinois.

Charles R. Swindoll, Div.D., is president of Dallas Theological Seminary and a speaker on the nationally syndicated radio program "Insight for Living." He has authored more than twenty-five books, including *Grace Awakening* and *Laugh Again* (both published by Word).

John Trent, Ph.D., is a licensed professional counselor and the president of Encouraging Words, a ministry committed to strengthening marriage and family relationships. He has authored and co-authored (with Gary Smalley) more than a dozen books, including *The Blessing* (Thomas Nelson) and *The Language of Love* (Focus on the Family).

Ed Wheat, M.D., and Gloria Okes Perkins have collaborated on a number of books, including *Intended for Pleasure, The First Years of Forever and How to Save Your Marriage Alone* (all published by Zondervan). Wheat is a retired physician and sex therapist in Springdale, Arkansas. Perkins is a writer and biblical counselor.

Everett L. Worthington, Jr., Ph.D., is a professor of psychology at Virginia Commonwealth University in Richmond, Virginia. He is the author of several books including, *To Forgive Is Human* (InterVarsity).

R. Kirby Worthington is a freelance writer living in Virginia.

H. Norman Wright is a licensed marriage, family and child therapist. He is the author of over 60 books, including *Quiet Times for Couples* (Harvest House) and *Simplify Your Life and Get More Out of It!* (Tyndale).

Cynthia G. Yates is a Montana-based freelance writer and the author of *1,001 Bright Ideas to Stretch Your Dollars* (Servant).